——GREAT——
Australian
YARNS

The Five Mile Press Pty Ltd
1 Centre Road, Scoresby
Victoria 3179 Australia
wwww.fivemile.com.au

First published 2004
This edition published 2011

Edited by Mara Sennett
Designed by SBR Productions Olinda Victoria
Cover design by Aimee Zumis

Printed and bound in China

Cover photographs: Frederick Bayley Deeming courtesy
   author collection; Tommy Woodcock and Phar Lap
   courtesy The Herald and Weekly Times Photographic
   Collection; Albert Griffiths courtesy National Library
   of Australia Collection; Donna Lola Montez courtesy
   author collection; Ned Kelly courtesy Victorian Police
   Historical Unit

The extract from Judith Wright's poem 'Jacky Jacky',
which appears on page 108, is from *A Human Pattern:
Selected Poems*, ETT Imprint, Sydney, 1996

ISBN 978 1 74300 148 6

GREAT
Australian
YARNS

PAUL TAYLOR

The Five Mile Press

Contents

Preface   8

1 **First Blood**   11
   Nightmare on the Coral Islands   12

2 **Cannibal Convicts and the Monsters Who Made
   Them**   23
   A Few Friends for Dinner   24
   And for Afters   34
   Slaughter on Vinegar Hill   37
   What the Cat Brought Out   40
   The Designer Death Camp   42
   The Most Loathsome Man in Our History   47
   The Death of the Devil   52

3 **The Best of a Bad Bunch**   61
   The Last Dance of Our First Australian Idol   62
   He Died WIth His Boots On, and a Portrait of Polly   69
   If Only Ned's Mother Had Been Sent to the
   Seaside …   76

4 **Half-forgotten Heroes**   93
   Jack and Murph's Three Weeks at Hell's Fun Fair   94
   The Man Who Stared Down Death   99
   In the Alien Arms of Jacky-Jacky   104
   Escape from the Stockade   109
   Something about Australia   112
   The Boy Who Set Sail with 200 Shady Ladies   118

5 G'day Sport! 123

Ashes to Ashes, the Never-ending War 124

No Medals for Our Fighting Boys of '45 129

The Day They Tried to Kill the Legend 134

The Last of the Bareknuckle Men 138

The Sweet Science's Fabulous Freak 141

This Sporting Strife 145

6 The Lady Killers 149

More Tea, Dear? 150

Killing Them with Kindness 155

And They Call Women the Weaker Sex! 162

Mrs Scott's Sad Mistake 166

7 The Ghosts and the Ghouls 169

Condemned by the Ghost on the Post 170

The Phantom of the Princess 173

Carnage at the Ice-cream Cart 175

Line Up, Line Up, for the Girl in the Bottle 178

The Hand in the Grisly Glove 181

8 The Gruesome 183

Norah, My Dear, Who Murdered You? 184

The Day Despicable Deeming Was Lost for Words 192

The Girl Who Spent Ten Years in the Bath 198

The Grim Reaper's Groundhog Day 202

The Shark That Coughed up a Killer 211

9 Three Odds and a Sod   *215*

Awful Arthur Orton, the Man Who Hoodwinked
Two Nations   *216*

Hats Off to Mr Whippy!   *227*

I Say, Christie, That Drunken Sailor Was You,
Old Man!   *234*

The Shock Horror Truth about John Norton   *240*

10 Wild, Wild Women   *247*

A Saturday Arvo's Entertainment with Sweet Nell
of Tooth's Brewery   *248*

You Always Hurt the One You Love   *255*

La Lola's Excellent Australian Adventure   *262*

The Days of Julia's Lives   *267*

Preface

A Ripping Yarn is a true story, or a purportedly true story, heard or read with the mouth agape. The lips move now and then, involuntarily. Awe, fear, astonishment, revulsion, excitement – sometimes even humour: the words that come out depend on upbringing, and the category of the Ripping Yarn.

Yarns that curdle the blood and send a shudder up the spine, such as the diabolical saga of the *Batavia* ... the convicts who ate one another ... the penal death camps, or sadistic serial killers, will draw instant, powerful responses – often expletives deleted in polite conversation.

Other yarns may be quirky and amusing. Lola Montez, the firecracker who flogged the Ballarat newspaper editor, or Percy Grainger the eccentric composer who flogged himself and his lady friends, trigger an irresistible titter. Heroic yarns of superhuman endeavour bring reverent responses. Tales of sporting derring-do stimulate our vernacular's you-little-beauty! reaction.

The Ripping Yarns in this book are true. But for the most part, sadly, they are not the stories history teachers tell. John Norton, it's safe to say, is someone few know. Yet the rambunctious life of this outstanding scoundrel sums up the best and the worst of Sydney at the turn of the 19th century.

The tales – or myths – of the romantic, and perhaps not coincidentally, handsome, outlaws Matthew Brady, Ben Hall and Ned Kelly, passed over in a few paragraphs in the history books, nonetheless vividly reveal the social structure, the morals, and the mores of their time, and help explain the legacy they have left us.

Other characters, such as the inimitable confidence trickster Arthur Orton, leave us marvelling at the gullibility of the Victorian era – but then invite us to reflect on the adulation we give to the Alan Bonds of our own day. John Giles Price, the inhuman commandant gratifyingly beaten to death by convicts from the hell hulks at Williamstown, reminds us of the cruelty that was so common – and is so frighteningly recent – in our society.

And then there are the minor players and stories from our tribal memory. The Pyjama Girl in her viewing bath and the Shark Arm mystery at the Coogee Aquarium ... the gangsters and their gun molls ... Fisher's Ghost which 'fingered' a killer, and Federici, the phantom of the Princess Theatre who some say still haunts the stage – these are people, events, incidents and shadows largely forgotten but integral to our extraordinary heritage.

The expression 'Ripping Yarn' was most likely born in the common rooms and musty dorms of the English public school in the late 19th century, inspired and nurtured by the adventurous and bloody expansion of the British Empire. The Ripping Yarns in this book, however, were Made in Australia, and can be summed up colloquially in that quintessential Australian exclamation: Ripper!

Paul Taylor

1 | First Blood

Nightmare on the Coral Islands

A century and a half before the arrival of the First Fleet heralded the white settlement of Australia in 1788, two young Dutchmen landed on the mainland of West Australia. Vile, treacherous, serial murderers, they were our first white settlers.

The two didn't choose to come to Australia. It was settle or swing. They settled, and the last the pair saw of the civilisation they left behind was a row of bodies, hands severed, dangling and fly blown on a barren, awful island of death. Jan Pelgrom de Bye and Wouter Looes, two of the 316 men, women and children who sailed on the Dutch merchant vessel *Batavia* were put ashore, marooned, in 1629 as punishment for their part in a mutiny – the bloodiest in history.

October 1629: traitors hang from gibbets on Batavia's Graveyard. Those who had signed their name to the pirate oath of allegiance first had their hand severed.

All told, 210 from the *Batavia* died on three tiny coral islands just off the coast of the mainland of Australia. But, life in the 17th century was cheap, and sea voyages were notoriously risky; mutinies, pirates, shipwrecks, fever and madness were common. What distinguishes the *Batavia* story from other stories of shipwrecks is the unremitting pageant of the worst of human nature it revealed on a vast, grotesque canvas: surreal savagery, lust, treachery, cowardice and – daily for week upon week – gruesome murder.

It was a nightmare that began almost as soon as the *Batavia* set sail from Holland in October 1628. The *Batavia*, the flagship of the Dutch East India Company, the finest Dutch East Indiaman afloat, was on her maiden voyage, leading a fleet to her namesake city in Java in the East Indies – Jakarta, in modern-day Indonesia. On board were sailors, soldiers and merchants and their women and children under the Fleet Commander, the Company senior merchant, Francisco Pelsaert. The *Batavia* was captained by Ariaen Jacobsz. In the hold were chests containing a fortune: a quarter of a million guilders in silver coin, a casket brimming with gold and jewels and 600 tonnes of wine, cheeses and cloth.

The *Batavia* looked a splendid vessel, as those who went aboard a meticulous reconstruction of the ship discovered when she sailed to Sydney in 2000. Built of Baltic oak, canvas sails fully rigged, her hull green and gold and with a red lion proud on her figurehead, she was, on deck and safe in sedate Darling Harbour, every inch a ship that would bring out the old sea dog in the most land-locked of lubbers.

Below decks it was a different story. In many places you had to stoop to move about among the huge winches, the cannons and the precipitous companion ladders that shared a stiflingly stuffy, cramped and claustrophobic area. There, in 1628, where more than 300 slept, bloated rats and cockroaches scuttled from stem to stern, faeces and urine disgorged from the bilges and it was foul going in the fairest of weathers for all but the ship's commanders: the captain, Jacobsz, and his superior, Pelsaert. These two were to sail the *Batavia* into waters never dreamed of, far more unpleasant than the cramped squalor below decks.

Pelsaert and Jacobsz were at odds with each other from the beginning. They had been together on a previous voyage to the Dutch East Indies colony and they disliked each other intensely. Jacobsz particularly resented the fact that it was company policy to put a merchant in command above him. Their hatred was exacerbated by a passenger, Lucretia van den Mylen, a beautiful and voluptuous young woman sailing to join her husband in the Dutch colony.

Jacobsz lusted after Lucretia, but Pelsaert took care of her – too much care, perhaps. Francisco Pelsaert was a dasher. At the gorgeous court of the Great Moghul in Agra, he had dallied with slave girls and seduced the wives of courtiers. On the *Batavia* he was in command and Captain Jacobsz had to make do with Lucretia's maidservant, Zwaantie Hendrix. Unlike her mistress, with whom she soon quarrelled and left, Zwaantie was all too willing.

On 14 April, after six months at sea, the *Batavia,* the other nine ships in the merchant fleet and the man-o'-war accompanying it reached the Cape of Good Hope and dropped anchor. While Pelsaert was occupied taking on provisions, Jacobsz and Zwaantie went on a 'ship crawl' – a belligerent drinking binge that took them from ship to ship docked in the port. With them was a former apothecary from Haarlem, Jeronimus Cornelisz.

A suave and cultured man, Cornelisz, the ship's Undermerchant and, as such, the third most senior company man on the *Batavia* after the commander and the captain, had become close friends with Jacobsz and his lover, Zwaantie. Cornelisz was a member of a cult that practised sexual orgies and sanctioned any crime because, its members said, man was made in God's image, and since God inspired each and every idea and action – even murder – He therefore must approve. In addition, Cornelisz proved to be a man with the rare and frightening persuasive power of a Charles Manson. Cornelisz could control those with weaker personalities.

When Commander Pelsaert came back on board and learned of the trio's rampage at the Cape, he gave Captain Jacobsz a public tongue-lashing. Hatred of Pelsaert now began to simmer. The mutinous cauldron began to boil when, three weeks later, Lucretia van den Mylen was stripped and sexually assaulted by a group and Pelsaert announced he would be taking one of them, the Bosun, in chains to Batavia.

It was Cornelisz who hatched a plot that would give the mutineers the *Batavia*, the treasure in her hold, and the woman he wanted – like Jacobsz he lusted for Lucretia van den Mylen. Cornelisz suggested to the captain that with help from fellow conspirators – a Lance Corporal and some of his soldiers, junior officers and most of Jazobsz's crew – they could kill Pelsaert and the rest of the soldiers, commandeer the *Batavia*, take its treasure and, using the heavily armed vessel as a pirate ship, prey on Dutch East India Company ships plying their rich trade.

On the eve of 4 June, the conspirators went to their bunks with weapons hidden and at the ready. Some weeks after leaving the Cape, a storm had separated the *Batavia* from the fleet, and two hours before dawn on 4 June the ship found itself alone in the Abrolhos group of islands, some 80 kilometres off the west coast of Australia.

Abrolhos is a Portuguese word meaning 'eyes wide open'. Francisco Pelsaert was a shrewd, resourceful man, but on the night of 4 June he was sick in his cabin, and Jacobsz, although he kept his eyes open, failed to keep them open wide enough. It was a bright, moonlit night and the sea glistened so much that he or the pilot mistook the reef's foaming fringe for moonlight reflection. The *Batavia*, with all sails set, smashed onto the coral rocks. Pelsaert rushed up on deck and roared for the cannons to be dumped overboard (where, exactly 334 years later on 4 June 1963, divers found many of them alongside remains of the ship.) Jettisoning the cannons made no difference. The ship kept striking, and now a new storm was brewing. Pelsaert ordered the anchor to be dropped and the mainmast cut down. Its loss only made matters worse.

The *Batavia*, Pelsaert saw, was stuck fast and breaking up. But, through the storm, he could see an island about three leagues away, with two smaller islands, little more than outcrops of rock, beside it. The islands were their only chance, and that morning Pelsaert ordered the women and children put ashore while the crew struggled to salvage all possible food and supplies. Foolishly, the crew ignored the fresh water on board, presuming there would be plenty on the islands, and took the opportunity to break into the grog.

As the storm raged, 180 people were safely landed on the main island and 40 on the smallest – among them the warring commander and the captain. Also landed were food and a few barrels of water. On the second day more crew and passengers, merchandise and some of the silver coins and jewels were taken off.

On the third day it was decided to take off Cornelisz and 70 others who were still on the *Batavia*. Heavy seas beat the crew back four times. With a heavy heart, Pelsaert later said, he left 'with the utmost grief, my lieutenant and seventy men on the very point of perishing on board the vessel.' Sink or swim. As conditions worsened 30 of them sank. Tragically, Cornelisz was not among them. Eventually, ten days later, he swam and survived – to be greeted as a hero when he at last made it to land.

In the meantime the castaways on the islands began to explore their new habitat. There were birds and fish but no fresh water, and Pelsaert knew the group would quickly die unless water was found. For the next three days he oversaw the hurried construction of two skiffs with covering decks built from timbers from the wreck of the *Batavia*. Intending to find water on the mainland, he set sail on 8 June with 47 others, among them Jacobsz, Zwaantie Hendrix and Jan Evertsz, the Bosun.

The rocky, barren west coast of the 'great south' mainland was guarded by high cliffs and treacherous breakers and the little ships sailed and were blown further and further north looking vainly for a safe landing. With just enough water to keep them going, and 1000 kilometres from the wreck, Pelsaert decided the best course was to keep going and make for Java and Batavia.

Without Commander Pelsaert the castaways began to die. They had soon drunk all the water taken off the *Batavia,* and about 20 had perished of thirst when at last rain fell and they collected the precious drops in sail sheets. Jerome Cornelisz made it to shore and by right of his Undermerchant title took command of the company. Immediately he began to resurrect his mutinous fantasy. This time he planned to restore and rehabilitate the *Batavia*, run up the pirate flag and seize the expected rescue ship from Java. Then, with the salvaged treasure and the merchandise in the hold of the new ship, he and his cohorts would be free to roam and rob.

Cornelisz demanded that his fellow conspirators sign a pirate compact: a solemn oath of allegiance with a list of regulations. He was to be the 'Captain General'. To ensure there were fewer mouths to feed and to satisfy his psychotic urges, he ordered the murder of all those who were not a party to the compact – men, women and children. Only the most comely women were to be spared. These would be shared by the mutineers. The beautiful Lucretia, however, was his alone: she was to be his concubine.

The killings began. At first they were covert and under cover of darkness. People would be killed at night and buried in secret, or taken out on rafts in search of water and drowned. Then the killings became open and increasingly orgiastic. Merchants, junior officers, soldiers – even cabin boys – hacked to death, drowned, bashed, beheaded or strangled men, women, children and infants. As the murders went on, day after day, week after week, the killers became drunk with bloodlust and, in a gorgeous uniform of red coats embroidered with gold and silver from material looted from the ship's hold, began a frightful game, hunting down their prey and contriving ever more sadistic ways to kill.

It seemed nothing could stop the atrocities until, on one of the smaller islands, Wiebbe Hayes, a soldier sent with an unarmed party of around 25 others to find water – in reality to get them off the main island –

noticed two pools of water that rose and fell with the tide. Was it salt water? He took a sip. It was fresh water, and in abundance. Wiebbe Hayes, unaware of the reign of terror on the main island, sent up the arranged smoke signal to Cornelisz: water found.

The shipwreck, the drownings, the indiscriminate daily slaughter: the Batavia horror, captured in this engraved vignette published 18 years later.

At the same time the first of a score or so of men escaped, swimming, to the smaller island. Hayes learned of the unspeakable atrocities on the other islands and knew that he had to prepare for an attack. He held the water supply. With those who had escaped, he and his men numbered 45, against Cornelisz and his mutineers – 36 men and five women. But Cornelisz's troops were armed with pikes, swords, adzes and muskets. Hayes's men hurriedly dug in, set up a stockade and began making pikes and morning stars from timbers and barrel hoops washed ashore. Then they waited for the inevitable attack.

On 27 July, Cornelisz sent to the island a cadet, Daniel Cornelissen, with a letter to the soldiers inviting them to join the mutineers. The soldiers promptly gave Hayes the letter, and he ordered the boy to be taken prisoner and sat back to wait for the attack. When it came the defenders beat it off, throwing rocks and stones and taking the fight to the invaders. A second attack came within a week, and this time Cornelisz was there to command it. Three boatloads of mutineers tried to land on the shore, but Hayes's men waded into the water and once again drove them back, taunting the mutineers whose muskets failed to fire.

Events now began to echo the chapter in Robert Louis Stevenson's classic pirate story, *Treasure Island*, and it is possible that Stevenson may have been inspired by the saga of the *Batavia*. In the novel the *Hispaniola* mutineers swear oaths of allegiance to their leader, Long John Silver, attempt to storm the stockade, and are repulsed. Silver tries to persuade the cabin boy, Jim, to desert, and leads a second attempt to take the stockade when this is rejected. On Wiebbe Hayes's coral island, Jeronimus Cornelisz, routed twice, decided to offer a small boat in exchange for wine and blankets. At the same time he once again secretly tried to bribe some of the soldiers into joining him.

Wiebbe Hayes was a man whose will was as strong as that of Cornelisz. He had no intention of bartering with the killers and, at his signal, his men fell upon and seized Cornelisz and five others, killed four and let slip Jacop Pietersz, who escaped back to the main island to join his fellow mutineers, lick wounds and plan the next attempt. Hayes, however, now had a boat.

Two weeks later, on 17 September, the mutineers tried a third assault. Four of Hayes's soldiers died from gunshots in the first rally and the situation was looking grim. Then, as the mutineers retired to re-load, the defenders saw beyond them, a ship, the *Sardam*, with Francisco Pelsaert aboard, making its way through the reef. At the same time the mutineers saw the *Sardam*. Both sides made a dash for boats and rowed furiously to be first to the rescue ship.

Aboard the *Sardam* Commander Pelsaert was about to step into a skiff loaded with bread when Hayes's ship came alongside and the soldier gasped out his incredible story. Pelsaert had just enough time to get Hayes and his men on board and order cannons primed and muskets at the ready when two boats came alongside manned by men bristling with weapons. They were dressed in Cornelisz's lavish embroidered 'uniform'. The men in the boats protested that they came as friends but refused to put down their weapons and asked to be taken on board to explain matters. Pelsaert instead gave them the choice of surrendering or being blown out of the water. The men put down their weapons. The remaining mutineers on the main island were quickly rounded up. Put in irons and tortured they confessed, one by one. The first man to break, John Bremen, confessed to murdering 27 men.

Pelsaert called a council. Rather than risk taking all back to Batavia for trial, the council decide to execute the most dangerous mutineers then and there. Cornelisz was the first to go. He had undergone five torture sessions before he confessed, but finally, on the morning of 2 October, Australia's first serial killer was taken to the island site of many deaths, Batavia Graveyard. First they brought Cornelisz to a block and hacked off his hands. Then he was dragged to a makeshift gallows. He had said under torture, 'Sometimes, circumstances force one to do a great many things one would rather not have to do,' but that was not the real Jeronimus Cornelisz speaking. His last words were much more in character. From his evil heart he roared in vain defiance: 'Revenge! Revenge!'

Then they strung him up.

Cornelisz was followed by seven men who once were simply soldiers, or carpenters, merchants or cabin boys, murderers such as Mattys Beer. A 21-year-old soldier, Beer confessed to killing, or helping to kill, nine people. He cut off the head of Coen Aldertsz to test the sharpness of a sword. Others were taken to Batavia to be executed, hanged, or broken on the block – bound to a cartwheel with their limbs shattered and left to die a slow, agonising death.

Cadet Daniel Cornelisson, who carried the message to Wiebbe Hayes and was held prisoner, had his right hand severed and was executed. Solomon Deschamps, a merchant, was forced to strangle a baby poisoned by Cornelisz. On the voyage back he was thrice keelhauled – dragged by ropes beneath the ship's keel – and outside Batavia Castle, on 31 January 1630, while a huge crowd watched, he and others like him were given 100 lashes and executed. The worst of them, men like Jacop Pietersz, who had escaped from Wiebbe Hayes and led the last of the mutineers, were 'broken from under upwards and the body exposed on a wheel'.

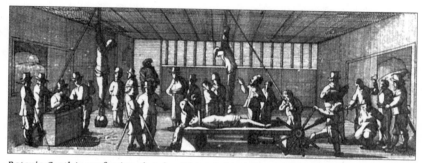

Batavia Castle's confession chamber. Wrists behind their backs, prisoners were winched high, then dropped, agonisingly dislocating their arms. Others were broken on the rack.

And on the coral island two others were spared. Jan Pelgrom de Bye, a cabin boy, 18, murdered another boy and helped kill a man and a woman. He had cried when Mattys Beer was given the honour of cutting off the head of Coen Aldertsz. He cried again when he was sentenced to hang and begged for mercy. Pelsaert gave it and ordered instead that he was to be marooned on the Australian mainland. Wouter Looes, a soldier, took part in killings and took command of the mutineers when Cornelisz was captured. But he had been kind to Lucretia van den Mylen, and Pelsaert consented to let him live. He, too, was marooned on the mainland.

The *Batavia* atrocity broke Fleet Commander Francisco Pelsaert. He was stripped of his commission and all his wages and possessions were confiscated. He died of malaria in Sumatra less than a year later. The *Batavia's* captain, Ariaen Jacobsz, was imprisoned and Jan Evertsz, the Bosun, hanged for his part in the rape of Lucretia. Wiebbe Hayes was hailed as a hero and promoted. The woman who was at the centre of this unimaginable horror story, Lucretia van den Mylen, never got to see her husband. He was dead when she reached Batavia. She returned to Holland, re-married and never spoke of the nightmare.

And of Jan Pelgrom de Bye and Wouter Looes marooned on the mainland, nothing more was heard. But, many decades later, there were reports of explorers encountering blue-eyed Aboriginal people, and it is feasible that one of their descendants may be reading these words at this moment.

2 | Cannibal Convicts and the Monsters Who Made Them

A Few Friends for Dinner

Man's flesh is delicious – far better than fish
or pork …

– Alexander Pearce

*A*lexander Pearce was unique. The only man to escape twice from the nightmare penitentiary Macquarie Harbour, he was Australia's first recorded serial killer. And he was that rare monster – a man-eater, a cannibal who relished human flesh.

Pint sized and pock marked though he was, Alexander Pearce's only known likenesses show a slight, fine-featured young man with tousled hair, a stubborn mouth and a pugnacious chin. Today he might be manning a call service or have a walk-on role in *Neighbours*. More likely he would lead an anonymous life of unsuccessful minor crime, turning up regularly in the Magistrate's Court to answer charges of burglary and drug dealing and, with any luck, getting off with bonds or community service orders.

But the little blue-eyed Irishman from County Fermanagh had the bad luck of living long before soapies or sit-coms, community service orders or stress counselling. He was born in 1793 at a time when stealing half a dozen pairs of shoes, as he did, could be fatal if you were caught, as he was. It was 1819, and the 26-year-old was destined for the gallows or for transportation to Van Diemen's Land, now known as Tasmania.

Avoiding the gallows, for the time being, Pearce arrived in chains in Hobart Town in 1820. Life in the penal colony was hard, but it could be worse, far worse, as Pearce knew. He was put to work in an open-plan penal camp and then as an assigned servant, where it was easy to abscond and take a refuge in a tavern. Pierce was a lazy, surly man who got into this habit despite the floggings he inevitably got after his

24

drunken hours of freedom. Then he graduated into forging currency and passing the notes off, and when this scheme was discovered, he fled into the bush. He was caught after two months hiding in the scrub around Hobart Town, and deemed in need of far sterner discipline at a place from which he could not escape – the newly established penal settlement at Macquarie Harbour on the south-west coast of Tasmania, where the Commandant, Lieutenant John Cuthbertson, wrote the standing orders for the gaolers: '… the constant, active and unremitting employment of every individual in very hard labour is the grand idea and main design. They must dread the very idea of being sent there… Prisoners upon trial declared that they would rather suffer death than be sent back to Macquarie Harbour. It is the feeling that I am anxious to be kept alive.'

At Macquarie Harbour, Pearce joined convicts who lived and worked on Sarah Island, a four-hectare island in the middle of Macquarie Harbour. Lived and worked in hell. By day the lucky ones laboured in the forests on the mainland, the wettest place in Australia, cutting down the huge pines for sale to local boat builders. The unlucky worked in chains under water, driving piles for the slipways to load the fallen timber. In winter, under dank grey skies and mists, the prisoners were forced to slave 12 hours, and in summer, it was 16 hours. And they did it on a daily ration of 500 grams of brine-cured beef or pork, two or three years old, 750 grams of bread and four ounces of oatmeal and salt. By night many of them quivered in agony from the floggings routinely administered for the smallest of infractions – for insolence, or rebelliousness, or singing, or refusal to work.

Prisoners would do anything – they would maim or murder by mutual consent – just to escape Macquarie Harbour and be sent to Hobart Town to be tried, or as a witness. One man killed just so that he could have a smoke. He was in a group of prisoners in single file when he smashed an axe onto the skull of the man in front. There was no tobacco on Macquarie Harbour, he explained later, and he missed smoking. He had killed so that he would be sent back to Hobart Town where he could at least have a twist of nigger-head shag tobacco before he was dangled.

The Hobart Town execution option became so popular that Commandant Cuthbertson decided to institute public hangings at Port Macquarie Harbour. Three condemned were marched to the gallows, but as Surgeon Barnes reported:

> ... their execution produced a feeling, I should say, of the most disgusting description ... So buoyant were the feelings of the men who were about to be executed, and so little did they seem to care about it, that they absolutely kicked their shoes off among the crowd in order, as the term expressed by them was, that they might "die game"; it seemed ... more like a parting of friends who were going a distant journey on land than of individuals who were about to separate from each other for ever; the expressions used were "Goodbye Bob" and "Goodbye Jack" and expressions of that kind, among those in the crowd, to those who were about to be executed.

This was Macquarie Harbour, and Pearce was not impressed.

How was Pearce to escape? 'The Western Hell' they called the Sarah Island settlement, and 'Hell's Gate', the narrow headlands of the harbour. Escape through Hell's Gate was impossible. For small boats the turbulent, boiling 100-metre wide bottleneck of rips and currents was impassable. Swimming was suicidal. Around the harbour grew thick, almost impenetrable bush. No one, the authorities believed, could abscond through the bush: the dubious refuge of Hobart Town was through dense, uncharted wilderness 225 kilometres away, and without a compass the chances of surviving were nil.

But Pearce and others thought it a chance worth taking. He had been at The Western Hell only a month when, with six others, Pearce overpowered the guards on the mainland, jumped into boats and rowed to a nearby coal works where another convict, Robert Greenhill, was waiting with stolen provisions. They scuttled one of the boats, rowed further down river in the other, and then started walking east to where they thought Hobart Town lay. There, they planned to steal a schooner and 'proceed home'.

This was a representative bunch of reprobate convicts. Matthew Travers, an Irishman under life sentence, and Robert Greenhill, who had been a sailor, had tried to escape from Van Diemen's Land and been punished by being sent to Macquarie Harbour. There was an ex-soldier, William Dalton, serving 14 years for perjury in Gibraltar; Thomas Bodenham, a highway robber; William Kennelly, alias Bill Cornelius, transported for seven years and sent to Macquarie Harbour for trying to escape; John Mathers, a young Scottish baker doing seven years at Macquarie Harbour for forging a 15-pound money order; and a man now remembered only as William 'Little' Brown.

Ahead of the group was some of the most rugged country in the world, mile after mile of mountainous steep rock faces and rotting ferns and creepers that make it impossible to keep a straight line. They struggled along from dawn to dusk, taking it in turns to head the file and hack a path. 'Little' Brown, Pearce related, 'was the worst walker of any, he always fell behind, and then kept cooing [sic] so that we said we would leave him behind if he could not keep up the better.'

Between them the eight had ten pounds of flour and six pounds of beef and, other than the convict uniforms they stood in, no protection against the bitter cold and endless driving rain. For a week, it poured with rain, a heavy, drenching rain, and then it turned to gales and sleet. They could not build a fire – their tinder was soaked and useless – and by the ninth day they had eaten their rations. They went another two days before Kennelly voiced what they had probably all been thinking: 'I'm so weak I could eat a piece of a man.'

No doubt Kennelly said this as if he meant it to be a weak joke, but the others brooded on it overnight, and Pearce tells,

> The next morning there were four of us for a feast. Bob Greenhill was the first who introduced it and he said he had seen the like done

before, and that it eat much like pork. Mathers spoke out and said it would be murder; and perhaps then we could not eat it. "I'll warrant you," said Greenhill, "I'll eat the first bit; but you must all lend a hand, so that we'll all be equal in the crime."

We consulted who should fall and Greenhill said, "Dalton, he volunteered to be a flogger, we will kill him."

We made a bit of a breakwind with boughs and about three in the morning Dalton was asleep. Then Greenhill struck him on the head with an axe and he never spoke again. Greenhill called Travers and he cut Dalton's throat to bleed him. Then we dragged him away a bit and cut him up.

They cut off the head and tore into the torso, too impatient to observe the niceties. 'Travers and Greenhill put his heart and liver on the fire and ate them before they were right warm. The others refused to eat any that night but the next morning it was cut up and divided and we all got our share.'

Brown was walking slower and slower. He was a liability, he knew, and he was bound to be next. Kennelly, too, was frightened and the pair fell behind until they had disappeared, slipped away to retrace their steps. They made it to Macquarie Harbour on 12 October, almost a month since their escape. But they were done in. Brown died on 15 October, and Kennelly, three days later.

Five convicts were now left. Pearce, Greenhill, Bodenham, Travers and Mathers were lost, with no idea where they were, or how far they were from Hobart Town. On the day that Brown died, it was Bodenham's turn to feed his companions. Greenhill pole-axed him with a sharp, violent blow to the back of his head, and Bodenham was dismembered, cut into smaller pieces, cooked and eaten.

For the next week the four ate while they stumbled and staggered through the bush. They covered only three or four miles a day, when, exhausted and despairing, they reached a small valley. 'A very fine country, full of many kangaroos and emus, and game of all sorts,' but they had no weapons and watched in mounting frustration as their meals bounded beyond their reach. So it was John Mathers's turn. The five stopped by a little creek to boil the last of Bodenham, but Mather, who had been squeamish from the beginning, could not eat his share. He gathered some fern roots and boiled them but 'he found it would not rest on his stomach ... which occasioned him to vomit to ease his Stomach & while in the act of discharging it from his Chest, Greenhill still showing his spontaneous habit of bloodshed seized the Axe & crept behind him and gave him a blow on the head.'

Mathers spun up and around, grappled with Greenhill and, stronger than him, came away, panting and wild eyed, holding the axe. The others stepped back. Pearce and Travers slowly calmed the other two. But all four knew it could not last. It was a standoff, and Mathers now had the killing tool. For safety they split in twos: Mathers sided with Pearce, and Greenhill went with Travers, and the two pairs eyed each other warily across the campfire. They took turns sleeping on the understanding that their partner would guard them.

Mathers made a poor choice in his partner. Pearce was secretly on the other side. 'We walked on till night, and then Travers and Greenhill collared Mathers and got him down. They told him they would give him half an hour to pray for himself, which was agreed to; he then gave the prayer book to me and laid down his head and Greenhill took the axe and killed him.' Now there were three. They had the remains of Mathers to keep them going, but human flesh, rich in protein, is lacking in carbohydrates that give energy, and they needed energy badly.

Four days later, when a snake bit Travers's foot, he knew his time was up. His leg swollen to enormous proportions, he begged to be allowed to die peacefully and for the other two to leave him there. Greenhill, the axeman, assured him he would not desert his mate, he would stay with him in the hope that Travers might rally and survive. And, with Pearce, he did stay until, six days later, Greenhill's patience ran out and he killed Travers with the now standard single blow from the axe. Travers 'only stretched himself in his agony, and then expired.'

One to go. They walked apart. When one stopped, the other stopped. When one squatted, so did the other. Greenhill never let go of the axe. Neither man slept. Finally, near dawn one morning, when Greenhill fell asleep at last, Pearce stealthily slid alongside, slipped the axe from his hand and despatched him with a number of blows to the head. 'I then took part of his arm and thigh, and went on for several days.'

Greenhill's part in the awful odyssey had been crucial. He had done the killings, but he had also taken the party, using his sailor's skills to navigate by the stars and the sun, almost directly due east across the island to the settled area. Without him they would certainly have wandered in aimless circles.

For the first time in almost seven weeks, Alexander Pierce was able to eat without fear. For the next four days, he settled down to recuperate while he feasted on Greenhill. Then, the first of a series of good luck occurred: Pearce stumbled into an Aboriginal camp. The tribe had been cooking when they saw him coming and fled at the apparition of this wild, bearded white man. There was kangaroo and possum on the campfire and he ate all he could and took the rest. A week later, he came across two ducks, strangled them and ate them raw. When he blundered on to some stray sheep in the bush and cornered and killed a lamb, he knew he was near a farm. This was confirmed when he heard a dog barking as he was enjoying the lamb and, turning round, found himself looking along the barrel of a musket.

Pearce told Tom Triffet, the man with the musket, a shepherd, that the wild, near-naked white man he saw before him, tearing into an uncooked lamb, was a convict, an escapee from the penal settlement on the other side of the island. Incredibly, he learned in return, he had made it to the outskirts of Hobart Town, much of it barefoot. He didn't tell Tom Triffet about the cannibalism: Triffet might not have been inclined to take Pearce back to his hut. Instead Triffet took him into his hut – he wouldn't turn in a fellow Irishman – and for 11 days, while the benevolent Triffet fed him and nursed him back to good health, and for several weeks afterwards while he stayed with other Irish shepherds, Alexander Pearce enjoyed the only peaceful period of his life since he was found with six pairs of stolen shoes four long years before.

One day when Triffet was away from the hut there came a knock on the door. Opening it, Pearce was confronted by two bushrangers, Ralph Cheetham and William Davis, like Pearce, escaped convicts. The three swapped yarns, and in no time at all Pearce had accepted their offer to join them. The little Irishman's talent for immersing himself ever deeper into his living nightmare was about to be reinvigorated. And his taste for cannibalism – and now it was truly a taste – was to be revived.

Pearce left Triffet a note thanking him for his kindness, and the trio disappeared into the dense bush forest. Their hide-out was well concealed and well provided with arms and food – a flock of 180 stolen sheep grazed around two huts. It was the Yueletide season, and the bushrangers, whether or not they were aware of it, celebrated Christmas Day with the customary roast lamb. It couldn't last and less than six weeks later it was all up for them. There was a ten-pound reward on the heads of his companions, and on 11 January 1823, the 48th Regiment of troopers who had been ordered to rid Van Diemen's Land of the growing bands of bushrangers surrounded the camp after a tip-off and took Pearce and Cheetham without any resistance. Davis tried to shoot his way to freedom but was cut down and, like the others, taken in chains into Hobart Town where, seven weeks later, in March 1823, Davis and Cheetham dangled from the gallows.

Incredibly, Pearce, the great survivor, didn't join them. He was not tried for bushranging but instead found himself returned to Macquarie Harbour, where the prisoners lauded him as a hero. More so when Pearce told the full story. He admitted to murdering Robert Greenhill and being a party to the murder of Dalton, Bodenham, Mathers and Travers. And he confessed that he had dined off them all.

It was, as it were, a deliciously macabre story, but the authorities wouldn't wear it. They had no doubt that Pearce was concocting this tale of culinary adventures simply to protect the missing convicts: they were undoubtedly still in hiding but would inevitably be flushed out and suitably punished. In the meantime, Pearce was flogged, of course, and put in solitary confinement; mild punishment by the standards of The Western Hell and one quite enjoyed by prisoners. He had escaped the noose and was not even given an additional year or two on his sentence. (He had by now served three years – minus the 113 days he had absconded – of his seven-year sentence.)

Now all Pearce had to do was to keep his head down and stay out of trouble while he served the remainder of his sentence. With any luck he would eventually be free to roister in the taverns of Hobart Town or grow old back in the Emerald Isle where he could terrify his grandchildren with tales of life in Van Diemen's Land.

Naturally, Pearce chose the other path: he escaped from Macquarie Harbour once more. This time he had only one companion, Thomas Cox. A young Shropshire lad, he had been transported in 1819, the year that Pearce was sentenced at the Armagh Assizes. Like the other convicts, Cox hero-worshipped 'Cannibal Pearce' as the man who had proved it was possible to escape from Macquarie Harbour and get to Hobart Town. But perhaps, like the penal authorities, Cox didn't really believe that Pearce ate the flesh of men. If so, he fatally deluded himself. Five days after the pair took to the bush, the schooner, *Waterloo*, cruising down Macquarie Harbour, saw smoke signals rising and a figure on the shore waving to alert them, and rowing ashore they were met by a man who needed no introduction: Alexander 'Cannibal' Pearce.

This time Pearce's story was simple. Cox had drowned, he said, trying to swim a river. He wanted to surrender. Then he was searched. In his packets they found enough food to keep him going for days. But, in one pocket, they found raw meat – human flesh. It was true, then. 'Cannibal' Pearce was true to his nickname.

Now Pearce gave up all pretence. A short distance away, in the scrub, they found Cox's body and Pearce readily agreed that he had killed Cox. 'And I am willing to die for it.' It seemed that the pair had been about to cross a river when Cox revealed that he couldn't swim. Pearce was furious, and a violent argument was settled when Pearce picked up – once again – an axe, and cut Cox down. Then, he later told the court in Hobart Town, he was overcome with the compulsion to feast on human flesh. 'I ate part of him that night and cut up the greater part of his flesh in order to take it with me,' he confessed.

By now Pearce was clearly demented, but not so much that his conscience couldn't be tortured by his grotesque crimes and, he said, he had signalled the *Waterloo* as a way of ending them. The court obliged, and on 20 June 1824, on a bitterly cold day in Hobart Town, with snow on Mt Wellington, the Chief Justice, John Pedder, sentenced Pearce to hang.

Alexander Pearce was a cannibal with a conscience – and a taste for eating others. On the morning of his death, he left posterity to ponder his answer to Coxswain Smith of Macquarie Harbour. In the yard of the Hobart Town gaol at 9.00 a.m., on 19 July, Smith asked Pearce what drove him to eat another. Pearce replied: 'No man can tell what he will do when driven by hunger.' And, then, he added: 'Man's flesh is delicious, far better than fish or pork.'

And for Afters

*A*lexander Pearce's successful escape from Macquarie Harbour inspired 90 convicts to try their luck in the next six years. Perhaps two dozen made it – among them the romantic and dashing Matthew Brady and a gang of 13. The rest perished. They starved, they were speared by Aborigines or … they were eaten.

'Cannibal' Pearce had set a gruesome example that was certainly followed by at least two other absconders, and the odds are that among the 65 or so convicts who disappeared never to be heard of again, more than a few finished up in the bellies of their fellow bolters. Some, like the absconders Mark 'The Monster' Jeffries, Hopkins and Russell would have drawn straws to see who was to be the Sunday roast. In their case, Russell lost the toss and was shot by Jeffries, as nasty a killer as Australia has known. Russell provided tucker for five days.

A government executioner and flogger, Mark Jeffries was known as 'The Monster' for good reason. With Hopkins he turned to bushranging and shot a stockman employed by a settler, Mr Tibbs. Then he shot Tibbs and captured Mrs Tibbs. When Mrs Tibbs's baby began squalling, 'the Monster' picked up the infant by the legs and dashed its skull against a tree.

Other freedom seekers such as Matthew MacAvoy, an Irishman, and Edward Broughton, an Englishman, who left us with an account of their man-eating ways, played a nerve-wracking game in which no one dared sleep for fear he would be served as the chef's special on the following day. MacAvoy and Broughton took to the bush on 8 October 1830 and came out again – congratulating themselves, no doubt – near where Pearce himself had emerged seven years before. That was as good as it got. Almost immediately, they managed to walk into a band of troopers, part of the infamous 'black line' devised by Lieutenant-Governor Arthur to push the Aborigines into a containable pocket.

The two were taken to Hobart Town and incarcerated while enquiries were made. A month later the news came through from Macquarie Harbour. Broughton and MacAvoy, it transpired, were among five men who bolted. Where were the other three?

Broughton and MacAvoy didn't know, they said, what had become of the others – William Coventry, Richard 'Up and Down Dick' Hutchinson and Patrick Feagan – and they stuck to that line until two days before they were to hang for absconding. Then they confessed. Their story, told in the *Hobart Town Courier* of 1831, follows much the same grisly path as Alexander Pearce's story. The five men overpowered their guard, took off into the wilderness and then, on the verge of starvation, plotted to kill and eat 'Up and Down Dick'. Broughton told the Reverend Mr Bedford, the gaol chaplain, that he killed Hutchinson with an axe and 'he was cut to pieces, and with the exception of the intestines, hands, feet and head, the body was carried with us. We lived some days upon his flesh; we ate it heartily. I do not know how many days it lasted.'

Then, like Pearce's party, they began the awful game of musical menu. 'We each of us feared that on going to sleep we would be dispatched by the others – we were always in a state of dreadful alarm.' They had every reason to fear each other. Patrick Feagan, an 18-year-old from Liverpool, 'a boy of the most depraved character', released the tension when he took the axe to Coventry, a 60-year-old man. But Feagan botched the job, and managed only to partially wound Coventry. While Coventry pleaded for his life, Feagan, for all his depravity, stood unable to finish the job. MacAvoy and Broughton had to step in. 'We lived upon his body for some days: we were not starving when we killed Coventry, we had only consumed the remains of Hutchinson the same day. We were not at all sparing of the food we obtained from the bodies of our companions; we eat it as if we had abundance.'

Feagan, of course, was next. Smaller and younger than the others, he was seated warming his toes in front of a fire when MacAvoy took to him. Broughton claims that he was shocked and affronted by this:

> I leaped up on my feet in a dreadful fright, and saw Feagan lying on his back with a terrible cut in his head, and blood pouring from it; MacAvoy was standing over him with the ax in his hand. I cried to MacAvoy, "You murdering rascal, you bloody thirsty wretch, what have you done?" He said, "This will save our lives." And then he struck him another blow on the head with the ax. Feagan then groaned and MacAvoy cut his throat with a razor, through the windpipe.

> Feagan's body we cut up into pieces and roasted it; we roasted all but the hands, feet and head.

Four days later they walked into the black line and captivity. They hanged on 5 August 1831, having consumed their way into a footnote in the story of Alexander 'Cannibal' Pearce.

Slaughter on Vinegar Hill

*I*n May 1798, 100 000 Irish rose in the revolt against the British Government. This was a time of a wave of revolutions sweeping across the European continent and the Irish rebels thought Britain could be next to fall. They were tragically wrong. In just three months, 30 000 were killed, most of them barbarically. Peasant farmers armed only with pikes and pitchforks went against the British cannons, women and children suffered atrocious reprisals and hundreds were saved from the gallows but imprisoned.

Among these political prisoners was 'General' Joseph Holt, who had won fame for his guerrilla war in County Wicklow, and who, in 1800, was among 235 political prisoners shipped in chains to Australia. The first of 50 000 Irish rebels who would be transported over the next four decades, they were, in the main, fine men, intelligent and passionately political. The uprising, however, had left hatred that persists to this day and distrust among the British and the Irish that was soon to be manifest in Botany Bay.

Governor King was rightly suspicious of these 'seditious people', as he described them in a worried report soon after he took over control of the colony. For the sake of safety, he wrote to the Secretary of State for the Colonies, he had sent some of the worst troublemakers to Norfolk Island and he had formed volunteer militia units in Sydney and Parramatta.

A few days later he learned – he believed – that his fears were founded. Evidence had been discovered, he wrote again, of a 'horrible plot' to overthrow the government, and acting on the advice of the Reverend Samuel Marsden, he established a court of enquiry. 'The Flogging Parson', as he was known, hated Catholics and was determined to find if there was any truth in the rumour that iron pikes had been made and hidden, ready for a Catholic uprising.

Joseph Holt was brought along to watch – and, no doubt, learn – as two men, Maurice Fitzgerald and young Paddy Galvin, were given a taste of the cat to loosen their tongues. [See What the Cat Brought Out, page 40]

A few months later, on 10 March 10 1801, King discovered a second plot 'more diabolic than the first'. Like the first, it led to 'severe corporal punishment' and the ringleaders were sent to Norfolk Island.

For a year or two things were quiet, thanks in large measure to James Dixon, a priest, who had been transported for life for his part in the 1798 rebellion. Dixon was popular with the Irish convicts and Governor King was so pleased that he disbanded the volunteer militia and allowed the Catholics in the colony to attend Sunday Mass. Until then they had to attend Anglican services, something they bitterly resented. Now, Catholics were able to meet with official sanction on Sundays and – inevitably, with the memories of '98 still alive – talk of an uprising grew among them.

It came on 4 March 1804, at the government farm at Castle Hill. The tolling of the 8.00 p.m. barrack bell was the spark for convicts to rush from their huts, overpower the guards and set a house alight, the signal for a general uprising in the area. The Castle Hill flogger was found trembling under a bed and taken outside for a taste of his own cat. Then, gathering recruits and arms as they went, the insurgents headed for the Hawkesbury, where they planned to march on and take Parramatta and then continue to Sydney, seize a ship and sail to freedom.

It was a fine plan but one without hope. Governor King reached Parramatta at 4.00 a.m. the following morning and declared martial law throughout the district. Major George Johnston, a man of action, arrived from Sydney with 56 men about an hour later. They were tired after their 15-mile march, but after only a brief rest Johnston had them on their feet and giving chase. At around 11 a.m., the troopers caught up with the rebels. They were on a hillside near Toongabbie that came to be known as Vinegar Hill, a reference to a famous slaughter of United Irish six years before.

Father Dixon was with Major Johnston and went forward to tell the convicts that King had declared martial law: they could be legally shot on sight. He advised them to surrender. They declined. Then Johnston and a trooper rode up and demanded to speak to their leader. Phillip Cunningham, a former soldier, and a man named William Johnson stepped out. What did the rebels want? he was asked. 'Death or liberty,' came the reply. 'I'll liberate you, you scoundrel,' Johnston barked back, clapped a pistol to his head and arrested him. Then, when the rebels continued to defy him, he ordered his troops to fire. Only a few shots were returned from the insurgents' ranks, and within minutes a dozen of them lay dead. The troops moved in with fixed bayonets. Another half dozen – among them Cunningham – were wounded, and 26 captured.

Although he was badly wounded, Cunningham, on Johnston's orders, was summarily hanged on a staircase, and two days later William Johnson and seven others swung. Nine were sentenced to floggings of between 200 and 500 lashes, and 34 were sent to the coalmines at Newcastle. Over the next few months King found footling reasons to order that several prominent Irishmen convicts should be banished to Norfolk Island, among them Joseph Holt, who survived it all to end his days a prominent and greatly respected citizen of Sydney.

Vinegar Hill, with Eureka Stockade half a century later, remains the only battle fought on Australian soil.

What the Cat Brought Out

*T*he Irish political prisoner, 'General' Joseph Holt, left this account of the Reverend Samuel Marsden's interrogation of two Irish Catholics. 'The Flogging Parson' hated Catholics and was determined to find out whether or not there was any truth in rumours going around that iron pikes had been made and hidden, ready for a Catholic uprising.

Holt was brought along to watch as two men, Maurice Fitzgerald and young Paddy Galvin, were given a taste of the cat to loosen their tongues. Holt's account strikingly illuminates the attitudes of the authorities and the men they were determined to crush.

'The place they flogged them,' Holt later wrote, 'their arms pulled around a large tree and their breast squeezed against the trunk so the men had no power to cringe ...There were two floggers, Richard Rice and John Johnson the Hangman from Sydney. Rice was a left-handed man and Johnson was right-handed, so they stood at each side, and I never saw two threshers in a barn move their strokes more handier than those two man-killers did.' Holt continued:

> The moment they began I turned my face towards the other side and one of the constables came and desired me to turn and look on. I put my right hand in my pocket and pulled out my pen-knife, and swore I would rip him from the navel to the chin. They all gathered round me and would have ill used me ... [but] they were obliged to walk off.
>
> I was to the leeward of the floggers. The flesh and skin blew in my face as it shook of the cats. Fitzgerald received his 300 lashes. Doctor Mason – I will never forget him – he used to go feel his pulse, and he smiled and said: "This man will tire you before he will fail –

go on!" During the time Fitzgerald was getting his punishment he never gave so much as a word – only one, and that was saying, "Don't strike me on the neck. Fight me fair."

When he was let loose, two of the constables went and took hold of him by the arms to keep him in the cart. I was standing by. He said to them, "Let me go." He struck both of them with his elbows in the pit of the stomach and knocked them both down, then stepped in the cart. I heard Doctor Mason say that man had strength enough to bear 200 more.

Next was tied up Paddy Galvin, a young boy of about 20 years of age. He was ordered to get 300 lashes. He got 100 on the back, and you could see his backbone between his shoulder blades, then the doctor ordered him to get another 100 on his bottom. He got it, and then his haunches were in such a jelly that the doctor ordered him to be flogged on the calves of his legs. He got 100 there and as much as a whimper he never gave. They asked him if he would tell where the pikes were hid. He said he did not know and would not tell. "You may as well hang me now," he said, "for you will never get any music from me."

They put him in the cart and sent him to the hospital.

The Designer Death Camp

*I*n 1774, when Captain James Cook discovered Norfolk Island, he described it as a 'Paradise'.

Half a century later it was hell on Earth. Today, Norfolk Island is a serene tourist attraction, and articles in the glossy magazines generally dwell on the Pitcairners – the descendents of Fletcher Christian and other *Bounty* mutineers who settled on Pitcairn Island and moved to Norfolk Island in the 1850s. But the rich soil of Norfolk Island holds a darker story. Botany Bay, Port Arthur, Port Macquarie, the dreadful Macquarie Harbour, Moreton Bay, Newcastle – all the penal colonies had horrific histories, but none could match that of Norfolk Island.

'Here was a place of perverted values where evil was reckoned to be good and where the unbelievable became the norm,' wrote the historian J. L. Robson.

To begin with, it was designed to imprison those who did not fear life in other penal colonies. From 1825, and for the next 30 years, the 2000 wretches confined on the island – bushrangers, cut throats, pirates, footpads, highwaymen, thieves, mutineers, political prisoners and old lags – men and women – all suffered in a surreal world of sadism. These hard nuts were to understand, the government said, that the island was ruled by the cat-o'-nine tails and that they should harbour no hope of ever returning to England.

'My object,' wrote Governor Darling, 'was to hold out that settlement as a place of extreme punishment short of Death.' And so it was. Worse, it was designed to make its victims long for death. The punishment for the most minor 'offence' – singing, for instance – was enough to break the toughest and most obdurate. You could be put in solitary confinement for 'Having some ravelling from a pair of trousers' – 14 days, or 'Being at the privy when the bell rang' – 14 days.

Torture was an art at Norfolk Island. Beatings were everyday matters and the walls and floors of cells were splattered with blood. 'A jet of blood from a prisoner's head reached, in one instance, as I recollect, as high on the wall as I could reach with my extended arms. The man had been struck by the bludgeon of one of the wardsmen,' wrote the chaplain. There were other forms of torture as well, sickeningly sadistic. But flogging was at the heart of the darkness on Norfolk Island. 'The steady rhythm of torment,' Clive James wrote in *Snake Charmer in Texas*. Men and women were flogged relentlessly. Some men so often that their spines were bared. A Catholic bishop who visited told of 'the state of the yard, from the blood running down men's backs, mingled with the water used when washing them when taken down from the triangle – the degrading scene of a large number of men ... waiting their turn to be tortured, and the more humiliating spectacle presented by those who had undergone the scourging ...'

How could men bear it? During the course of the rule of a succession of tyrannical commandants, it was not uncommon for convicts to arrange for one to kill the other so that both the dead man and his murderer could be released from their living hell and try their luck in the afterlife. There are a number of such instances, but few as pathetic as the fate of 16 men convicted of mutiny. In January 1834, they and others planned, at the dawn muster, to rush the guards, capture the commandant and the 18-pound cannon, hang all the informers, constables and soldiers who would not join them and seize the next ship that hove to. Then they would skin the commandant by his own cat and hang him for three days, distribute the convict women and the gaolers' wives, and sail for New Caledonia.

It was an audacious plan and it almost succeeded. On 15 January, as a downpour of rain swept the settlement, a pack of convicts in the hospital attacked their guards, struck off their irons, armed themselves and waited for soldiers returning from the road gang. Thirty-eight of them crouched in the doorway of the hospital and waited for the road gang to return, 30 men escorted by a dozen soldiers. At a signal, the road gang turned on their guards and the hospital convicts rushed out. In the hand-to-hand fighting the guards began shooting and their shots alerted the barracks.

Meanwhile, convicts at another camp had been alerted by a convict who ran to them crying, 'Turn out my lads – now is the time for liberty!' But, by now, the Redcoats had formed ranks and sent a volley into their midst. Outside the hospital, Captain Foster Fyans, the Acting-Commandant, had rallied soldiers from the 4th Regiment. Fyans gave the order, 'Fire!', and 15 rebels fell. The others ran for it, into the sugar cane. The troopers followed. 'The men were very keen after these ruffians,' Foster Fyans, in his autobiography can almost be heard chuckling. 'It was really game and sport to these soldiers ...Come on to out, my Honey – with a prick of the Bayonet through both thighs or a little above.'

It was all over. Five rebels were left dead and about 50 wounded. Two soldiers, mistakenly shot by their fellows at a night search the following day, died. The youngest ringleader, Dominick McCoy, bayoneted repeatedly, lay dying. He was still alive, however, when he was taken to hospital – Captain Fyans ordered him to be chained and dragged there across 200 metres of stone.

The retribution was appalling. At the best of times Fyans was a monster. 'Daily he would have a ward at a time paraded before him in the barrack yard with the triangles rigged and some six or seven floggers with a bag full of "cats" attending him, when without rhyme or reason he would call anyone that his eyes met out and give him a hundred," one surviving Norfolk Island convict wrote. (He survived, although he played a ringleader's part in the mutiny, because he was an informer.)

This time Fyans's floggings literally wore out the cats and the prisoners were chained in irons triple the usual weight. Judge William

Burton who came to the island in June, was horrified and moved by the sight of the prisoners – wizened, grey, shuffling, aged far beyond their years – and sentenced 13 to death. Yet he had originally sentenced 29 to the gallows and changed his mind when one of the men begged, not for mercy, but for a last chance to see a priest. 'To appeals like these the human heart could not be insensible,' the judge wrote.

Yet those the judge spared had no cause to thank him. One of the 13 doomed men said: 'Sentence has been passed upon us before, and we thought we should have been executed, and prepared to die, and wish we had been executed then. It was no mercy to send us to this place. I do not want to be spared on condition of remaining here; life is not worth having on such terms.' Three months later the Catholic priest, Father Ullathorne, came to comfort the men in their last week. His memoirs tell, yet again, of how the convicts saw death as a blessed release:

>...The turnkey unlocked the door and said, "Stand aside, Sir." Then came forth a yellow exhalation, the produce of the bodies of the men confined therein ... I entered and found five men chained to a traversing-bar. I spoke to them from my heart, and after preparing them and obtaining their names I announced to them who we reprieved from death and which of them were to die after five days had passed. I thus went from cell to cell until I had seen them all. It is a literal fact that each man who heard his reprieve wept bitterly, and that each man who heard of his condemnation to death went down on his knees with dry eyes and thanked God.

When the day came, the first seven, each dressed in white, were led to the gallows while every convict on the island looked on. The Commandant had told them: 'If any of you attempt to move or show any signs of resistance the officer in the stockade has my positive order to open fire at once.' The seven were composed and prayed quietly, prayers they had learned from Father Ullathorne in their last week. The hangman, who had been brought from the mainland, recognised one of the seven. 'Why, Jack, is that you?'

Jack turned and said: 'Why, Bill!'

'Well, old friend,' said the executioner, 'it can't be helped,' and pulled the lever. The seven dropped.

The next day the awful scene was repeated with the other six.

There was to be one more major mutiny, on 1 July 1846, over – ostensibly – the deprivation of cooking pots and kettles. Four guards were slaughtered before it was put down. Fourteen men were charged and 12 condemned to the noose. Another five were hanged in the following days. Drastic measures, clearly, needed to be taken and a new superintendent and commander of Norfolk Island was appointed – the most feared, the most hated and the most contemptible man in Australia's history – John Giles Price.

The Most Loathsome Man in Our History

John Giles Price was asking for it and he got in spades. And sledgehammers and crowbars and chains and boots and rocks – anything that came to hand and that could rip and crush and bludgeon him into a bloody pulp.

It was not what he wanted, but Price was certainly asking for it, and had been ever since his arrival, in 1846, as the Commandant of Norfolk Island.

John Giles Price was the very model of countless monsters of fiction and film who followed him: the galley slave driver; the Boss man of the Deep South chain gangs; the heartless warders in a hundred movies and more. And, as Commandant Frere, he himself was thinly disguised in Marcus Clarke's *For the Term of His Natural Life*. One of 14 children of a penniless Cornish baronet, Price even looked the part of the callous prison warder. Central casting could hardly do better.

Price was 53 at the time of his arrival on Norfolk Island. The father of five lived with his wife and children on the hell island. He could be charming and some said he was brave. He would often go unescorted into the midst of an angry crowd of 500 convicts, intimidating them by sheer will. Once, when a lag snatched one of his pistols, Price didn't blink. He looked the man down, sneered at him, called him a cowardly dog, and the man fell to his knees, offering Price the pistol. He gloried in his power, and his bravery was more a blend of bravado, foolhardiness and a maniacal contempt and hatred of convicts. But Price could show fear. When he came under the pressure of an official report highly critical of him, he burst into tears and begged its author, Bishop Willson, to

47

suppress it. He was frightened that he might be sacked from the job he so much enjoyed.

Price introduced himself to the convicts on Norfolk Island with great relish: 'You know me, don't you? I am come here to rule, and by God I'll do so and tame or kill you. I know you are cowardly dogs, and I'll make you worry and eat one another.' In his claim that 'You know me...I know you,' Price may have been speaking the literal truth. In later years convicts claimed that somehow Price had once been on the 'inside' – he knew the language of the underworld and he knew how the criminal mind worked. They believed that he frequently visited criminal dens in Hobart Town, where he had been the Police Magistrate, mingling as if he were himself a criminal.

In his biography of this mysterious and contradictory man, John Barry wrote:

> He was strangely fascinated by their viciousness and attracted by the evil in them even as he was repelled by it. It was a psycho-pathological love-hate relationship. He regarded them as less than human, with no claim to justice in a civilised sense, but his vanity nevertheless demanded that they should move in a submissive terror of him. At the same time a peculiar warped strain in his nature made it necessary for him to have their reluctant regard and grudging respect as a "fly" man ... one who but for the accident of circumstances might have been a king among them.

In 1849, the former chaplain on the island, whom Price had lobbied to be relieved, wrote a blood-curdling account of life under the Commandant. The Reverend Thomas Rogers, Chaplain of Norfolk Island during Major Childs's time and part of John Price's rule, was the man on whom Marcus Clarke based his character, Reverend North, in *For the Term of His Natural Life*. Rogers, who died aged 99 in Melbourne in 1901, wrote a damning indictment of Price. In his book *Correspondence*, published in 1849, he talked of 'the ground on which the men stood at the triangles ... saturated with human gore, as if a bucket of blood had been spilled on it covering a space three feet in diameter and running out in various directions in little streams of two or three feet long. I have seen this.'

Rogers also wrote:

> A man named Dytton was chained down to the floor of the hospital and gagged for getting up to the window in the hospital cell for air. He had been ill at the hospital for six or seven weeks, has never been well since a beating he received whilst in the chain gang.
>
> He had abused a constable for removing pegs on which hung his clothes and rations, so was gagged, taken to the New gaol, chained down and dreadfully beaten by several constables. He lay in a puddle of blood. Next day a constable came in and jumped on his chest.

Rogers told the heart-rending story of Lloyd, a man of 27 who was just a boy when he was transported. Sentenced by Price to nine months' extension in gaol, he tried to hang himself in his cell but was discovered while still alive and brought before Price. Price ordered an immediate 50 lashes, but the surgeon intervened and said he believed it might kill Lloyd. That would not do: Price could not allow him to escape that easily. He ordered Lloyd to be strapped down and he was kept in that position for six weeks. Rogers wrote:

> The chaplain who visited him told me that he looked more like a pale distended corpse than a human being, and his voice was so weak it could hardly be heard.
>
> One day the chaplain, seeing his lips moving, leaned down to put his ear to the man's mouth, and at length distinguished the words "Loose me – loose me."
>
> The chaplain replied, "No Lloyd, I dare not do that." A deep sigh followed the refusal, and the tears trickled down the culprit's emaciated face.

And, finally, an incident that was of no great moment in Price's life but demonstrates his supreme inhumanity:

> A man whose age prevented his employment at heavier occupation than that of a gatekeeper was one day eating his dinner; he had a mouthful of salt beef and maize left. A fellow prisoner happened at that moment to pass by, and was asked if he would have the morsel of bread and meat, it was instantly accepted.
>
> While he was eating, a constable who had been watching the giving rushed up and took the two men into custody. Mr Price sentenced them, the one for giving, the other for eating the morsel of food, to a month's detention on the Island, which detention might prolong their sentence for several months.

Price's cruel punishment – in effect also extending the sentence of the old lag who had offered another a morsel of food – had an ironic, fatal echo a few years later. In 1853, after more than six years of unrelenting cruelty, Price left Norfolk Island and returned to Tasmania to retirement on a farm. But, the following year, he was invited to be Inspector-General of penal establishments in Victoria, and he was pleased to have the whip hand once again. He should have stayed on the farm. On 26 March 1857, he was at the quarry at Williamstown where convicts from the five prison hulks were moored nearby.

The hulks – where Ned Kelly was later to spend a year – were, Robert Hughes says in *The Fatal Shore*, 'a new byword for ferocity. The worst of Norfolk island had come to the mainland: the tube gagging and spread-eagling, the bludgeon handle jammed in the mouth in tobacco searches, the rotten victuals, the loading with irons, the beatings, ringbolts and buckets of sea water. Before long, a warship had to take up station next to the hulks, its guns double-shotted so that, if the prisoners motioned and the guards had to flee, it could sink the hulk and send its ironed men to the bottom.'

The working parties in the quarry must have been relieved to be given work out in the open, away from the misery of the rotting pensioned-off war ships, a feeling that would have vanished once the word spread that John Price was coming. Price strode into their midst with his usual arrogance. When a convict named Dan Kelly asked him if his recent three-day solitary sentence would affect his imminent ticket-of-leave to freedom, Price responded exactly as you would expect. Like the old lag who had offered food to a fellow convict, Kelly's sentence certainly would postpone his day of freedom.

It was too much for Kelly. 'You bloody tyrant, your race will soon be run!' he shouted. And he was right. As convicts milled about him, and one threw a clod of earth, Price did run. He was almost through them when he stumbled and they got to him. He lingered, unconscious, and died a day later. John Giles Price was, Robert Hughes said, 'one of the durable ogres of the Antipodean imagination for more than a century.'

The Death of the Devil

*T*he convict keeper John Giles Price was himself captured and remains for all to see in a vivid account written by a notorious prisoner, Henry Beresford Garrett. Garrett was transported to Norfolk Island for ten years for burglary and, on his release, with three others, held up the Bank of Victoria in gold rush Ballarat in 1854. The gang escaped with 14 300 pounds and 250 ounces of gold.

Garrett was arrested in London and sentenced to ten years hard labour in the hulks. Mr Justice Barry consoled Garrett, who had protested his innocence: 'If you are really innocent, the thought that you are so will be some consolation to you during the term of your punishment.' (Just four months later and not far away, Ned Kelly was born. He, too, would be sent to the hell-hulks at Williamstown, and he, too, would face the supercilious and merciless Mr Justice Barry.)

Garrett wrote of Price in his last years. In an unpublished manuscript, 'The Demon', he paints a memorable portrait of the monster he called John.

> John's features were not ill-formed. They were as far from ugly as beautiful. They were not what is called strongly marked, yet to those about him they had a most repellent effect. His cold grey eyes had a ferocious glitter. On one of them he wore a glass, not from any defect of vision, but from what he in another would have termed flashness. It became him about as much as a frilled shirt would have a sweep as his working dress.

> To the disposition of a Nero he joined the frame of a Hercules. Over six feet in height, he had a round bullet head of the true Legree type, a light complexion and hair, the last almost sandy and slightly inclined to curl, a rather large but well-shaped mouth, a thick bull

neck, square massive shoulders, no waist but ribbed down to the hips like an Atlas, legs strong and slightly bowed, his whole frame as indicative of immense strength as his face was of ferocity. How his presence would affect others unacquainted with his name and deed I know not, but to all who knew him it was most unpleasant. Prisoners, warders and his own children felt and spoke of him alike, and from prisoner servants we learnt that his wife feared him worst of all. The same sternness ruled the home as the barracks.

When Price arrived on Norfolk Island, he mustered the prisoners. Garrett was among them, and his description of that defining moment shows us the man in all his naked fear and hatred of humanity:

The yell of defiance from 500 throats rather startled him. He turned tail. It may have been either fear or anger. He stepped back a couple of paces, looked round at his attendants and up at the soldiers in the gallery and nodded. The soldiers brought their rifles to the ready and the snick of the locks were audible. Every man around him drew his cutlass and pistol and things began to look ugly.

Let me describe him as he then stood. He was dressed something after the style of a flash gentleman. On his round bullet head a small straw hat was jauntily stuck, the broad blue ribbon of which reached down between his shoulders, a glass stuck in one eye, a black silk kerchief tied sailor fashion, round his bullneck, no vest but a bobtail or oxonian coat, or something like a cross between this and a stableman's jacket seemed to be bursting over his shoulders. A pair of rather tight pants completed his costume, except for a leather belt, six inches broad, buckled round the loins. In the belt two pepperbox revolvers were conspicuously stuck.

The yells subsided and, assured by the presence of the soldiers and the guard, he struck an attitude by placing his arms akimbo, and again spoke.

"You know me, don't you? I am come here to rule, and by God I'll do so and tame or kill you. I know you mean cowardly dogs, and I'll make you worry and eat each other." What else he would have said was lost in another burst of yells ...

Price quickly instituted an efficient system of floggings for the least offence.

> Under John flogging became an art. Men were trained to it as to a trade. Sheets of bark were stretched on the triangles and the novices made to practice on them. It became a task, too, as rigidly enforced as the task of field labour, and woe to the flogger whose victim's back did not show the desired amount of mutilation. He was sure of the same number of lashes as the other had received, laid on, too, by the severest of floggers.

> ... Men's backs, ragged and bruised from the lash, were baked in the sun like crackling pork. They swarmed with flies and maggots, with not a drop of water to moisten them. They used to make poultices of lemon and lime pulp, and where these could not be got they poured their urine on to each other. Each was like a naked fire to their backs. Men ill with dysentery, their trousers wet with discharge and smothered with flies and maggots, and weak from disease, starvation and punishment, staggered to and from labour, until, no longer able to do so, they laid down and died, or committed suicide. The stench of their festering backs in those packed dormitories and their groans were horribly offence to smell and pitiable to hear.

And here is Garrett on the hulks – and John Giles Price's inevitable murder:

> At this time there was in full play that atrocious hulk system which brought disgrace to the Government, misery to thousands and death to himself [Price]. Five of these swung at their moorings in Hobson's Bay and to these dens were sent all men sentenced to more than five years.

As all who have seen them might know and as all who have worn them can testify a pair or irons riveted round the ankles and worn day and night for years is no small punishment, and intended as a secondary one only to be inflicted by a Magistrate for some grave offence, yet every man sent to those hulks was placed in irons weighing from 14 to 40 lb.

This could not be for safety for aboard or in the quarries the men were guarded by warders armed with double-barrelled rifles and had there been none of these clean-shaven faces and close-cropped heads and the branded prison dress would have made escape all but impossible, and though there could be shown a necessity for ironing those at work, there could be none for ever fettering those who never quitted the hulks. It was sheer love of cruelty which did this.

On the breaking up of these floating hulks on John's death many had the opportunity of seeing what they were like. One enterprising fellow bought one and exhibited it at a shilling a head, but for the information of those who did not see I may describe it. There were 42 separate cells on each of the two decks. The floor of the lower one being 5 ft. below the water, the only light and ventilation to which was through a hole of 4 in. by 8 in. covered with perforated iron and within 2 ft. of the water.

Through this in rough weather the water used to wash, and make sleeping on the floor impossible. To sit on the night tub was the only remedy.

The bedding was one small blanket or rug, never washed, aired or changed till worn out, and so loathsome from dirt and vermin.

Along the seawalls of the cells about 3 ft. from the floor was a row of massive ringbolts. To these men were handcuffed with their hands behind their backs for punishment. To sit or lie down was impossible, the crime which caused this being a word or reply to some taunt or threat, other crimes being all but impossible. The time of punishment varied from one day to a week and to reply while on this ringbolt was to ensure bludgeoning and gagging often into insensibility and beyond it.

The bludgeoning they called warming you and then the cooling down came in the shape of sundry buckets of cold sea water to wash the blood off you, leaving you hanging on the ringbolt to dry.

While thus suspended your food, a pound of bread, would be flung in on the floor among the salt water, urine, blood and excrement. To reach it except with your foot was impossible and any entreaty to have it held while you gnawed it was jeered at. If gagged they would not even remove it, but ten minutes after flinging the bread in would fling it out again, saying, "You haven't eaten it and don't want it." A word of expostulation ensured the warming and etceteras. Often for a week, night and day, men have been thus suspended and treated. Complaints but continued it.

One fellow did complain to John who said: "Ah, you don't like it. Can't meet it. You're not half a pebble. Keep him on it."

From complaining the man protested, was bludgeoned and gagged. The men heard the blows and shouts, and yelled their detestation.

"Just go round," he said, "and mark the doors of the most noisy of those fellows, and when we have done with this one we'll have this one out and a dozen or more one by one served the same way." Still the rest yelled cursed and groaned.

As at Norfolk I kept myself still but it did not save me from the bludgeoning and the ringbolt. He shouted out that he sentenced the whole ship to a month's bread and water and no beds and they yelled louder than before and at the end of the month on his next visit they greeted him with a storm of yells. All that month at certain hours the men kept up these yells, night and day at intervals they burst out. The river and bay steamers used to pass regularly by. Ever as they did so a chorus of yells would greet them with cries of "Murder", "Starvation" etc.

They covered up our ventilation holes to stop the sound. Still the cries arose and some who had heard them wrote to the Press, saying something wrong must be going on and urging visitations and inquiries.

John replied that the prisoners were mutinous and dangerous and that the guards feared an outbreak and massacre, and the Government moored the old guard ship, Sir Harry Smith, opposite, loaded and double-shotted the guns with orders to sink us if the officers gave the signal by flight.

It was very cheerful to starve and see the guns looking at you which any moment a treacherous and cowardly flight might open upon and sink us. We fully expected that this would have been done and learnt that fear of trusting each other alone prevented it.

And here is how Garrett – from a distance – saw Price's murder. His account varies from those who were closer to the incident. Garrett claims that the prisoners plotted to kill Price and that the uprising was not spontaneous. But Garrett's claim that the prisoners intended to lure Price to his death was supported by the *Argus* newspaper on the Tuesday after his death. It reported that the murder was 'premeditated and planned' and that Price was to be hanged from cross bars outside a tent used by the convicts from the hulk Success – Garrett's hulk.

Both gangs knew he [Price] had been sent for and were on the watch for his appearance. His fate had already been decided. Several of the men knew what awaited them aboard – the ringbolt, gag and bludgeon and flung back into the President during his pleasure. Death was preferable. They had nothing but life to lose, but he had much to lose. Death to them was an escape from misery. To him it was the loss of everything that makes life desirable. His death was no impulsive act but the calculation and determination of hours of cool thought. Only the manner of it was different to what they meant it should be.

In each quarry was a large tent formed of the sails and spars of the dismantled hulks and over the yard forming the ridge pole his executioners had passed a well-greased rope with a noose. He should die the death of a dog or of capitally sentenced criminals. He was to be inveigled or dragged in the tent and hung.

What must have been the misery these men suffered and anticipated to make them thus coolly throw their lives away? Let all ask themselves what amount would induce them to do a similar act.

The whole quarry of 100 men knew what was going to be done, saw the rope and knew its purpose. All were not to take a part but all approved. But out of that 100 men surely there is one traitor who for a hope of a pardon will warn and save him? Not one. All had such a thorough hatred that his death was preferable to a pardon. Not one would whisper to the officers the warning which would have saved. Perhaps one reason for this was his deceit to those who had served him and been cheated again and again of a promised reward. Nothing is more certain than that had he had the goodwill or confidence of one man he must have been warned.

About two o'clock he was seen coming up the raised tramway leading from the quarry to the jetty. With him were three or four hulk officers. The men were gathered in a crowd near the tent. All work in our gang was immediately suspended, the men mounting the quarry bank and walls so as to have a view of the others.

I and four others were employed dragging stones from the top of the quarry to the top of the embankment midway between the two quarries and commanding a good view of both.

On descending into the quarry he ordered the men to fall in. They refused and surrounded him, crying "To the tent, to the tent", and fifty hands were raised aloft with the day's allowance of offensive bread, the owners shouting "Look at this", and some who could not get near flung them at him.

"To the tent, to the tent," cried others and began to hustle him towards it, but as if smelling danger there, or he may have got a glimpse of the rope and guessed its purpose, he began to struggle and elbow his way from it.

He is surrounded by seven officers who are surrounded by 100 men, twelve to one, fearful odds, but many men were unequally matched have fought their way to safety, and the odds are not so great as appears. Not more than 20 of the 100 will do aught but shout and so the odds are reduced to 2½ to 1, and armed as some of them were with pistols and all with life preservers, well fed, with the law on their side the 8 men ought to be able to resist the 12 unarmed men, fettered and weak from starvation.

As soon as he felt himself being borne towards the tent he began with his immense muscular strength to elbow and push him way from it and he finally succeeded in clearing the surging mass, flinging them aside as a vessel dashes aside the water from her bows.

He rushes up the embankment not 40 yards from where my cart party are looking on. He is alone. His seven dastardly officers have already turned tail and fled. After him rush about a dozen infuriated men who have snatched up shovels, picks, hammers and stones.

On gaining the top of the embankment he paused a moment to look where he should rung. He had a wild frightened look. How one would like to know his thoughts and feelings at that moment? Men drowning are said to have a lightning-like view of their past lives. Had he aught of this? Did he then think of one of his many crimes and which? Did he feel the presentiment he had uttered not three hours previously? One thing at least he saw – that like a nobler man, all his friends and servants had deserted at the first sniff of danger.

Had he run into our gang he might have escaped, but seeing them all looking on and my party direct in the way he may have thought we were only waiting to bar his passage.

Some of his pursuers have cut off his retreat down the tramway.

The rest are mounting close to him and he dashes down the other side towards the bay. He has hardly reached the bottom when a stone flung from the top strikes him between the shoulders and knocks him on his face in a shallow water hole. He never rises again. Before he can do so his enemies are upon him and we lose sight of him. All we can see is a confused scramble, blows of shovels, pick handles and hammers and it put one in mind of the hounds worrying a fox.

Yes, the strongman is down in the crush of his self-made foes who will show him the same mercy he showed them. He had no time to ask for other mercy. Whether he would have done so I have often wondered but what no plea on his part could have done (saved him) a little effort on the part of his seven cowardly officers must.

I have often heard John spoken of as brave and fearless. He may have been so but I never knew one act of his life which would have entitled him to be thought so. To bully and torture the defenseless is generally held a trait of cowardice as well as cruelty. If, as is said, the brave are ever humane, and again, if as is said, cowards are cruel, then judging him by his acts he has written his own epitaph by his own acts.

When backed by armed force as he was it needs not a brave man to bully, strike and swagger. The veriest coward that crawls can and none but such do it.

If his life was cowardly his death was still more so. A brave man would have died with his face to his foes and fighting. He fled from them and fell as a fool and coward falls.

3 | The Best of a Bad Bunch

The Last Dance of Our First Australian Idol

*M*atthew Brady, our first popular idol, took his final bow on a grim stage on 1 May 1826. Brave, chivalrous and handsome, gallant to the ladies and something of a blowhard, but with a charm that eluded only the authorities, he was, said a contemporary, 'a born leader of men and a conqueror of women'. Contemporary images of him show a young, amiable version of the Russell Crowe or cricket captain type: 'a robust young man, muscular and well made, with an innocent face with bright eyes and a good wide forehead,' wrote a man who played a role in rounding up the Brady gang. Matthew Brady cost the lives of men on both sides of the law, but he broke the hearts of many more women.

When his 22-month reign as the monarch of the wilds came to its inevitable end on that May day, Brady danced his last on the gallows at Hobart Town while below him a crush of ladies sobbed inconsolably. The manner of his going was calculated to turn on the waterworks. Right to the end Brady had a style and a grace that found a later echo in Ben Hall and Ned Kelly, and because of it all three, rightly or wrongly, are remembered today in a romantic hue while their pursuers and persecutors are misty, murky figures, long forgotten.

There are resonances of Butch Cassidy in Matthew Brady's tale. Like the American outlaw, Brady had his own 'Hole in the Wall', a hide-out from which he would ride out with his gang, attack a settlement or a stagecoach, and then vanish into the craggy peaks of Tasmania's Great Western Tiers. Like Butch he had a sense of humour. And, like the movie version of Butch Cassidy's end, he was relentlessly pursued until finally he was trapped and resigned himself to his fate.

Matthew Brady was born in Manchester, England, to poor Irish parents and sentenced at the Quarter Sessions at Salford on 18 April 1820, to transportation for seven years for stealing what we might accidentally leave at the supermarket and not bother to go back for: a grocery basket of bacon, butter and rice. In December that year, he was assigned to work for a Hobart Town free settler and made several attempts to escape what was virtual slavery. Each time he was caught and given a taste of the cat. In all he was whipped 350 times in three years, and he determined that there would be no more. In 1823, Brady stowed away on a ship to England, but he was discovered and delivered instead to Macquarie Harbour, the dreaded penitentiary for convicts who committed crimes while still under sentence.

Here, at Macquarie Harbour, the slightest misdemeanour brought 100 lashes, and Brady could see himself very quickly exceeding the 350 he had accumulated in Hobart Town. Escape from Macquarie Harbour was simple: you just stepped into the bush wilderness where you could quickly disappear. The problem was that you then either starved to death, or were speared by Aborigines. Then 'Cannibal' Pearce and the six men he devoured showed that it was possible to escape and cross the endless mountain ranges to the other side of Van Diemen's Land where lay Hobart Town and some hope of escape to the mainland and freedom.

On 9 June 1824, 11 days before 'Cannibal' Pearce was sentenced to death, Brady and 13 others at work on a vegetable patch away from the island settlement overpowered their guard. The commandant, who had been inspecting the garden with the surgeon, managed to jump into a boat and escape, but the convicts held the surgeon and called for him to be flogged, as they customarily were while he looked on. Typically, Brady stopped them. He was not bloodthirsty, and the surgeon had once showed kindness to him. In any case there was not time to lose. The 14 scrambled into a whale boat, crossed the sandbar at Hell's Gate under fire and, pursued by a boatload of redcoats, headed into the open sea and the blackness of the night.

The bolters, led by James Crawford, a former Royal Navy navigator, steered for Derwent 320 kilometres away and, ten days later, came ashore. At once they robbed lone travellers on the road, took their guns and provisions and struck inland. There, among the peaks, the 14 holed up in the wild mountains above Arthur's Lake, a virtually impregnable hide-out – still known today as Brady's Lookout – from which they would periodically venture to rob and plunder.

The gang was led at first by James Crawford, but when a hold-up went wrong and Crawford was shot, captured and promptly hanged, Brady took charge. A born leader, he was audacious and clever and the gang was quickly celebrated as Brady's Bunch. In March 1825, Brady's boldness almost led to his end. Visiting a receiver of stolen property, Thomas Kenton, he found instead that the door was flung open by two redcoats pointing muskets in his face. Brady was battered with a musket butt and bound, and while Kenton, who had betrayed Brady, kept watch on him, they went for reinforcements.

When the redcoats had gone, Brady asked Kenton for water. There was none in the small hut. Possibly to salve his conscience, Kenton took a bucket and went to a nearby creek. He had no sooner left the room than Brady dashed to the fire, plunged his bound hands into it and, biting back the agonising pain, kept them there until he could snap the ropes. Kenton returned to find Brady armed with his gun.

Brady let him live. He was famous for deploring murder. But, a year later, he and Kenton met again, this time in the Cocked Hat Inn on the Launceston-Hobart Road. Kenton, Brady heard, had been claiming that Brady had shot two troopers in cold blood. When Brady burst in on him, Kenton was upstairs in bed. Kenton, knowing Brady's reputation, sneered at the bushranger, told him he would end on the gallows and announced he was walking away. As he went for the door, Brady shot him dead. It is believed to be the only deliberate murder by Brady.

Governor George Arthur had long issued a proclamation declaring Brady an outlaw and calling 'in the most earnest manner' for all citizens and their convict servants to shoot him and his gang on sight or to assist the Crown to bring him to justice. Now the appeal was bolstered by the offer of a reward of 100 guineas on the head of Matthew Brady. Brady countered with his own reward poster, pinned to the door of the Royal Oak Inn at Cross Marsh a week later:

Mountain Home. April 25th.

It has caused Matthew Brady much concern that such a person as Sir George Arthur is a large. Twenty gallons of rum will be given to any person that will deliver his person to me.

Brady's sense of humour never deserted him – but sometimes it could go awry. He burned wheat stacks and barns and houses of people he disliked and sent them prior notice. Once he ordered an assigned servant to leave his master's house and join the gang. The man refused, and Brady went to the sideboard, filled a wine glass with rum and told the man to drink it. The man, a teetotaller, said he never took strong liquor. 'Well, you do now,' Brady laughed, cocking his gun and putting it at the man's temple. The servant drank it, staggered from the house and was found dying, calling for water, the next morning.

Brady could also fly into a rage at brutality. He loathed the cannibal child killer, Mark Jeffries, and had to be restrained from trying to free Jeffries from gaol so that he could string him up. When McCabe, his friend and partner, threatened to rape a woman, Brady shot him through the hand, flogged him and expelled him from the gang of 30. McCabe was run down and captured, and, remorseful, Brady made a desperate attempt to free him. He failed, but McCabe went to the gallows refusing to disclose the secret of Brady's hide-out in the mountains.

Brady and his boys were dogged for almost their entire time at large by the formidable Lieutenant William Gunn. An ex-officer and farmer, Gunn was a gigantic man, fearless and a fine bushman. The gang had held up Gunn's servant not long after they escaped, and Gunn had gone after them, never far behind until finally he and his men fell on them, forcing Brady and some of his gang to flee and capturing five who were duly hanged.

Lieutenant Gunn's farm was near Sorell, a pretty little town that Brady attacked late one night 14 months later. The gang overpowered the gaol guards, set the prisoners free and locked them up with the citizens. Brady was in high spirits. The day before he had held up a nearby homestead, ordered dinner to be cooked and served by the servants and discussed politics with his hapless hosts, the Bethunes, before taking their cash, jewellery and valuables. He was feeling impregnable, and on an apparent impulse, he had decided to visit Sorrel.

Brady's plan worked perfectly ... almost. In the careless way of free spirits, Brady was not given to great attention to detail, and while he held court Mr Laing, the head gaoler, escaped, went over a wall, mounted a horse and rode for Lieutenant Gunn. Gunn had suspected that Brady was in the district and, with his men, had spent the day in driving rain searching for the Brady boys. Now, with Dr Garrett, a magistrate, and his men, he rode to the little town to surprise the boys. The surprise, however, was short lived. The foolish Garrett rushed into the gaol, gun in hand, and was made prisoner, joining the troopers in the cells. Gunn, meanwhile, was stealthily making his way to the cells when two of the gang sprang from behind trees. In the shoot-out Gunn was wounded. Shot in the arm – it was later crudely amputated – the giant kept on coming, blood gushing from his wound. Gunn's men were moving, too, and it was too hot for Brady. The bushrangers scattered, leaving a calling card outside the gaol – a trooper's shako cap atop a log of wood.

It was a close call, and although Brady defied all Governor Arthur's attempts to capture him for the next year, one by one Brady's boys were picked off, killed or captured. He had to get off the island.

Inevitably, Governor Arthur's mounting reward offers – 300 guineas or 300 acres of land to the settler who brought in Brady or his head or, for convicts, a pardon and free passage to England – proved irresistible to men who once would have given Matt Brady food and shelter.

In December 1825, Brady tried to escape from the island. He planned to seize the ship *Glory* at anchor in the Tamar, but foul weather and the gang's reluctance to go with him forced Brady to retreat. His time was running out, he knew, but his magnificent bravado had not deserted him. Now he drew up an ultimatum to Governor Arthur demanding safe conduct out of the colony. If the Governor declined, Brady promised to capture one of the most prominent settlers, Richard Dry.

Governor Arthur dismissed the ultimatum as just another of Brady's impudent sallies. But Brady was true to his word, and when the day of the ultimatum had passed, he and his gang made their way to the settler's house, held up the guards and took Dry, his family and guests, prisoner. Just as Ned Kelly was to do, Brady made his hostages feel welcome in their own homes. He charmed the women, dancing with them and singing ballads at the piano. In the midst of this jollity, a servant slipped away and went for help. Colonel Balfour and his troops surrounded the house, and Brady and his men had to shoot their way out. Brady rode off with his few remaining gang members, wearing Balfour's hat, shot from his head in the opening exchange of gunfire. But Brady, too, was shot. A ball had gone into his calf and out the back of his thigh.

The colony was in ferment, and the cry went up for the giant, Lieutenant Gunn, to track down Brady once again. Instead, Brady was to fall by treachery from within. Governor Arthur had planted a convict named Cohen into the gang. Cohen's escape, with broken iron fetters on his legs, had been connived so that he was found by the Brady boys and invited to join the gang. With them, he distinguished himself in a number of raids and skirmishes with the troops and won Brady's confidence. Finally, however, Cohen betrayed the gang's hiding place to Lieutenant Williams of the 40th Regiment.

About 60 men of the 40th closed with the gang and several were killed on both sides. Brady escaped, but his wound hampered him and he left a trail easily followed by a skilled Aboriginal and the bounty hunter, John Batman. Batman, a farmer turned man-hunter – later to be the man who 'founded' Melbourne – had already captured 'the Monster' Jeffries, and now he followed his wounded, prize prey 4000 feet up the Tiers. He found Brady at first light, hobbling through the trees on a makeshift crutch.

Batman called on Brady to surrender. Brady spun round, cocked his gun and called out, 'Are you an officer?'

'I'm not a soldier,' said Batman. 'I'm John Batman and if you raise that gun I'll shoot. There's no chance for you.'

'You're right,' Brady said. 'My time's come. You're a brave man and I yield, but I'd never give in to a soldier.'

On 17 March 1826, draped in chains, Brady was taken to Hobart along with – to his disgust – Jeffries. Brady refused to sit on the same side of the cart as 'the Monster'. Seven weeks later, Brady was to hang alongside Jeffries and eight others, all bushrangers.

Brady was given his Last Communion and mounted the steps of the gallows. His cell had been filled with flowers and fruit and letters from well-wishers, and now the colony had come out to see him off. Women sobbed and threw nosegays, and men shouted encouragement to him. Matt Brady bowed to the crowd, straightened and dropped into history. He died, wrote a witness, 'more like a patient martyr than a felon'.

He Died with His Boots On, and a Portrait of Polly

*B*illy the Kid, Jesse James, Wyatt Earp, Doc Holliday, Butch Cassidy and many more Americans became Wild West legends in the three decades from 1860. In Australia during the same period, a succession of outlaws had careers just as just as bloody and just as wild.

But, with the exception of Ned Kelly, the last of the outlaws, the names and the deeds of bushrangers such as Captain Thunderbolt, the Clarke brothers who shot dead five policemen, mad, bad Dan Morgan and 'The Reverend' Captain Moonlight are fading. Internationally, they are known not at all. They deserve to be remembered, at least by Australians. Frank Gardiner, for instance, and his partners, Johnny Gilbert, a Flash Lad and likeable with it, and Ben Hall, whose photograph shows a wistful sensitive face that tells its own tragic story, have a tale that is every bit as engrossing as their American cousins.

Frank 'Darkie' Gardiner started his career as a horse thief, was caught at the age of 20 and sentenced to 15 years in Cockatoo Island penitentiary on Sydney Harbour. After a few years, he was given a ticket-of-leave and quickly turned to robbing banks, mail coaches and travellers. He was a man who liked the ladies, a good horse, and poetry. Darkie kept a copy of Byron's poems in one pocket and his pistol in the other. A flamboyant man, Darkie Gardiner, like many of his breed, enjoyed taunting the authorities with impudent letters and giving himself a regal title. He called himself 'Prince of Tobymen'.

Frank Gardiner's first partner was on old 'schoolmate', John Piesley, another ex-convict from Cockatoo Island. Together, they enjoyed success holding up coaches and robbing gold miners until troopers wounded Gardiner in a shoot out at Lambing Flat and later captured and hanged Piesley for murder. Gardiner then teamed up with two partners, Gilbert and Hall, and the story of the gang began to take on its spectacular shape. Johnny Gilbert, a Canadian, came to the goldfields in 1852. Cheeky, cheerful and a dashing dresser, Johnny Gilbert was noted for his audacity. Ben Hall is simply the most enigmatic of all Australian bushrangers, in many ways the most romantic of all the bushrangers.

Ben Hall was charged in 1862 as an accessory in a minor hold-up by Gardiner. He was almost certainly innocent, but he was kept in gaol for a month before his trial and quick acquittal. Then Hall rode home to Cubbin Bin on Sandy Creek, in the Lachlan district of western New South Wales. Ben Hall's home was a rough slab hut, with an earthen floor, but it was on a selection of 16 000 acres, enough to carry 600 cattle a year. His heart was high. He was going home, a free man, to his wife and baby ... you'll know what happens next. Ben Hall found his humble home burned to the ground and his cattle scattered. Ben's wife, Bridget, too, was gone. She had run off with an ex-policeman, taking their young son Harry with her.

Ben Hall bought a gun and swore vengeance. First, he joined Darkie Gardiner's gang, then he stole the horse of the man who had charged him, the unpopular English baronet in charge of the police at Forbes, the arrogant and pompous Sir Frederick Pottinger. And then he took part in a robbery that, until Melbourne's Great Bookie Robbery more than a century later, was unequalled in Australia.

In June 1862, at Mandagery Creek, a tributary of the Lachlan, Ben Hall, Frank Gardiner, Johnny Gilbert and five others pulled red scarves over their noses and rode out from their cover at Eugowra Rocks. Guns in hand, they bailed up teamsters driving two bullock wagons loaded with stores for the goldfields and made them turn their wagons to block the road. Then, right on time, came the Ford & Company mail coach.

John Feagan was driving the four-in-hand coach. Beside him was the guard, Police Sergeant James Condell. Inside the coach were three armed troopers and 14 000 pounds in gold and banknotes on its way from Forbes to Sydney. Feagan acted quickly, braking and trying to wheel his horses when he saw the roadblock, and then eight men firing in a volley. Horses reared, Feagan jumped to the ground, but Condell, wounded in the side by a bullet, dropped his rifle and fell as the horses broke free from the overturned coach. While some of Gardiner's men kept the troopers covered, the others lashed the bullion to the coach horses and rode off to the safety of their hide-out high in the Whoego Mountain. There, they divided the shares at their leisure, while Sir Frederick Pottinger, pursuing a hunch, led his men 300 miles south to Hay.

Things began to go awry when one of the gang, Dan Charters, took it into his head to visit his property. When he came across a party of police, Charters panicked, spun his horse and rode furiously for the safety of Whoego. But the police had with them Billy Dargin, a renowned black tracker, and with Dargin working on the run, they reached the summit not long after the gang had fled leaving some of the gold bullion behind. The gang now went their ways. Gardiner and his mistress, Kate Brown, headed for the Queensland border. Gilbert fled to New Zealand. Ben Hall buried his gold in a hiding place that is still to be discovered and went back to his homestead.

Charters, however, was captured and was soon talking, giving Sir Frederick the names of all but one of the Eugowra gold-robbers. To Pottinger's rage, he refused to give up Ben Hall. Pottinger rode out, nevertheless, to arrest Hall, ordered his troopers to burn the Sandy Creek homestead to the ground once again and took Hall to Orange where, once again, he was freed for lack of evidence. Charters was given a job breaking horses and as a groom for the police, and for many years after, he lived anonymously and under police protection. But Henry Manns, Alec Fordyce, Jack Bow and Johnny O'Meally were charged along with Hall. The charge against O'Meally, like Hall's, was dropped for lack of evidence, and Fordyce and Bow were sentenced to life imprisonment. Henry Manns got the death sentence.

Henry Manns was hanged – twice. Manns had gone to the gallows composed and ready to meet his Maker. When the sheriff gave the signal and the hangman pulled the lever, the horrified onlookers saw that the noose of the rope had slipped over the chin and Manns hung suspended by the middle of his face. For ten minutes, they watched the body writhing and swaying in agony until the surgeon stepped forward, raised Manns's body and the hangman adjusted the noose, this time around the neck. Then the surgeon let fall the body and Mann swung, strangling, until the surgeon pronounced him dead.

For the next three years, Ben Hall and a new gang under him ranged the Lachlan with Johnny Gilbert and Johnny O'Meally, robbing banks, mail coaches and the homes of squatters. They were outlawed, with a price of a thousand pounds on their head and were liable to be shot on sight. But they operated with a carefree audacity that caused the Yass Courier to note: 'Ben Hall has obtained a lease of the main southern road.' And after a hold-up in which Hall captured three police officers who had pursued him and the gang, stripped them of their uniforms and tied them to trees, Bell's Life of Sydney ran the story under the headline, 'Narrow escape of police'.

Sixteen months after the great escort robbery, Ben Hall and his gang of four returned to Eugowra and Coonbong Rock to repeat their raid on the gold coach. You can never go back ... The coach had no gold and, in frustration, Hall decided to visit an old enemy – Henry Keightley of Dunn's Plain, near Bathurst. A giant of a man, Keightley was active in organising civilian volunteers to track and capture the bushrangers. A crack shot he boasted that if they ever came near his place he 'would turn them over'. Keightley quite expected the bushrangers to come calling. His house was barricaded and fitted for a siege.

On 24 October 1863, Ben Hall and his gang made their way through the bush to Keightley's home. It was twilight. Keightley saw them coming and thought they were police. 'Here come the bushrangers!' he called facetiously to a friend. Then, as the five dismounted and Hall bellowed, 'Stand or we'll fire!', Keightley realised his error. He ran for a shotgun as he called to his wife to barricade the doors and windows. In their haste, Mrs Keightley locked out her little sister, Lily Rotton, and the child wandered laughing as gunfire broke out from both sides. One of the gang, a young boy named Mickey Burke, ran for the house, a revolver in each hand, firing as he went. Keightley cut him down with a charge of buckshot while Lily watched horrified. Burke groaned, 'They'll never take me alive,' and shot himself in the head.

Hall called on Keightley to come out or he'd burn down the building with all in it. When he had surrendered, Hall told Mrs Keightley that he would hold her husband to ransom for 500 pounds and gave her 24 hours to raise the money. She and Keightley's friend, a doctor, harnessed a fast trotter to a gig and set off for Bathurst, 26 miles away. At four o'clock on a Sunday morning, they woke the manager of the Commercial Bank, told their story, swore him to secrecy, and gave him a cheque for the money. On her return she handed the money to Hall, who thanked her, congratulated her for her courage, and rode off.

Johnny Dunn, a prominent jockey, had joined Hall and Johnny Gilbert and took part in a number of hold-ups and raids on stations until, during the Gundagai mail coach hold-up at Black Springs, Gilbert shot and killed Sergeant Parry. In January 1865, Dunn shot another policeman and a few months later, robbing the Araluen escort, shot Constable Kelly.

Hall made plans to leave the country, visited his wife and got her promise that his son, Harry, would get his property and any money he could send from overseas. He never got there. 'Coobong' Mick Connolly, who promised Ben he would see his wishes carried out, is thought to have led the police to him. On 6 May 1865, Billy Dargin, who had tracked Dan Charters to the Gardiner gang's hide-out, was at the head of a party of six police who surrounded Hall's camp while he slept. Dargin slid on his belly through the grass towards the sleeping Hall until a horse snorted and Hall jumped to his feet. Dargin shot him in the chest. Hall clutched the wound, saw Dargin whom he had known all his life, and gasped, 'So it's you, Billy – at last! Shoot me dead, Billy, don't let the traps take me alive.'

Troopers fire a blood lust fusillade that left Hall's body cruelly tattered.
Capture and Death of Ben Hall the Bushranger, *wood engraving by*
Oswald Campbell, 1865
National Library of Australia Collection

Billy Dargin obliged. Then the police, out from cover now, joined in, firing volley after volley into Hall's body. In all, 27 bullets crashed into his corpse. Ben Hall died with his boots on and 74 pounds in his pockets. He was 27. With him he carried three revolvers, a gold watch, three gold watch chains and a gold locket holding a miniature portrait of his sister, Polly. He was buried the next day. In the three years he roamed at large his gang had raided 21 towns and homesteads – once, at Canowindra, they had occupied the town for three days – bailed up 10 mail coaches, and shot dead two policemen.

In his *Ned Kelly. A Short Life*, author Ian Jones makes the point that 11-year-old Ned Kelly probably read the bushranger's obituary in his local paper, the *Kilmore Free Press*. 'With all his crimes he has never been accused of being bloodthirsty, nor did he directly kill any of the victims he robbed ... such then, in brief, are some of the incidents of the early life of a most desperate bushranger, who has eluded the grasp of a strong and active police force for three years, and who was ultimately captured, but not until his body was pierced with bullets and slugs from his feet to the crown of his head.'

Johnny Dunn and Johnny Gilbert were soon tracked down. The pair was hiding out in a hut at Binalong when Dunn's grandfather told police where to find them and helped them further by dampening their cartridges. Four police kicked down the door of the hut and shot Gilbert dead. Dunn, wounded in the foot, escaped but was captured near the Queensland border and hanged.

Frank Gardiner had already served a year of his 32-year imprisonment with hard labour when Hall was gunned down. He had been discovered at Apis Creek, 100 miles west of Rockhampton, when his mistress, Kate Brown, wrote to Hall's wife, Bridget, telling her how, as Mr and Mrs Christie, they were the part-owners of an inn, and doing very well. The police read the letter with interest and Gardiner was taken without a shot fired. After 20 years in gaol he was given clemency on condition that he exile himself.

Gardiner sailed in the barque *Charlotte Andrews* for China and ended his days running the Twilight Saloon on Keaney Street, San Francisco. In 1903, he was shot dead in a poker game. It is tempting to believe he was holding the same 'Dead Man's Hand' – a pair of eights and a pair of Aces – dealt to Wild Bill Hickock when he, too, was shot dead at the card table. Hickock, in any case, would have respected Frank Gardiner and Ben Hall as two men every bit as wild as any who came out of the American West.

If Only Ned's Mother Had Been Sent to the Seaside ...

*H*ad Ned Kelly's mother been sentenced to spend six weeks at the seaside, her son might have been a footnote in the short and violent history of bushranging: 'Edward (Ned) Kelly. Horse thief. Apprentice, 1870–1871 to Harry Power (see Power, Harry, last of the noted bushrangers.)'

Mrs Ellen Kelly, battling to bring up her family in appalling poverty, certainly could have done with a holiday. But it was her, and the Kelly family's, ill fortune to come up against a man with an implacable hatred of the Catholic Irish. Here was a hanging judge with a fear that unless the bog Irish Catholics were kept in check they could rise up – as they had back in Ireland when he lived there – and overthrow the established order. Sir Redmond Barry was the Protestant Irish son of a British General, the senior judge in the colony named after the ruling British monarch. Barry knew the Kellys: he had sentenced Ned's uncle to be hanged for arson.

Now Barry was sitting in judgment on what the Crown said was the attempted murder of a policeman – but what was, in fact, little more than a farce. A fracas in a tiny crowded kitchen that was almost comical, the sort of slapstick scene that 30 years later had silent movie audiences in stitches. A villainous, lecherous landlord enters, gleefully twirling a wicked moustache. His eyes light up as a fair maiden comes within his grope. The heroine's sweetheart/brother/mother, outraged, come to her rescue, and the rounds of the kitchen ensue, with the villain, beaned by a frying pan as the piano accompanist supplies the sound effects, executing a slow, stiff-as-a plank pratfall.

Tragically, the rounds of the kitchen at the Kellys led to the gaoling of Ned's mother and drove Ned and his brother to become fugitives. That, in turn, led to the shootout at Stringybark Creek and that led to the bank hold-ups, the creation of the very first superhero outfits and the Last Stand at Glenrowan. And that, finally, led to the legend of Ned Kelly.

It all happened for Ned Kelly in 26 mostly tumultuous years. But, long after his execution at Melbourne Gaol in 1880, he continues to fascinate. For some, he is simply a blowhard full of the worst aspects of his Irish blood, a thug who became a killer who intended to kill scores more. There is truth in that. But, there was another side to Kelly. And it is the combination of that side – his charisma, with its Irish charm, foibles and blarney, his chivalry and his bravery, and the fact that he was, as he claimed, 'a widow's son wronged' – that has kept the legend of Ned Kelly alive. That and the helmet, of course.

But it all was triggered by the rounds of the kitchen and the shoot-out that followed at Stringybark Creek.

At Jerilderie, a town he held captive for two days, Ned handed over his 8300-word manifesto, an autobiographical document addressed to the Premier of the State, giving his side of the story. It told of the affray in the kitchen of his home and of the Stringybark killings and why Ned was adamant that he shot in self-protection. And it railed against the persecution he and his family had always suffered from 'the cowardly conduct of a parcel of big ugly fat-necked wombat headed big bellied magpie legged narrow hipped splay-footed sons of Irish bailiffs and English landlords which is better known as officers of the Victorian Police.'

At Jerilderie, we see the side of Ned that has inspired a Booker Prize novel, one of scores of fiction and non-fiction books, a $40 million Hollywood movie, numerous other television dramas and movies, including the first feature film ever made, and Sidney Nolan's famous sequence of 27 Ned Kelly paintings. At Jerilderie, Kelly was a charmer – men and women agreed – a fine figure of a man, with, the schoolteacher recalled, 'a lot of Don Quixote ... a dreamer in his own way.'

Standing at the bar of the pub, Ned put his revolver down beside his glass. 'There's my revolver,' he told the assembly. 'Anyone here may take it and shoot me dead, but if I'm shot Jerilderie shall swim in its own blood.' Ned Kelly was not a heavy drinker, but he sometimes talked like one. He was foolhardy and, sometimes, foolish. 'I am a widow's son outlawed' is a memorable statement, but Ned continues, 'and my orders must be obeyed!' and the noble note of defiance becomes shrill and absurd.

Ned Kelly is an enigma. A braggart and a cool-headed killer. A brave man who came back to save his mates when he could have saved his own skin. (Had he been born 35 years later, Dame Mabel Brookes wrote in her autobiography, Ned might have won a Victoria Cross at Gallipoli.) An articulate and intelligent man who might have saved his life had he chosen to speak in his defence at his trial. A man who took his last walk, to the gallows, and talked about the flowers on the way. A man who wanted to start a revolution that would establish a Republic in north-east Victoria, but who had nothing to say at the last but a mumbled, 'I suppose it had to come to this.'

The Melbourne Gaol's Protestant Minister, John Cowley Coles, visited Ned, at Ned's request, shortly before his execution. 'The man by no means looked a ruffian,' Coles wrote. 'He had a rather pleasant expression of countenance. He was one of the most powerfully built and finest men that I ever saw. He treated me with great respect, listened to all I had to say, and knelt down by my side when I prayed ... He answered me, "I have heard all you said this morning referring to the address [a sermon Coles preached within Kelly's hearing, the text being Prepare to meet your God]. I believe it all. Although I have been bushranging I have always believed that when I die I have a God to meet." He added, "When I was in the bank at Jerilderie, taking the money, the thought came into my mind, if I am shot down at this moment, how can I meet my God?" I knelt down in the cell and prayed with him, he kneeling by my side.'

The foremost authority on Kelly, Ian Jones, best sums it up in *Ned Kelly. A Short Life*.

Because Ned Kelly was what he was, and did what he did, Australians will always speak and write about him in terms of their own gods or their own demons. This is the Kelly phenomenon today as in 1880. This is perhaps Ned Kelly's tragedy, yet it is also his triumph and the seed of his immortality.

Ned Kelly's parents, John 'Red' Kelly and Ellen Quinn, were married in the little church of St Francis, still standing in the heart of Melbourne, on Monday, 18 November 1850. Red had been a convict, ostensibly transported from Ireland for stealing two pigs. The reality may have been much darker. There are good reasons to believe that Red was an informer who caused two of his mates to be apprehended for cow stealing – one of them had been shot dead trying to escape.

In December 1854, at Beveridge, 40 kilometres north of Melbourne on the road to Sydney, Edward 'Ned' Kelly was born, the eldest of 11 children Ellen would bear. Ned grew up a conscientious scholar who came second in his class and excelled at all games. He was a natural leader, his classmates remembered, and a brave boy. In 1862, aged 11, Ned heroically rescued a small boy from drowning, and in gratitude, the parents presented young Ned with a splendid green silk sash with a commemorative inscription. Ned was wearing that sash beneath his armour when made his Last Stand at Glenrowan.

A year after Ned's brave act of rescue, Red Kelly died and 12-year-old Ned became the man of the house, looking after his mother and six siblings. In 1867, the family moved to an 88-acre property on the Eleven Mile Creek near Greta in Victoria's north-east, where Ellen's family and her in-laws, small selector farmers, were frequently before the courts on charges of stock theft.

The north-east of Victoria was a bitterly divided community: squatters against selectors. The squatters, a small group of men who controlled the land from the founding days 50 years before, considered themselves the rightful owners and fought against any proposal to allow others to settle. From 1860, however, any man or single woman could select up to 320 acres and pay it off over time, provided that they lived on the land and cultivated it. Neither side was satisfied with the arrangement. The selectors, with reason, were bitter at the way the squatters, once they realised land reform was inevitable, had secured the best lands on their runs and entrenched themselves in positions of power. The police inevitably favoured the squatters.

At Greta, Ellen was among her family, the Quinn clan, and her in-laws, the Lloyds. Here, Ned first got into trouble with the law. In 1869, at 14, he was charged with assaulting a Chinese man but the charge was dismissed. And, at Greta, the last of the notable bushrangers, Harry Power, recruited young Ned as his apprentice. A year after the assault charge, Ned was up before the magistrate at Benalla charged with being an accomplice of Power, but again the charge was dismissed. Then, he was gaoled for six months for throwing a hawker into a creek. Up to this point, Ned could be seen as a larrikin, something of a bully, but the sort of likely lad that can still be found in country towns. At heart, they are decent enough and almost invariably go on to distinguish themselves in the town football and cricket teams before marrying and disappearing into the mists of domesticity.

In 1871, however, Ned, now a strapping youth, was found with a stolen horse and, when he resisted arrest, was brutally pistol-whipped. Ned claimed, and it was certainly true, that he hadn't realised the horse was stolen (he'd borrowed it from a friend), but he was sentenced to three years' hard labour at Beechworth, Pentridge and the *Sacramento*, a convict hulk moored at Williamstown. He came out at 19 probably intending to stay out of trouble and spent three years working in a variety of jobs, but then he went back to horse stealing on a large and sophisticated scale.

The pivotal moment in the story of Ned Kelly arrived one April afternoon in 1878 when Constable Alex Fitzpatrick came to Greta to arrest Ned's 16-year-old brother Dan. Fitzpatrick had no authority to do so and was going against orders that stipulated that police officers were never to go alone to the Kellys. He was also going there after stopping, he admitted later, for 'some brandy and lemonade' at a pub on the way.

What happened next will never be known. Fitzpatrick, the Kellys claimed, made a pass at 15-year-old Kate Kelly and a brawl broke out. Mrs Kelly whacked Fitzpatrick with a shovel and, Fitzpatrick claimed, Ned appeared and shot him in the wrist. Ned claimed that he was many miles away at the time, but in any case the wound was so slight that a doctor testified that it 'might' have been caused by a bullet grazing the skin. The likelihood is that Ned was there and that Fitzpatrick, as he said, was grazed by a bullet from Ned's gun in a scuffle. But, whatever the truth – and Fitzpatrick was later dismissed from the police force because 'he could not be trusted out of sight' – the trouble in the kitchen was footling. Mrs Kelly bandaged the graze and Fitzpatrick rode off, seemingly at peace with the clan. Instead Mrs Kelly found herself charged with attempted murder.

At the trial, Sir Redmond Barry sentenced Ellen Kelly to three years' hard labour. On the same charge, he sentenced two other men said to be in the Eleven Mile Creek area to six years' hard labour. The gaoling of his mother outraged Ned. He and Dan headed for the hills after the incident in the kitchen and hid out in the Wombat Ranges, where they set up a gold-mining camp and a whisky still to raise money for their mother's legal costs.

They also offered to give themselves up if their mother was released. Instead, the police set out to find – and kill, as some of the police had publicly promised – the Kelly brothers.

On 25 October, a party of four police, disguised as prospectors, camped at Stringybark Creek, close to where the Kelly boys had their hide-out. Two friends, Joe Byrne and Steve Hart, were with Ned and Dan when, the next day, they discovered the police camp and set out to disarm them and take their horses. Two of the troopers were relaxing around the campfire when the four emerged, and Ned barked: 'Bail up! Throw up your hands!' One of the troopers, McIntyre, surrendered immediately, but Constable Lonigan, a man who had once 'blackballed' Ned (grabbed and dragged him by the testicles), dived behind a log and came up gun in hand. Ned had once promised: 'If I ever shoot a man, Lonigan, you'll be the first!' As Lonigan raised his head, Ned shot him in the eye. Crying 'Oh Christ, I'm shot!', Lonigan fell dead across the log.

Now the Kelly boys and friends waited for the other two policemen. When Sergeant Kennedy and Constable Scanlon rode back into the campsite, they were met by McIntyre who told them, as Ned had ordered, that they had better surrender as they were surrounded. Scanlon laughed at the joke. His laughter died suddenly when Ned stepped out and called, 'Bail up! Hold your hands up!' As the other three members of the gang ran out calling on the police to bail up, Scanlon swung the barrel of his Spencer carbine and fired at Ned. Ned shot him off his horse, and Dan, probably, fired the shot that killed him. Kennedy had rolled off his horse and McIntyre sprang on it and rode for his life. Kennedy, firing as he went, followed on foot, dodging behind trees and reloading as he went. Ned came after him and shot him. Kennedy, Kelly considered, was mortally wounded, and he shot him again to finish him.

'I put his cloak over him,' Ned later said, 'and left him as well as I could and were they my own brothers I could not be more sorry for them. This cannot be called wilful murder for I was compelled to shoot them or lie down and let them shoot me. It would not be wilful murder if they packed our remains in, shattered into an animated mass of gore to Mansfield. They would have got great praise and credit ... Certainly their wives and children are to be pitied, but they must remember those men came into the bush with the intention of scattering pieces of me and my brother all over the bush.'

With the deaths at Stringybark Creek, the Kelly Gang was born – four outlaws, with a price on their heads.

Six weeks later, with the colony still in ferment, the Kelly Gang pulled off their first, audacious hold-up. On the outskirts of the small town of Euroa, on the road to Sydney, the Kelly Gang invaded the Faithfull Creek homestead and locked up the station hands, a passing hawker, a selector and his son and others. Ned talked for hours to his captive audience about his life and the Mansfield Murders, as the shoot out at Stringybark was now known. Some of the hostages slept, others stayed awake absorbed by his account, and some, sympathetic, offered him money, not knowing the gang was about to get their hands on a fortune very shortly.

The next morning, the gang cut the telegraph lines, burned their clothes and changed into new suits from the hawker's wagon. That afternoon, they bailed up another nine men, locked them with the others at the homestead under Joe's guard and went into Euroa's drowsy Binnie Street. At 4.00 p.m., Ned walked into the National Bank. Steve and Dan came in through the back. They bailed up the manager, Mr Scott and, after taking 2000 pounds, had so put him at ease that he shared a whisky with them. Scott was later to give evidence at Ned's trial that Ned was a gentleman and treated Mrs Scott well. The manager's wife was even more impressed. She told the police that Ned was 'a much more handsome and well dressed man than she had expected and by no means the ferocious ruffian she had expected him to be.'

Mr and Mrs Scott, along with her mother, nanny, maid, baby and younger children, were taken for a buggy ride that ended back at the Faithfull Creek homestead. By now the audience had now grown to 37 men, women and children, and the gang treated them to an exhibition of trick riding before departing, warning them not to go for help for three hours. One of the admiring audience reported:

The horsemanship displayed by Ned Kelly is something surprising. He maintains his seat in the saddle in any position, sometimes resting his legs at full length along the horse's neck, and at others, extending his whole body till his toes rested on the tail, dashing along at full speed.

It was a hold-up that had hurt no one and entertained all. 'The bushrangers,' noted the Melbourne *Herald*, 'played with the women and boys and treated everyone with the greatest civility.' The government, however, was not amused. It increased the reward for the gang's capture to 1000 pounds – dead or alive.

Eight weeks later, across the border, the Kelly Gang held the town of Jerilderie captive for two days and took another 2000 pounds from the Bank of New South Wales. Once again, the event was cavalier and clever – this time the gang bailed up the entire town, including the police, stayed two days and left a lasting impression that, almost all agreed, was admirable. Ned, looking splendid in a police uniform, encountered the bank manager in his bath, bought drinks for the bar, made menacing boasts and showed his superb horsemanship. To one of his captors, Constable Richards, 'he was the gamest man I ever saw.' And, to another, who heard him make blood-chilling threats, 'it was only a matter of bluff ... from first to last.'

Ned came to Jerilderie with a written manifesto, 8300 words he had dictated to Joe, a virtual history that rambled and ranted in many places but which succinctly explained his side of the story of Stringybark. He wanted the letter to be published, but like an earlier version he had written at Euroa it was kept from public knowledge.

The Kelly Gang then disappeared for four months. Despite the most intensive police operation ever mounted in the colony – rounding up and gaoling Kelly sympathisers, putting their houses under close watch and bringing Aboriginal trackers from Queensland – the gang could not be found. While they laid low, the gang forged suits of armour from plough steel, inspired, it is conjectured, by a Chinese warrior's suit of armour they would have seen in Beechworth's Burke Museum (where it still can be seen), or perhaps by an armour-clad character in *Lorna Doon*, the then popular novel about an outlaw family in the late 17th century.

Above all, Ned and the gang spent this time planning a spectacular uprising – one that would change the map of the British Empire. The uprising, Ned fantasised, would result in the establishment of a Republic in the north-east of the state – something he had forecast in the Jerilderie Letter: 'to show some colonial stratagem which will open the eyes not only of the Victoria police and its inhabitants but also the whole British Army.'

While the Kelly Gang eluded the police, Aaron Sherritt, a close friend of Joe, had been working as a double agent, informing the gang and the police of their respective movements, but always managing to keep the police one step behind. It was a dangerous business. When, finally, Joe Byrne suspected that his best mate had turned traitor, he shot Aaron at the door of his home while three police, there to guard Sherritt, cowered under the bed. Knowing that the killing of Aaron would bring a trainload of police to the murder site, Ned held up the tiny town of Glenrowan and got some railway-plate layers out of bed to tear up the railway line. The train would be derailed, the police would be killed, injured or unable to defend themselves and his supporters would fall on them. The north-east republican uprising would begin.

The train did set out, but not until 30 hours had passed. The police under the bed had been too frightened to leave the hut and raise the alarm. In the meantime, the Kelly Gang, in their fashion, had rounded up the townspeople – many of them sympathisers – and entertained them with a party at the Glenrowan Inn that went on until the early hours of Monday, 28 June 1880. It bore all the Kelly trademarks – generosity, civility, wild threats and songs and dance.

Then, as the police train neared Glenrowan, it was stopped by the local schoolteacher, Thomas Curnow, a man whom Ned, believing that he was a sympathiser, had released a few hours earlier. The police and their horses poured out of the train carriages and took up positions around the hotel. The Kelly Gang's last stand was at hand. Within the first few minutes of a pitched gun battle, Ned had wounded an old adversary, Superintendent Hare, but in return and despite his armour he had been badly wounded. He struggled on to Music, Joe's horse, got through the inadequate police cordon and went to warn his supporters that the plan had failed. Then he went back, coming in behind the pub just as a volley of shots hit Joe in the groin and he fell dying. Ned called for Steve and Dan to follow him. In the confusion, Ned went out alone and, in the bush, weak from loss of blood, passed out.

Just before dawn, Ned came to, got to his feet and made one last attempt to rescue Dan and Steve, trapped inside the inn. In the early morning mist, his helmeted figure, towering and black, emerged shooting at the cordon of police and taunting them: 'Good shots, boys. Fire away, you buggers, you cannot hurt me!' The truth was they had hurt him; he was reeling and staggering like a drunken man. Then Joe's horse, Music, saddled and bridled, came up to Ned from the trees. Kneeling by now, Ned let Music pass and she was shot.

Finally, it was over for Ned. After 30 minutes, the gunfight ended when he was brought down, close to death, with 28 bullet wounds. A Catholic priest, Dean Matthew Gibney, heard Ned's confession and, believing he was near death, gave him the last sacraments. Inside the inn, now set ablaze, Ned's mates were indeed dead. Father Gibney, showing incredible bravery, went into the burning building and came out as it was about to collapse, announcing: 'They're all dead!' Joe's body was dragged from the flames, but those of Steve and Dan were burnt beyond recognition. A young boy and two men had also died in the siege, fatally wounded by police bullets.

On 28 October 1880, at Melbourne's Supreme Court, Edward Kelly went to trial, charged with murdering Constable Thomas Lonigan at Stringybark Creek. He told his lawyer, David Gaunson:

All I want is a full and fair trial and a chance to make my side heard. Until now the police have had all the say, and have had it all their own way.

If I get a full and fair trial, I don't care how it goes; but I know this – the public will see that I was hunted and hounded on from step to step; they will see that I am not the monster I have been made out. What I have done has been under strong provocation.

(The truth of Ned's comments emerged the following year at the Royal Commission into the police called as a result of the Kelly affair. Superintendent Nicholson admitted that the police had instructions that they 'should endeavour, whenever they commit any paltry crime, to bring [the Kellys] to justice and send them to Pentridge even on a paltry sentence, the object being to take their prestige away from them.')

Ned Kelly may have wanted a fair trial, but the counsel who represented him, Bindon, failed to ensure it. Bindon called no evidence on Kelly's behalf, stopped the Jerilderie Letter from being admitted as evidence and advised Ned not to give sworn evidence, or even an unsworn statement. In doing so he brought the question of guilt down to one man's word. McIntyre, who had escaped the shootout at Stringybark, would tell the jury that Kelly shot Lonigan in cold blood, denying that Lonigan had raised his head from behind a log and was about to take aim when he was shot.

But would it have mattered? The trial was before Sir Redmond Barry, the Irish-born Protestant, a renowned hanging judge who had sentenced Ellen Kelly, Ned's mother, to three years' hard labour. At that time, it was later said, Barry told her and the court that he regretted that her son was not in the dock alongside. 'I'd have given him 21 years.' Now he had her son before him. And, said John H. Phillips, former Chief Justice of Victoria, in his book, *The Trial of Ned Kelly*, 'The conclusion is inescapable that Edward Kelly was not afforded a trial according to law.'

Kelly had always claimed he shot Lonigan and the other police at Stringybark in self-defence. 'It is all very well to say that we shot the police in cold blood. We had to do it in self defence,' he told John Tarleton, the Jerilderie bank manager. And, in the letter he handed over at Jerilderie, he said:

> He [Lonigan] had just got to the logs and put his head up to take aim when I shot him that instant or he would have shot me as I took him for Strahan the man who said he would not ask me to stand he would shoot me first like a dog.
>
> ... This cannot be called wilful murder for I was compelled to shoot them or lie down and let them shoot me ... Remember these men came into the bush with the intention of scattering pieces of me and my brother all over the bush.

[The police parties had gone into the Wombat Ranges in search of Ned and Dan disguised as prospectors. Their horses carried long and stout straps to carry bodies out of the bush. And some had boasted that if it came to bringing the brothers back dead or alive they'd opt for the latter option.]

Nonetheless, Barry directed the jury to find Ned Kelly guilty or not guilty on the charge of murdering Lonigan and would not allow them to consider returning a finding of manslaughter – a verdict that would have agreed that Kelly had killed in self-defence. This ruling, that the jury could not consider a verdict of manslaughter, was plainly wrong, Justice John Phillips has said. Sir Redmond Barry, Phillips said, 'should have told the jury that it was for them to decide whether the police [at Stringybark Creek] were acting as ministers of justice or summary executioners' and 'should then have reviewed for the jurors the evidence relative to this issue. Instead the matter was put to the jury in terms that were conclusive in favour of the Prosecution ... Whether the result would have been any different had the jury been correctly directed is, of course, entirely another matter.'

The Australasian Sketcher *shows Kelly confronting Barry with his argument that the charge of murder was false. He was probably right, but Barry had the last word.*

Without the possibility of considering a verdict of manslaughter, the jury took just 30 minutes to find Kelly guilty of Lonigan's murder. When Sir Redmond came to pronounce the death sentence, he was intensely nettled when Kelly argued that the charge of murder was false. But, Kelly conceded, the way that the evidence was presented meant the jury had no choice other than to find him guilty. It was his fault. 'It is not that I fear death; I fear it as little as to drink a cup of tea ... I do not blame anybody – neither Mr Bindon nor Mr Gaunson: but Mr Bindon knew nothing about my case. I lay blame on myself that I did not get up yesterday and examine the witnesses, but I thought that if I did so, it would look like bravado and flashness, and people might have said that I thought myself cleverer than Counsel. So I let it go as it was.'

In a famous exchange in which Kelly clearly got the better of the judge, he said, 'A day will come at a bigger court than this when we shall see which is right and which is wrong.' Then Sir Redmond pronounced that Edward Kelly would be taken 'to a place of execution, and there you will be hanged by the neck until you are dead. May the Lord have mercy on your soul.' And that should have been the last word. Ned, however, came back with, 'I'll go further than that, and say I will see you there where I go,' and two weeks after the hanging the judge suddenly died.

The date for the execution was set for 11 November 1880. In that short time – 13 days after the verdict of guilty – a petition for clemency went around Melbourne. The city's population was 300 000. More than one in ten signed it, a phenomenal figure, pro rata, which has probably never been matched. (Unofficial figures for the petitions that came in too late put the total at above 60 000.) Four thousand people packed a public meeting at the Hippodrome and another 2000 to 3000 massed in the street outside. In today's terms, these figures would translate to a petition signed by 300 000 and a mass meeting of around 60 000 to 70 000 – a respectable figure for a modern-day football final. It was 'humiliating,' said one newspaper, 'to have to admit that a great number of respectable working people were present.'

The petition's appeal for a reprieve was rejected by the Governor, and on the day before Ned was to die, his mother, Ellen, said goodbye to her eldest son. She was brought from her wing of the gaol, where she was still serving her sentence in the prison laundry. Traditionally, she is said to have told Ned, 'Mind you die like a Kelly, son,' but Ian Jones believes it far more likely that she said, 'I mind you'll die like a Kelly, son.' Ned also farewelled his brother Jim and his sisters, Kate and Grace, that day.

On the evening of 10 November 1880, Ned Kelly enjoyed his last

Arms pinioned, canvas hood on his head, Ned faces his executioner, Upjohn. 'I mind you die like a Kelly,' his mother had told him, and he did.
Originally published on the cover of the Australasian Sketcher.

meal – roast lamb with green peas and a bottle of claret – softly sang hymns and such songs as 'The Sweet Bye and Bye' and slept soundly till 5.00 a.m., when he got up, went down on his knees and prayed silently for 20 minutes. Then he went back to sleep. He awoke at 8.00 a.m., and the blacksmith came to take off his leg irons. Escorted from across the prison yard, Ned passed the cart waiting to take his corpse but simply nodded at some flowers growing by the wall. 'What beautiful flowers,' he said.

At the Melbourne Gaol, Ned was taken into a small holding cell a few metres from the gallows and given Extreme Unction, the church's solemn last rite, by Dean O'Hea, the priest who had baptised him as newborn, 26 years before. Then Upjohn the hangman, a huge, forbidding brute, pinioned his arms. 'There is no need for tying me,' Ned said. Unperturbed, Upjohn put a canvas hood on his head and, preceded by three priests and an acolyte, Ned walked the few steps to the gallows. He is said to have sighed: 'Ah, well, I suppose it had to come to this.' Then Upjohn slipped the noose around his neck, Ned shifting his head to make sure the knot was below his chin, and dropped the canvas cap over Ned's face. Almost in the same movement, the hangman sprang back and pulled the lever to the trapdoor.

'Death must have been instantaneous, beyond a slight twisting of the shoulders and spasmodic quiver of the larger limbs, no motion was visible,' an observer later recorded.

Ellen Kelly was cared for until her death in 1923 by her son Jim, the last of her 11 children. As a 14-year-old, Jim had been gaoled for three years for the theft of four cattle. That term in prison stopped him becoming a member of the Kelly Gang. When Kate died in 1898 – she was found drowned – Ellen and Jim raised her three children. Ellen Kelly, the diminutive matriarch, tough as iron bark, who held the family together, lived on and died, a well-respected woman, at the age of 90. Jim Kelly died 23 years later, in 1946. He was 87.

The legend of Ned Kelly, however, lives on.

4 | Half-forgotten Heroes

Jack and Murph's Three Weeks at Hell's Fun Fair

*O*ne day he was just young Jack, the boy who looked after the donkeys at the seaside penny rides. The next he was Jack the Lad, a brawny young bloke who jumped ship in Perth and humped his bluey around Australia. Then he was Simpson, the man with the donkey, the hero of the heroic troops at Gallipoli. A guardian angel who saved scores of soldiers. A man resigned to the certainty that he would sacrifice his life for others.

Simpson was English, but Australians have always counted him as their own. His happy-go-lucky demeanour, his disregard for authority, and his cheerful acceptance of a beer or a fight – a stoush – stamped him, as dinki-di. Simpson lost his stoush with death, but he always knew he would. Would he then have cared if he knew that his extraordinary bravery would be officially unrecognised? He should have won half a dozen Victoria Crosses. Albert Jacka, Australia's most famous VC winner, got his at Gallipoli a week before he went out on his last rescue. Jacka single-handedly killed seven Turks in a few furious seconds of trench fighting. Simpson risked his life day after day saving dozens of Anzacs.

Your brother landed with us from the torpedo boat at daylight on 25 April so taking part in the historic landing. He did excellent work during the day. He discovered a donkey in a deserted hut, took possession and worked up and down the dangerous valley carrying wounded men to the beach on the donkey.

This plan was a very great success so he continued day to day from morning to night and became one of the best known men in the division. Everyone from the General down seems to have known him and his donkey which he christened Murphy. The valley at the time was very dangerous as it was exposed to snipers and also was continuously shelled. He scorned the danger and always kept going, whistling and singing, a universal favourite. So he worked for three weeks.

On the night of 18 May as you will have read in the papers, the Turks made a heavy attack on our position. Early in the morning as usual your brother was at work, when a machine gun played on the track where he was passing. The days of his almost miraculous escapes were past, for he fell on the spot, shot through the heart. He truly died doing his duty.

We buried him that night on a little hill near the sea-shore known as Queensland Point, Chaplain Green, reading the service. The work your brother did was so exceptionally good that his name was mentioned in the orders of the day. He gave his life in the performance of a gallant and cheerful service that has been excelled by none.

That was how John Kirkpatrick's family, of South Shields, Tyneside, England, learned their boy was dead. The family knew him as their young Jack who used to work at the seaside holiday attraction, Murphy's Fair, putting little kids up on donkey rides for a penny a ride. From early morning, Jack looked after the donkeys until, late at night, he would ride one home.

Jack and the donkeys had a rapport. He was gentle with them. But, when his father died, Jack, now 17, put Murphy's Fair and the donkey rides behind him and looked forward to a life … well, he had no idea. Certainly no idea of his destiny – to die in battle and be commemorated on the currency of a country half a world away.

On 12 February 1910, Jack Kirkpatrick joined the crew of the *Yedda* as a stoker. The *Yedda*, bound for Australia, had hardly docked in

Newcastle when Jack jumped ship and, for the next few years, humping his bluey around the country, got work cane cutting, cattle droving, coal mining, gold mining and working on coastal ships. He was in Fremantle on one of these ships when, three weeks after war was declared, he jumped ship once again and, under the name of Simpson, enlisted in C section, 3rd Field Ambulance, 1st Australian Division, Australian Imperial Force.

Jack liked a laugh, he liked a drink, and he wouldn't walk away from a fight. In Australia, he had plenty of that, and at Gallipoli he got the fight of his life. Just before dawn, at about 5.00 a.m., on Sunday, 25 April 1915, 'C' section rowed from the transport *Devanha,* and the men leapt from the boat and waded ashore. The first into the water was killed immediately. The third man died beside him. Simpson was the second man in the water. Of the 1500 men in the first wave, 755 remained in active service at the end of the day. The rest – half of the landing force – were killed or wounded.

By dawn on the second day, the Turkish troops on the high ground looked down their gun barrels at the Anzacs, pinned to 500 acres, threatened from almost every angle except the sea at their backs. Working all day, stretcher parties under constant rifle and artillery fire carried the wounded, slipping and sliding, down the steep slopes to the beach at Anzac Cove. It was exhausting, agonising and dangerous work. Then, late on that day, Simpson, struggling under the weight of a heavy, wounded Digger, saw a donkey grazing in a hollow, oblivious.

Bullets buzzed around him, but for an instant Jack was back on the beach at Murphy's Fair. He made a head stall and lead from bandages and field dressings, lifted the wounded man on to the donkey – Murphy, or Murph, Simpson called him – and got the digger down safely.

From then on, Simpson and Murph did things their way. As he did not report back to ambulance headquarters for instructions for a few days, he was technically a deserter. No one cared about that.

Simpson and Murphy would start their work early, just as he and the donkeys did when he was a kid. From around 6.30 a.m., they would go to and fro the two kilometres up Shrapnel Gully, the main supply route to the front line, into Monash Valley and onto the deadly zone around Quinn's Post where the opposing trenches were just 20 metres apart.

To the left of Quinn's Post was Dead Man's Ridge, held by the Turks and from where they were able to snipe right down Shrapnel Gully. Through this sniper fire and shrapnel, Simpson would bring water for the wounded, leave Murph under cover while he tended them, and then carry them to the donkey.

Then they'd go back – a dozen or more times a day and into the night. Simpson would often continue until as late as 3.00 a.m. He made the two-kilometre trip through sniper fire and shrapnel, and dismissed all warnings of the certain death he faced with the reply, 'My troubles', an early version of the classic Australian expression, 'She'll be right, mate.'

Simpson lasted just 25 days. C.E.W. Bean, the official war historian, said:

On the night of April 25th he annexed a donkey, and each day, and half of every night, he worked continuously between the head of Monash Valley and the beach, his donkey carrying a brassard around its forehead and a wounded man on its back. Simpson escaped death so many times that he was completely fatalistic; the deadly sniping down the valley and the most furious shrapnel fire never stopped him. The colonel of his ambulance, recognising the value of his work, allowed him to carry on as a completely separate unit. He camped with his donkey at the Indian mule camp, and had only report once a day at the field ambulance. Presently he annexed a second donkey. On May 19th he went up the valley past the water-guard, where he generally had his breakfast, but it was not ready. "Never mind," he called. "Get me a good dinner when I come back."

He never came back. With two patients he was coming down the creek-bed, when he was hit through the heart, both the wounded men being wounded again. He had carried many scores of men down the valley, and had saved many lives at the cost of his own.

The Man Who Stared Down Death

A young Aboriginal woman with a mile-wide smile crosses the 400-metre line, arms outstretched and a nation jumps to its feet. A first ball from an unreconstructed young man, plump, and with blonde dyed hair, cuts behind the English skipper, scatters his stumps and another Australian immortal is born. A teenager with abnormally large feet ploughs his way up and down a pool and is hailed as demi-god. A horse bobs its nose and wins the Cup by a whisker. The horse joins a long line of equine Aussie legends.

In Australia, if you can kick a football straight and far, swim fast, whack a cricket ball or crisply put away a cross court volley, you may forever be remembered as heroic. But, shuffle on hands and knees across blizzard-swept ice and snow, day after day, desperately ill, with the soles separated from your feet and with every expectation that you will join the men who died with you a day or so ago, and, ah, that's a horse of a different colour! You may be disappointed at how you are remembered.

Douglas Mawson set an example of courage and endurance that stands alone. Yet, for decades, his incredible feat went relatively unnoticed by Australia, and it remains completely ignored by the world. While his contemporary, Ernest Shackleton, is celebrated in feature films and television documentaries for his doughty survival in the Antarctic, Mawson's far more daunting story remains in dusty, unopened history books.

Slowly, we are coming to appreciate Mawson. His face was on Australia's $100 note. But this honour was a long time coming. Australians, mostly, have a vague idea that the image of a granite-jawed man with piercing eyes and a knitted balaclava represents a hero, but few could tell you what this man did that was heroic. The fact is that Mawson deserves his place because he was both a hero and a remarkable scientist. When Amundsen and Scott of the Antarctic were vying for the empty glory of being first to the South Pole, Mawson was contributing far more to the understanding of the region than all other expeditioners up to that time. His scientific achievement is considerable, but his personal saga of survival is astonishing, and for today's generations, almost unbelievable. Ernest Shackleton's saga, travelling 1500 kilometres in an open boat with five companions, is justly renowned. But, it pales beside Mawson's lone epic of endurance.

Douglas Mawson graduated with a degree in geology from the University of Adelaide and joined Shackleton's *Nimrod* expedition to the Antarctic in 1907. Then he returned to Australia and began planning an expedition that would reveal the mysteries of the Antarctic's western coastline. In 1911, he sailed to Antarctica with a scientific party on the steamer *Aurora*. The party set up a base at what Mawson named Commonwealth Bay, 'the Home of the Blizzard' as he was later to dub it. It was set on a stony beach flanked by ice cliffs that led to a featureless landscape where black-draped guideposts were needed to help sledge parties find their way back, and where the wind whipped through you at 400 kilometres an hour.

On 10 November 1911, Mawson left the base and led five sledging parties exploring the coast. Mawson, with two others, a Swiss mountaineer, Dr Xavier Mertz and Lieutenant Ninnis of the Royal Fusiliers, left the other four parties to strike out on their own. They were in good spirits, singing songs as the sun came out for the first time in months.

Disaster struck suddenly.

Mertz, on skis, was breaking a trail for the sledges when he stopped at one of the many bridged crevasses the party had to cross. He gauged the danger and ran quickly across the chasm. Mawson did the same.

They looked back to check on Ninnis, who was bringing up the rear, and were shocked to see no trace of him. On the entirely featureless landscape, he had vanished. The pair retraced their steps. They came to a circular hole, four metres wide, in the bridge over the crevasse. Mawson and Mertz knelt and peered into it. Fifty metres down, on a ledge, they could see dead dogs and part of the rations being carried on Ninnis's sledge. The young soldier himself, the sledge and the other dogs had plunged into the unfathomable abyss.

Mawson and Mertz were now faced with getting back to base, 315 kilometres away. The sledge with almost all the food, their main tent and equipment was with Ninnis, beyond all reach. They had enough food for ten or 11 days, they were in a land where the wind could reach 400 kilometres an hour, where icy darkness reigned, and where the peril of crevasses was ever-present. It was a race with death, and Mertz lost it. Two weeks after they left the fatal crevasse, both men were suffering from violent diarrhoea, scaling skin and sores and infected fingers and toes. Mertz was in agony from abdominal pains. The pair were killing and eating the sledge dogs as they went, and scientists believe that their illness was caused by eating the livers of the dogs.

Mertz collapsed in convulsions and Mawson packed him on the sledge and tried to pull him. At the end of an exhausting day, they had covered just two kilometres. That night, Mertz fell into a coma and died. Mawson gave himself little chance of survival. In his *Journal,* he recorded, 'As there is little chance of my reaching human aid alive I greatly regret inability at the moment to set out the detail of coastline met with for three hundred miles travelled and observations of glacier and ice-formations etc; the most of which latter are, of course, committed to my head.' Then, he wrote:

> On 11 January, I set out over a good surface with a slight down grade. From the start my feet felt lumpy and sore. The sight of my feet gave me quite a shock, for the thickened skin of the soles had

101

separated in each case as a complete layer, and abundant fluid had escaped into the socks. The new skin underneath was very abraded and raw.

I did what appeared to be the best thing under the circumstances; smeared the new skin with lanoline, of which there was a good store, with bandages, and bound the skin soles back in place ...

Mawson had six pairs of thick woollen socks, and these he put on. Then, fur boots and crampons. Then he took off almost all his clothes and basked in the rare 'glorious heat' of the sun. He continued on, and then, a week later, crossing a glacier, he himself plunged through the ice and into the abyss. His sledge, however, jammed at the lip, and Mawson, attached to it by a rope, found himself dangling, alive, but with the sledge slowly slipping towards the edge. Mawson recounts these supposedly last seconds:

[I] ... had time to say to myself, "so this is the end", expecting the sledge every moment to crash on my head and all to go to the unseen bottom – then thought of the food uneaten on the sledge; but the sledge pulled up without letting me down, thought of Providence giving me another chance. The chance was very small considering my weak condition. The width of the crevasse was about six feet, so I hung freely in space, turning slowly around.

Mawson strained to reach a knot in the rope. And then another. Painfully, he hauled himself close to the surface. He was home free! Then part of the lip gave way and he plunged down once more. He hung there in despair and briefly contemplated the option of just giving up and falling into the blackness. But Mawson was not the man to do that:

It was the occasion for a supreme attempt. New power seemed to come as I addressed myself to one last tremendous effort. The struggle occupied some time, but by a miracle I rose slowly to the surface. This time I emerged feet first, still holding on to the rope, and pushed myself out, extended at full length on the snow – on solid ground.

Then came the reaction, and I could do nothing for quite an hour ... On the 19th it was overcast and light snow falling. I resolved to "go ahead and leave the rest to Providence."

He rested – and once again he was tempted to continue lying in his sleeping bag, sleeping and eating until the food ran out. He thought of the philosophy of Omar Khyam, *Unborn tomorrow, and dead Yesterday/ Why fret about them if Today be sweet!* He decided, he tells us in the *Journal*, 'to plug on'.

Ten days later, Mawson was down to his last kilogram of food and at least a week from base when, in an incredible stroke of fortune, he spotted black bunting on a snow mound and beneath it a bag of food left by a search party from Commonwealth Bay. With the food was a note telling him that 23 miles away he would find more food in 'Aladdin's Cave', and that the *Aurora* would wait for him until the last moment. It also told him that Amundsen had reached the Pole, and Scott was planning a second winter at his base on Ross Sea. Scott was to die that winter, in his tent, blizzard bound and with two companions.

Mawson, by all the odds, should have shared his fate. But, with food and the knowledge that his companions held out hope for him, he now believed he had a slim chance. On his hands and knees, pulling his sledge, he made it to the cave three days later. He had hardly thrown himself into the warmth of its shelter than a hurricane hit and raged for a week while he gathered his strength. A week later, he reached Commonwealth Bay. The *Aurora* had just left for Australia before winter set in, but five of his companions had volunteered to stay on to wait for the return of Mawson and his party.

Ten months later, the *Aurora* steamed back to Commonwealth Bay. Douglas Mawson sailed back to Australia where he was knighted and showered with honours. But, the fascination with the Antarctic, which had so absorbed the world, had ebbed now that nations were on the brink of war, and Douglas Mawson's epic story of courage and endurance has remained relatively unsung from that day.

In the Alien Arms of Jacky-Jacky

*J*acky-Jacky was a familiar name to generations of Australian school children until the last decades of the 20th century when, it seemed, his heroism was an embarrassment to black and white Australians. Here was an example of those who used to be called 'the noble savage', a black man devoted to a white explorer – and both hunted relentlessly by murderous Aborigines. The explorer, Edmund Kennedy, died in Jacky-Jacky's arms, and perhaps this poignant and telling moment is the final nail in the coffin in which Jacky-Jacky's heroism lies deeply buried.

Kennedy had led a party up the east coast of the peninsula of Cape York when, in July 1848, little more than six weeks after the party had left Rockingham Bay, its members began to experience the first of a mounting series of troubles that would end, six months later, in Kennedy's death by spearing. Ten men of the 13 who set out failed to come back: murdered or dead of starvation. Jacky-Jacky – his real name was Galmahra – gave this account of Kennedy's last day and of his own desperate escape from the killers:

> … We went on in the afternoon half a mile along the river side, and met a good lot of blacks, and we camped; the blacks all cried out "powad, powad," and rubbed their bellies; and we thought they were friendly, and Mr Kennedy gave them fish-hooks all round; every one asked me if I had any thing to give away, and I said no; and Mr Kennedy said, give them your knife, Jackey; this fellow on board was the man I gave the knife to; I am sure of it; I know him well; the black that was shot in the canoe was the most active in urging all the others on to spear Mr Kennedy; I gave the man on board my knife; we went on this day, and I looked behind, and they were getting

up their spears, and ran all round the camp which we had left; I told Mr Kennedy that very likely those blackfellows would follow us, and he said, "No, Jackey, those blacks are friendly"; I said to him, "I know those blackfellows well, they too much speak."

We went on some two or three miles and camped; I and Mr Kennedy watched them that night, taking it in turns every hour all night; by-and-by I saw the blackfellows; it was a moonlight night; and I walked up to Mr Kennedy, and said to him there is plenty of blackfellows now; this was in the middle of the night; Mr Kennedy told me to get my gun ready; the blacks did not know where we slept, as we did not make a fire; we both sat up all night; after this, daylight came, and I fetched the horses and saddled them; then we went on a good way up the river, and then we sat down a little while, and we saw three blackfellows coming along our track and they saw us, and one fellow ran back as hard as he could run, and fetched up plenty more, like a flock of sheep almost; I told Mr Kennedy to put the saddles on the two horses and go on, and the blacks came up, and they followed us all the day; all along it was raining, and I now told him to leave the horses and come on without them, that the horses made too much track.

Mr Kennedy was too weak, and would not leave the horses. We went on this day till towards evening, raining hard, and the blacks followed us all the day, some behind, some planted before; blacks all around following us. Now we went into a little bit of a scrub, and I told Mr Kennedy to look behind always; sometimes he would do so, and sometimes he would not look behind to look out for the blacks.

Then a good many blackfellows came behind in the scrub, and threw plenty of spears, and hit Mr Kennedy in the back first. Mr Kennedy said to me, "Oh! Jackey, Jackey! shoot 'em, shoot em." Then I pulled out my gun and fired, and hit one fellow all over the face with buck shot; he tumbled down, and got up again and again and wheeled right round, and two blackfellows picked him up and carried him away.

They went away then a little way, and came back again, throwing spears all around, more than they did before: very large spears. I pulled out the spear at once from Mr Kennedy's back, and cut out the jag with Mr Kennedy's knife; then Mr Kennedy got his gun and snapped, but his gun would not go off.

Relentlessly hunted, Kennedy and Jacky-Jacky might have survived in the open, but trapped in the mangroves in tropical rain they found their firearms useless.

The blacks sneaked all along by the trees, and speared Mr Kennedy again in the right leg, above the knee a little, and I got speared over the eye, and the blacks were now throwing their spears all ways, never giving over, and shortly again speared Mr Kennedy in the right side; there were large jags to the spears, and I cut them out and put them into my pocket.

At the same time we got speared, the horses got speared too, and jumped and bucked all about, and got into the swamp. I now told Mr Kennedy to sit down, while I looked after the saddlebags, which I did; and when I came back again, I saw blacks along with Mr Kennedy; I then asked him if he saw the blacks with him, he was stupid with the spear wounds, and said, "No"; then I asked him where was his watch? I saw the blacks taking away watch and hat as I was returning to Mr Kennedy; then I carried Mr Kennedy into the scrub, he said, "Don't carry me a good way;" then Mr Kennedy looked this way, very bad (Jackey rolling his eyes).

I said to him, "Don't look far away," as I thought he would be frightened; I asked him often, "Are you well now?" and he said, "I don't care for the spear wounds in my side and back," and said, "I am bad inside, Jackey."

I told him blackfellow always die when he got spear in there (the back); he said, "I am out of wind, Jackey."

I asked him, "Mr Kennedy, you are going to leave me?" and he said, "Yes, my boy, I am going to leave you"; he said, "I am very bad, Jackey; you take the books, Jackey, to the captain, but not the big ones, the Governor will give anything for them." I then tied up the papers, he then said, "Jackey, give me paper and I will write." I gave him paper and pencil, and he tried to write, and he then fell back and died, and I caught him as he fell back and held him, and I then turned round myself and cried: I was crying a good while until I got well; that was about an hour, and then I buried him; I digged up the ground with a tomahawk, and covered him over with logs, then grass, and my shirt and trousers; that night I left him near dark. I would go through the scrub and the blacks threw spears at me; a great many; and I went back into the scrub.

Then I went down the creek, which runs into Escape River, and I walked along the water in the creek, very easy, with my head only above water, to avoid the blacks, and get out of their way. In this way I went half-a-mile. Then I got out of the creek and got clear of them, and walked all night nearly, and slept in the bush without a fire.

Jacky-Jacky survived and 13 days later – with the hostile natives hot behind – he was rescued by a ship sent to pick up Kennedy's party. He returned with an expedition to find the other two survivors, Kennedy's body and that of the other nine men. In gratitude, Governor FitzRoy gave Jacky-Jacky 50 pounds and a brass breast-plate. Kennedy had a tablet erected in his memory in St James Church, Sydney.

Jacky-Jacky went back to his tribe near Muswellbrook, but he could never again be Galmahra. He took to the drink and died when he fell drunk into a camp fire.

Faithful – the way these wretched blacks should be,
but seldom are – a model for your people,
who sit in their wurlies and mope
and are ungrateful
for our busy invasion, our civilised example.

They too should love and help us. So we gave you
a special medal to be worn for the rest of your days,
and fifty pounds in the Bank for approved expenses;
and we spoke of you with pleased uneasy surprise.

Yes, something, some faintly disgusted incredulity
clouded our commendation. How odd of Kennedy
to die on so black a breast, in arms so alien.
It seemed somehow to betray a lack of dignity.

But you, Galmahra? I try to see into your eyes,
as frank and dark as the depths of your Hunter River.
You loved him, certainly; you wept as you buried him,
and you wept again, when your own escape was over.

From 'Jacky Jacky' by Judith Wright

Escape from the Stockade

*I*t was all over in 20 bloody minutes. But those 20 minutes 'freed Australia at Eureka long ago,' wrote Henry Lawson. And, for Mark Twain, 'I think it may be called the finest thing in Australia's history. It was a revolution – small in size but great politically; it was a strike for liberty, a struggle for a principle, a stand against injustice and oppression … the people knew it and are proud of it. They keep green the memory of the men who fell at Eureka Stockade, and Peter Lalor has his monument.'

Twenty-two diggers and six soldiers died on Sunday, 3 December 1854 at the barricade hastily flung up by Ballarat gold miners protesting against oppressive licence fees. The miners were led by Peter Lalor, one of a dozen wounded in the fighting. Henry Gyles Turner, in *Our Own Little Rebellion*, recounted how Lalor was able to escape, later to be pardoned and elected to the Victorian Parliament:

> (George) Black, who had been called Lalor's Minister of War, lay in hiding for a day or two with some friendly miners, and then after carefully disguising himself started off at nightfall, accompanied by Kennedy to find his way to Geelong, by a back track, over the Mount Misery ranges. They got bushed and suffered much hardship, but were generously treated by some diggers they fell in with, who saw through their disguise. Finally Black succeeded in reaching Melbourne, and remained in seclusion until the general amnesty enabled him to show himself.

> But the escape of Peter Lalor has more interest, because he bulked larger in the Colony's affairs afterwards, and was so widely personally known.

When the last of the Police had finally cleared away, after removing the dead bodies, some miners, whose claims were within the Stockade, discovered Lalor, helpless in his burrow. With very great caution they succeeded in smuggling him out into the bush across the Melbourne Road, and there they procured a horse, on which they held him while he made for the hut of an acquaintance in the ranges.

The man was absent, and Lalor distrusting the offer of the man's wife to go in search of him, preferred to spend the night in wandering at large in the bush. At daybreak next morning, in great pain, and faint from loss of blood, he made his way to the hut of a mining mate, Steve Cummins, where he was given food and rest, and an attempt was made by Mrs Cummins to bandage his wound.

His host, however, at once saw that the injury was too serious for amateur treatment; moreover, he knew that the Police were aware of his friendship with Lalor, and felt that the reward offered for his apprehension would stimulate them to search his place. So he consulted the Reverend Father Smyth as to the best means of securing both surgical assistance and safety for his friend.

The generous priest at once assured him of both if he would bring Lalor to the Presbytery under cover of night. This was successfully done, and in that sanctuary Drs Doyle and Stewart in consultation, amputated the arm from the shoulder joint, for the long delay in dressing it, and the rough usage it had received, destroyed all hope of saving it.

The suspicions of Cummins about the police were fully justified, for at the very time the operation was in progress, the troopers were ransacking his dwelling for traces of the man who was worth £200 to them. As soon as Lalor was able to get about after the operation, he was transferred to the secret custody of a friendly storekeeper at Brown's Hill, with a view to getting a passage to Geelong in some of the return drays trading there.

The opportunity at last presented itself, and he was safely conveyed to his destination by a carrier named Michael Carroll and his son, who knew the risk they were running, and scorning the temptations of the reward, which obtruded themselves by placards all along the route, were satisfied to have done a friendly turn to a man they admired, without seeking any pecuniary recompense.

They rigged up a tilt over one of their drays, and Lalor passed most of his time under that, for his wound was still unhealed and he was very weak. They encountered several troopers on the road, but the carrier was well known, and no attempt was made to search. But they had one narrow escape. While halting for supplies at Meredith, two diggers seeking a lift to Geelong, took a look under the tilt and recognised Lalor.

One of them immediately proposed that they should follow up the dray until they got close to Geelong, and then lay the police on to it, and get the reward. The other, whose name was Burns, and therefore probably not a countryman of Lalor's shrunk from the baseness of earning blood money, but fearing that if he refused his mate might make the disclosure at once, pretended acquiescence.

He suggested that the prospects were good enough to shout a bottle of whisky on. This was procured, and Burns generously allowed his companion to drink three-fourths of it. When it had taken effect he went to the carrier, to whom he was known, and said, "For God's sake get Lalor away as soon as you can; my mate wanted to lay the police on to you. I'll keep him drunk till you get well away."

The advice was acted upon, and shortly after midnight, the proscribed rebel was safely landed in Geelong at the home of Miss Dunn, the school mistress, to whom he had been long engaged, and afterwards married. With affectionate solicitude she secured his convalescence, and when the abortive trials of the insurgents collapsed, Lalor returned to Ballarat unmolested, and the emancipated diggers not only received him with enthusiasm, but subscribed £1,000, to enable him to start in business.

Something about Australia

*T*here was something about Australia – dreadful though it was – that Mary Bryant must have liked. Something that caused her to carry a nostalgic souvenir of the penal settlement she escaped from when she began her 3254-mile journey in an open boat. She took the souvenir with her in that boat. In fetters, she took it with her to Batavia. And she had it close when, finally, she landed under guard back in England facing a frightening prison sentence.

Mary Bryant's souvenir was a packet of dried Australian 'sweet tea' – sarsaparilla leaves. At the end of her remarkable story, she presented the packet in gratitude to the man who gave it a happy ending: Dr Johnson's biographer, James Boswell.

Mary was born Mary Broad in 1765, the daughter of a Cornish sailor. Twenty-one years later, she was convicted of street robbery with violence – stealing a cloak from 'a spinster' – and sentenced to death. The sentence was commuted to transportation for seven years, and Mary Broad was sent for a year to the *Dunkirk*, a prison hulk, and then put on the *Charlotte*, one of the ships of the First Fleet carrying just over 1000 men, women and children to an unknown land on the other side of the world.

On 13 May 1787, the *Charlotte* set sail. By the time the ship had reached Cape Town, Mary had given birth to a daughter, probably the child of one of the warders on the hulk. She called the child Charlotte, and on 10 February 1788, four days after landing at Sydney Cove, she married a convict who had been with her on the voyage – William Bryant.

Byrant was a fisherman and, like Mary, from Cornwall. He had been convicted of 'resisting the revenue offices when they attempted to seize

112

some smugglers' property' and was serving a seven-year sentence. Bryant fathered Mary's second child, Emanuel, in April 1790, by which time, said one Botany Bay officer, 'famine was approaching with gigantic strides and gloom and dejection overspread every countenance.'

Food was in such short supply that an invitation to dine with Governor Arthur Phillip was invariably accompanied by the injunction: 'Bring your own bread'. Guests would be ushered to the table at Government House and take a loaf from their pockets and place it on the table beside them. The ships of the First Fleet had brought enough food for two years and Phillip had been assured that, long before this supply ran out, it would be replenished. But the reality was that the food was of poor quality, the livestock died or wandered off into the bush, and convicts knew nothing of farming the infertile land around Botany Bay.

Famine's shadow was over the penal colony, and stealing food was a capital offence. On one day in March 1789, six marines who had been helping themselves to the food store were publicly hanged. In this desperate situation a fisherman was invaluable, and Bryant was given charge of the boats that hauled in the fishing nets each day. This was an important post, and 'Every encouragement was given to this man to keep him above temptation; an hut was built for him and his family; he was always presented with a certain part of the fish which he caught; and he wanted for nothing that was necessary; or that was suitable to a person of his description and situation,' Judge Advocate David Collins recorded.

Smuggling was in Bryant's blood, however, as it was in many a Cornishman's, and despite every encouragement to keep him above temptation the chance to sell some of the catch before it got into the hands of the authorities was too much for him. Inevitably, he was caught and given 100 lashes. He was allowed to stay on as a fisherman, but his rank was reduced, and he now began to consider escape. Bryant talked it over with Mary. Just a year ago, William Bligh and the 'loyalists' had been set adrift in a longboat by the mutinous crew of the *Bounty* and in six weeks had rowed from Tahiti to Timor. Mr and Mrs Bryant thought that, if Bligh could do it, they could do it too. They would need a boat, a compass and provisions.

In October 1790, the Bryants got what they required. A Dutch East Indies trader came to Port Jackson loaded with stores and with the sort of equipment Bryant needed. Bryant somehow persuaded a Dutchman to give him a compass, a quadrant, muskets, a chart, and some food, and he hid the contraband under the floorboards of his hut. In the following five months, he and seven male convicts, four of them with some experience at sea, stole and hid a considerable amount of food: 25 pounds of flour, 25 pounds of rice, three pounds of pork and 10 gallons of water, along with cooking utensils, bedding and fishing lines and sarsaparilla leaves for making tea. They also had their eye on a boat: the governor's cutter, a six-oared boat in excellent condition that Bryant used to go fishing.

The Judge Advocate Collins, however, was aware that Bryant was thinking of escape. He recorded that, with five other convicts, Bryant had been 'overheard consulting on the practicability of carrying off the boat in which he was employed.' This circumstance being reported to the governor, it was determined that all his proceedings should be narrowly watched and any scheme of that nature counteracted. The following day, the cutter was caught in a squall, overturned and badly damaged: enough for Collins to note that 'the execution of his project was for the present prevented'. While the cutter was being repaired, the conspirators continued hoarding and hiding food and Mary went on gathering sarsaparilla leaves from vines that grew on the foreshore of the harbour.

In the early moonless hours of 29 March, with the only ship capable of overhauling them on its way to Norfolk Island, the Bryants, their two infant children and their seven convict companions stole the governor's cutter and rowed, with oars muffled, for Timor. It was the start of a journey that was to take Mary halfway around the world.

What impelled the group to undertake such a journey? John Easty, a marine private at Botany Bay, wrote in his diary: 'It's a very Desperate attempt, to go in an open boat for a run of about 16 or 17 hundred Leags and in pertucular for a Woman and 2 small Children the eldest not above 3 years of age – but the thoughts of Liberty from such a place as this is Enough to induce any Convicts to try all Schemes to obtain it, as they are the same as Slaves all the time they are in this Country.'

William Bryant kept a journal of the voyage, since lost. It would have told a story of hair-raising escapes at sea and on land, mountainous seas where they bailed desperately expecting every minute 'to go the bottom', and, on land, close shaves with natives – 'very Stout and fat and Blacker' – who pursued them, firing arrows from their canoes, off the eastern tip of the Gulf of Carpentaria. Somewhere on the coast of Arnhem Land, the group drew breath and set course for Timor, where they tied up on the Koepang wharf on 5 June 1791. There, they explained that they were survivors of a shipwreck, a perfectly common and feasible story, and for some months they enjoyed freedom. For an inexplicable reason, however, there was a quarrel, which caused tongues to wag. The upshot was that Bryant confessed all to the Dutch governor, and they were put in detention until the unexpected arrival in the port of HMS Captain Edward Edwards.

Captain Edwards had been in command of HMS *Pandora*. He had been chasing the Bligh mutineers and had picked up 14 in Tahiti and chained them in a cage made for the purpose when his ship struck a reef off New Guinea and he and 98 survivors – 10 mutineers among them – had made their way to Timor in the ship's pinnace, longboat and two yawls. On 5 April, the escapees and the mutineers were sent in shackles aboard a Dutch tub, the porous *Rembang*, charted by Edwards to take them to Batavia. They made it – just. Six days out they ran into a frightening storm. 'In a few minutes every sail of the ship was shivered to pieces: the pumps all choked and useless,' wrote Surgeon George Hamilton, 'and she was driving down with all the impetuosity imaginable, on a savage shore, about seven miles under our lee. This storm was attended with the most dreadful thunder and lightening we have ever experienced. The Dutch seamen were struck with horror, and went below; and the ship was preserved from destruction by the manly efforts of our English tars.'

The *Rembang* limped into Batavia on 7 November 1791. The city was a notoriously unhealthy port. Twenty years before Captain Cook had written, 'We came in here with as healthy a ship's company as need go to sea, and after a stay of not quite three months, left in the condition of a hospital ship besides the loss of seven men.' In Surgeon Hamilton's opinion, 'all the mortality of that place originates from marsh effluvia, arising from their stagnant canals and pleasure grounds,' and within a month Mary's husband and youngest child had died of 'the pestilence' – dysentery or malaria. Three more of the Port Jackson escapees died before the ship reached Cape Town, where Mary and Charlotte and the three surviving convicts were transferred to a British man-o-war conveying soldiers returning from a tour of duty in Sydney. Among them was marine Captain Watkin Tench, who had come out on the *Charlotte* with William and Mary, and who wrote sympathetically:

They had miscarried in a heroic struggle for liberty; after having combated every hardship, and conquered every difficulty. The woman, and one of the men, had gone out to Port Jackson in the ship which had transported me thither. They had both of them been always distinguished for good behaviour. And I could not but reflect with admiration, at the strange combination of circumstances which had again brought us together, to baffle human foresight, and confound human speculation.

Eighteen months after their 'heroic struggle for liberty' began, Mary, Charlotte and the four fellow convicts were taken ashore when the ship docked at Portsmouth on 18 June 1792. They were removed to Newgate Gaol where they were condemned to remain on their former sentence until they should be discharged 'by due course of law'. Effectively this meant that they might be incarcerated for many years.

The sentence was cruel, but the prisoners themselves had said that 'they would rather sooner suffer death than return to Botany Bay,' and they were lucky to escape hanging, the usual penalty. In the meantime, the press had taken the story to its heaving bosom. 'The Girl From Botany Bay' – the headline writers were trembling on the verge of claiming her as 'Our Mary' – had the journals in a lather of excitement. 'The resolution displayed by the woman is hardly to be paralleled in the annals of ancient Rome,' pronounced the *London Chronicle*. The *Dublin Chronicle* topped that. The escape, it said, was 'perhaps the most hazardous and wonderful effort ever made by nine persons (for two were infants) to regain their liberty.'

James Boswell, the man the world is indebted to for his unsurpassed biography of Dr Samuel Johnson, read the newspapers with mounting interest. A barrister, he was in the habit of brilliantly defending at times without payment, and he fought for a pardon for Mary and her four companions. On 2 May 1793, Mary was discharged, and six months later Boswell came home to find four men on his doorstep. They were the convict escapees, finally pardoned, and waiting to thank him.

Mary thanked Boswell with her gift of the packet of Australian 'sweet tea' leaves and went home to Cornwall where she disappeared into history.

The Boy Who Set Sail
with 200 Shady Ladies

'*A*fter committing sundry rows and breaches of the peace, such as blowing up the seat of the privy and bringing rum in to school in coconuts ... I got expelled and sent to my Guardian, Mr Hay.' The opening lines of the memoirs of James Montagu Smith set the tone for his extraordinary recollections of life in Australia in the 1850s, the most colourful and turbulent decade in our history. Smith's *Journal* reveals an adventurer whose fierce love for his adopted country and his understanding of its unique virtues at a time when the colony was considered little more than a dumping ground for convicts – albeit rich in gold – qualifies him to be accepted as one of our forgotten heroes.

James Montagu Smith was sent to sea by his guardian shortly after he was expelled from school. The night before he sailed, 'I dined at the Governor's house [*his guardian's*] and thought I could not be a sailor unless I drank freely. Accordingly did, and got outrageously drunk and had to be carried home.' In 1852, the teenage boy found himself with 220 women convicts and half a dozen children, sailing from London's St Katherine's Docks to Hobart Town. Among the women was Mary Petty, who came on board cradling Sarah, her three-month-old baby.

A century and a half later, the lives of the 15-year-old midshipman and the convict mother again intersected – unearthing James Montagu Smith's enthralling real-life records, four notebooks, leatherbound and with the word 'private' on the cover of each. The notebooks remained that way for decades, known only to his descendants, until in 1996 they were chanced upon by Barbara Cuffley, a descendant of Mary Petty, and wife of social historian and author, Peter Cuffley. Cuffley edited the journals, and they were published in 2002 by The Five Mile Press as

Send the Boy to Sea: The Memoirs of a Sailor on the Goldfields.

James Montagu Smith's memoirs cover his life from the age of 14 to 21, from 1851 to 1857. Just seven years, but what years! Before he was 21, James had made three voyages halfway round the world. On his first, on board *The Lancastrian*, bound for Melbourne, the 14-year-old quickly found himself in trouble again. 'The Bosun was an arrant thief and soon taught us to be as bad as himself … the more we stole the better the Bosun liked us.' But the boy and another his age were caught and punished: tied to the topgallant rigging. When that ordeal was over, 'We were called down and made to walk the forecastle with a couple of handspikes on our shoulders; but we were released by the intercession of the solicitor's daughter, who was about 12 years old, and said she was quite sure "the pretty boy" (that's me) would not steal any more wine.'

The girl's father was Albert Read, who set up practice in Melbourne and sometimes defended the teenage Ned Kelly. Read's grandson was Judge Albert Read, and his great grandson, Richard Read, is a Melbourne Crown Prosecutor.

Shipboard life, for the boy, was dreary, often brutal, and always dangerous. On the return voyage, off New Guinea, Smith fell overboard in waters where the crew had caught an 11-foot shark. '"Man overboard!" thrilled through the ship, I saw the huge bulk glide past me, pale anxious faces up and down from the rails; ropes were thrown as I passed, and then she gradually receded and left me alone in the deep.' Miraculously, the ship turned and found him in the near dark.

James disliked the sailor's life, and on his next voyage, he and the first mate – who thought James 'too knowing and cheeky for me, that young shaver is' – came to blows. James was handcuffed to the mizzenmast in freezing weather and then locked up in the Black Box. 'This was a box made like a coffin standing on its end – one can neither sit or lie, nor indeed stand comfortably – with little holes at the top to breath through. It is anything but a pleasant place.' The ship, the *Sir*

Robert Seppings, was bound for Tasmania, transporting 220 women convicts. 'The sailors soon became intimately acquainted with them, and I was frequently employed to write love letters for the old salts.'

Sailing ship of the 1850s when James Montagu Smith made his voyages. On the first, aged 14, he was punished by being lashed to the rigging of the top sails.
Collection: Barbara Cuffley

James landed in Hobart Town – and in more trouble. On the word of the captain, a callous magistrate summarily found him guilty of insubordination and ordered him to be put on the treadmill. At sea again, he sailed from Norfolk Island – 'a perfect little paradise inhabited by demons' – on a ship with 300 convicts below deck –

[a]ll men who had been twice convicted of the most heinous crimes, and rendered desperate by the most horrible cruelty and ill usage. A more villainous looking herd of wretches I never saw. They

were all in irons, one leg being fastened to the other by a chain just long enough to allow them to walk.

A conspiracy was formed to take the ship before we had been many days out. They removed the fore-scuttle although it was well fastened down by some iron bars; and by that means they got into the hold.

But, there, a cabin boy spotted one of them in hiding, and, shades of *Treasure Island's* Jim Hawkins, kept quiet until he could alert the captain. A savage melee with the sailors and marines ended with the marines firing blanks into the convicts' midst.

Returned to Hobart Town, James escaped his ship by getting the watchman drunk but was caught at gunpoint and returned to the penitentiary and solitary confinement: 'the punishment most dreaded ... a stone cell, perfectly dark, very cold – only one blanket allowed at night ... and ... half a pound of bread per day ... Let the fools who talk of death being the greatest punishment try the slow starvation and solitary system.' It was 1853, a gold rush year. Along with thousands of others, James again deserted ship when it docked in Port Phillip Bay and walked 130 kilometres to the diggings, from Melbourne to Castlemaine. He found gold. Others, like his mate, Jimmy Barr – the Hairy Wee Man – died of starvation in the quest.

James, whose politics had been called 'radical humbug', was with the miners in their fight against the goldfields' arrogant, corrupt troopers and warned that 'some time or other they [the Troopers] would repent.' In support of the miners, he 'wrote a lot of bills which were stuck up on trees along the highway – very seditious they were too.' He left the goldfields nine days before the slaughter at Eureka Stockade. (At the same time, 100 kilometres from Ballarat, Ned Kelly was born.)

James held his native England – 'the Old Country' – in contempt. He felt suffocated by its stuffiness and hypocrisy. He despised the way young English middleclass women were kept powerless – used as objects for profitable marriage matches, knowing little and doing less. 'Those folks who write about women's rights should … point out the road by which they can right themselves by teaching them to be women and not things.' He loathed the English climate and 'the cold virgins of the north', and he loved Australia's sunny skies and warm women. There was 'a very pretty little girl about seventeen stopped there from Sydney. Her name was Ellen. … I was not long in making desperate love to her … Oh the joys of pure love in a genial climate!'

James also sympathised with and admired the Aborigines. 'They are happy and contented, or at least were so before the white man came and stole their country … They have tasted freedom and prefer God's canopy to Man's, and for this they are called barbarians; and for this they are despised. Pshaw! The European has much to learn, although he thinks of himself so very wise.'

Bushrangers, transportation, rebellion, gold fever – the penal colonies of Australia were in dramatic ferment. From it, as these vivid memoirs make clear, a distinct Australian identity was emerging. Tall, easy-going yet always ready for a stoush, a fervent believer in mateship and a fair go, a democrat with a radical political bent and passionate about his adopted country, young James Montagu Smith was the archetype of the new, unique and heroic Australian man. His like would land at Gallipoli half a century on.

5 | G'day Sport!

Ashes to Ashes, the Never-ending War

S outh Americans literally kill for football. North Americans love baseball. Canadians go crazy for ice hockey. But sport – in almost all its manifestations – cements Australia as it does no other country, and of all sports it is cricket that most obsesses us. Football is followed with a fearsome passion. Hundreds of thousands mourn if the Magpies lose a premiership or Queensland wins the State of Origin. But only cricket – and only a cricket match between Australia and England – has the capacity to plunge the entire nation into gloom or send it off to work on Monday morning with a glad heart and a song on its lips.

The cricket rivalry between Australia and England is unparalleled in international sport. Soccer has bitter rivalry but nothing to match the vintage of the struggle for the Ashes, a legacy that goes back to the day when England cricket was said to have died, at the Oval on 29 August 1882. On that day, for the first time, Australia beat England at its own game on its home turf. It was a famous victory, a thriller that caused one spectator to have a fatal heart attack and another to gnaw through the handle of his umbrella.

England began the match as firm favourites, and at one stage the odds on them winning were 60 to one on. They might have justified those odds but for the 'great man of cricket', W. G. Grace, a batsman who could charitably be called a cheat. W. G. was a colossus among cricketers, a man who believed he was a law unto himself. He'd bluff or bully umpires and opponents into letting him bat on when he was palpably out, and he had no respect for the spirit in which the game was supposed to be played. On the second morning of the Test, when

Australia was batting for the second time, Grace did something that has never been done since.

At the tail of the Australian innings, with the team struggling, the skipper, Lloyd, hit a ball to leg and he and his partner, Sam Jones, ran a valuable single. Jones safely crossed his crease and then, believing the ball to be dead, stepped outside the crease. Grace, who had the ball and was standing close to the stumps, dashed the bails off and bellowed: 'Howzat?' Jones, technically speaking, was out: the ball was still in play and the umpire had no option but to lift his finger. The Australians were furious. Spofforth, the bowler known as 'The Demon', swore the English would pay for such unsportsmanlike behaviour.

The English came out needing only 85 runs to win. But Spofforth was opening the bowling. Soon he had two wickets in two balls, but England now needed only 70. A partnership developed between Ulyett and Grace, and they took the score to 51 before The Demon struck again. Ulyett was caught from a ball by Spofforth, and then Grace went. Now they needed 32 and had six wickets in hand. Spofforth snared another. Nineteen runs needed, five wickets standing. Spofforth took the next two wickets, both for a duck.

Now the English spectators began to shudder. Silence shrouded the ground as Spofforth steamed in with and bowled Lucas. Ten to win and two wickets left. Now one man began sinking his teeth into his umbrella handle. Now it was too much for another's heart. The English failed by five runs. Spofforth took seven for 44 and in his last 11 overs four wickets for two runs. In all, Spofforth took 14 wickets for 90 runs. The reverberations of the nail-biting win have never really ceased.

The *Sporting Times* published an obituary: 'In affectionate remembrance of English Cricket which died at the Oval on 29th August 1882. Deeply lamented by a large circle of sorrowing Friends and Acquaintances. NB – the body will be cremated and the Ashes taken to Australia.' (The physical Ashes, of a stump, sealed in an urn and presented to the victorious touring English cricket team the following year, went home to England with the team and have stayed there ever since.)

Murdoch's team returned to Australia for one of the grandest home-coming processions the nation has known. Melbourne turned on a torch-lit procession headed by 700 fire-fighters; there were bands the length of Collins Street; and when, at the Melbourne Cricket Ground, the team was introduced one by one, the fireworks and the celebrations went on for hours.

But Melbourne crowds also cheered themselves hoarse for other sports, one of them a code of football that was played nowhere else in the world. Two years before the famous Ashes test took place, they were playing 'footy' – Australian Football – to huge crowds. Nat Gould, the American sports author and historian, was amazed at the fervour for Australian Football. 'It is no uncommon thing on a Saturday afternoon in Melbourne, when the famous clubs meet in a Cup Tie, to see from 25 000 to 30 000 spectators present. Considering the population [200 000] as compared with some great English cities, this I think, is an extraordinary attendance.'

Richard Twopenny, an English visitor, too, was astonished by the size of the crowds and thrilled by the new Australian game. 'The best game of football has been found, in Melbourne,' he wrote. He continued:

In corroboration of my opinion I would point to the facts that, while Sydney is at least as good at cricket as Melbourne, there are not a dozen football clubs in Sydney (where they play Rugby Union), as against about a hundred in Melbourne; that the attendance at the best matches in Sydney is not one-third of what it is in Melbourne; that the average number of people who go to see football matches on a Saturday afternoon in Sydney is not one-tenth of that in Melbourne; and that in Sydney people will not pay to see the game, while in Melbourne the receipts from football matches are larger than they are from cricket matches.

The quality of the attendance, also, in Melbourne is something remarkable; but of some 10,000 people, perhaps, who pay their sixpences to see the Melbourne and Carlton clubs play of an afternoon, there are not a thousand who are intensely interested in the match, and who do not watch its every turn with the same intentness which characterises the boys at Lord's during the Eton and Harrow match.

A good football match in Melbourne is one of the sights of the world. Old men and young get equally excited. The quality of the play, too, is much superior to anything the best English clubs can produce. Of course it is not easy to judge of this when the games played are different, but on such points as drop-kicking, dodging, and catching, comparison can be made with the Rugby game; and every 'footballer' (the word, if not coined, has become commonly current here) knows what I mean when I say, that there is much more 'style' about the play of at least half a dozen clubs in Victoria, than about the 'Old Etonians' or the 'Blackheath,' which are the two best clubs I have seen play in England.'

The Australian football code invented in 1858 and at first peculiar to Victoria had, within 20 years, spread to South Australia, Queensland and Tasmania, and in 1880 Victoria played against New South Wales. Victoria won with ease, and *Punch* magazine perceptively said the code would never be popular in Sydney as long as it continued to be called Victorian Rules Football: 'Victorian Rules ... had they dubbed the game Scandinavian Rules, well and good, but VICTORIAN – perish the thought! The sooner the game is altered to Australian Rules of Football the better!'

Sydney – indeed all of Australia – took the Melbourne Cup to its heart, although at first there had been some hesitation. In 1885 (Sheet Anchor's year), the *Sydney Morning Herald* railed against this 'worst occasion and cause for a national gathering, that is naturally allied to more that makes directly for human degradation than any other public sport or pastime that could be named.' Alarming, but alas, far too late.

The Cup had been a blazing success from the first, 1861 (Archer's year), and two decades on, it had established itself as an extraordinary sporting event, involving most of the community in a social celebration without peer.

'It is the Melbourne Cup that brings this multitude together,' Mark Twain wrote after his 1895 (Auraria's year) tour of Australia. He continued:

> Their clothes have been ordered long ago, at unlimited cost and without bounds as to beauty and magnificence, and have been kept in concealment until now, for unto this day are they consecrate. I am speaking of the ladies clothes, but one might know that.
>
> And so the grandstands make a brilliant and wonderful spectacle, a delirium of color, a vision of beauty. The champagne flows, everybody is vivacious, excited, happy; everybody bets and gloves and fortunes change hands right along, all the time. Day after day the races go on, and the fun and the excitement are kept at white heat; and when each day is done the people dance all night so as to be fresh for the race in the morning.
>
> And at the end of the great week the swarms secure lodgings and transportation for next year, then flock away to their remote homes and count their gains and losses, and order next year's Cup-clothes, and then lie down and sleep two weeks, and get up sorry to reflect that a whole year must be put in somehow or other before they can be wholly happy again.

Of course, Mark Twain was exaggerating, wasn't he ...?

Buried face up in shallow soil on Batavia's Graveyard, the skeleton of a tall man in his 30s, struck down by a vicious sword blow that left a deep cut on his skull. The absence of cuts to the forearms indicates that the man was taken by surprise and had no chance to ward off the blow, or, more likely, was held by Cornelisz's men. Felled, he was probably stabbed to death or had his throat slit and was then perfunctorily buried. There he lay, undisturbed for three centuries. *The* West Australian *Photographic Collection*

Matthew Brady was, said a contemporary, 'a born leader of men and a conqueror of women'. Another described him as a 'robust young man, muscular and well made, with an innocent sort of face, bright eyes and a good wide forehead'. No wonder, then, that when the Prince of Bushrangers was tried a year after this pencil portrait was done, The Hobart Town *Gazette* was forced with 'regret to state that the court was crowded with sympathising ladies who wept at the recital of Brady's sufferings'. *Mitchell Library Collection, State Library of New South Wales*

The suggestion of an under-bite and the hint of a knowing smile in this post-mortem pencil sketch provoke ironic reminders of Alexander 'Cannibal' Pearce's fondness for human flesh. At his trial the judge said: 'This case is too inhuman to comment on,' and then sentenced Pearce to be hanged and his body dismembered, in keeping with the horror of his crime. On a chilly August morning in 1824 a large and enthusiastic Hobart Town crowd was on hand for the proceedings. *Mitchell Library Collection, State Library of New South Wales*

He could be a Victorian-era philanthropist, a Lakes District poet, or perhaps an archdeacon, but Norfolk Island Commandant John Giles Price lived up to his family crest: 'a dragon's head in whose mouth is a human hand, dripping blood'. The monocle was pure affectation as is his benign pose for the camera. In reality he was terrifying. A cultured brute given to wearing a brace of pistols in his belt, Price was huge, immensely strong, supremely contemptuous of the convicts over whom he held the power of life and death, and probably a psychopath.

John Price, Inspector General of Penal Establishments, died Williamstown, Victoria, 1857, Tasmanian Museum and Art Gallery Collection

Hall and his gang attacked the Gundagai mail coach, shooting dead one of the police escort a few months after *Attacking the Mail, Bushranging NSW*, a chromolithograph from a drawing by S.T. Gill, was published in 1864. Accounts of the Ben Hall Gang's Gundagai shoot-out would have been listened to in awe by nine-year-old Ned Kelly. *National Library of Australia Collection*

On the trail of the Kelly Gang. For 26 months the fugitives eluded their pursuers with ease. Once, Aboriginal trackers took troopers to thick scrub where the Gang's horses had left fresh tracks. No one ventured further. Another time Ned got word back to his trackers that he had watched them lunching beside a creek, and accurately described the scene. This wood engraving was published in the *Australasian Sketcher*.

In convict linen jacket and corduroy trousers, Ned Kelly poses against a bluestone wall of the Melbourne Gaol. One of two photographs taken for his family by the gaol photographer, it captures the man as his admirers still see him. Strong, despite his many wounds – his shattered left arm, now shrivelled, holds a chord attached to leg irons and his crippled right hand is supported on his hip – Ned looks out at us, handsome, calm, and with the manly dignity he showed to the end, 21 hours later.
Victorian Police Historical Unit

ABOVE: How good was Young Griffo? Try his trick of plucking flies from the air, or standing on a handkerchief and defying anyone to hit you. The leader of a 'Push' from Sydney's then notorious Rocks area, he went to America, fought for the world lightweight title, won easily – but lost the decision: the referee incorrectly added the points. *National Library of Australia Collection*

OPPOSITE: 'He was a lovely animal to do anything with. Beautiful horse. He used to follow me around like a puppy dog. Followed me everywhere.' Tommy Woodcock, Phar Lap's strapper as a young man, talking affectionately half a century later about the horse he called Bobby. Seventeen hands high and weighing more than 700 kilograms, Phar Lap had a heart twice the size of a normal racehorse's. His stuffed hide (pictured with a middle-aged Tommy Woodcock) has been the most popular exhibit at the Melbourne Museum for 70 years. *The Herald and Weekly Times Photographic Collection*

Head ducked to avoid the camera, petite Jean Lee is led into Russell Street police headquarters. She denied ever going to 'Pop' Kent's until shown a page from her diary found in his room. Still defiant, she said: 'You can say what you like, Bobby won't make a statement and I'm not saying anything.' In a nearby room her lover Bobby Clayton had signed a statement – the next piece of paper she was shown. She immediately tried to save him by taking sole responsibility for the murder, but then recanted.
The Herald and Weekly Times Photographic Collection

'The fun of the world,' she called her trial, and serial poisoner Caroline 'Aunt Carrie' Grills revelled in it. *Truth* described the diminutive butterball as 'completely self-possessed, smiling and waving at the intervals to women who jostle for seats in the back of the court. She has enjoyed her forays with the cameramen.' When, after just 12 minutes, the jury returned with a guilty verdict, 'Aunt Carrie's' sunny disposition disappeared and 'Aunt Thally' emerged. Her fingers drummed angrily on the rail of the dock and she looked ready to reach for the thallium. *Newspix*

ABOVE: Shortly after his execution Deeming's corpse was subjected to the scrutiny of phrenologists, 'scientists' then in vogue who theorised that the shape and size of the head accurately correlated to a person's mental state and character. The measurements of his head were also taken for this wax model destined to be the object of delicious shivers when it was exhibited in the Chamber of Horrors at Madame Tussaud's, London.

OPPOSITE: 'Not quite a gentleman,' as one man recalled him, Frederick Bayley Deeming is seen on the cover of this 'Penny Dreadful' acting in a decidedly ungentlemanly fashion. Having cut the throat of his second wife Emily, he is preparing to entomb the body just as he had his first wife and their four children. Two years before, Jack the Ripper had hung up his razor and now Deeming, with one more victim than the Ripper, held the dubious title: The Criminal of the Century.

THE CRIMINAL

OF THE

Century

THE WINDSOR AND RAINHILL MURDERER.

The body of small-time Sydney crook James Smith (right) was never recovered – apart from one arm, which was regurgitated by a shark at Coogee Aquarium – and no one was ever convicted of his murder. Reginald Holmes, (below left) a well-known North Sydney boat builder involved in an insurance scam with Smith, told police that Patrick Brady (below right) had dumped Smith's body 'in a tin trunk outside Port Hacking'. But Holmes was shot before he could give evidence.

The Herald and Weekly Times Photographic Collection

Arthur Orton, photographed above before he bloated out to gargantuan proportions) and Sir Roger Tichbourne (photographed in Santiago in 1853, a few months before he sailed from Rio de Janeiro, never to be seen again) were palpably different. Their height, their weight, the color of their hair, their accents, their education their demeanour and their personality were totally at odds. But Orton audaciously claimed they were one and the same person.
Newspix

Percy Grainger and his wife Ella Strom. A strikingly handsome and outstanding eccentric, Percy's flair for living still has the capacity to cause dropped jaws. Completely self-centred, he nevertheless worked much of his life to provide for his mother and half a dozen others. Ella was a poet, 'as lovely as the morning to look upon,' Percy said, 'and a regular Amazon to walk, run, swim and dance, and play games.' They deserved each other.

The Grainger Museum,
The University of Melbourne

Australia's real life precursor to fiction's Sherlock Holmes, John Christie here looks extremely pleased with himself, and with good reason. Handsome, handy with his fists, intelligent and resourceful, Christie established his reputation with the Victoria police force for work stamped by his fondness for solving crimes in unorthodox ways. Most of all he enjoyed masquerading – dressing up and acting a part, male or female, to catch the many criminals of Marvellous Melbourne. *Victorian Police Historical Unit*

Donna Lola Montez's dark beauty and fiery temperament were utterly beguiling to four husbands and a string of infatuated men such as the composer Franz Liszt, the novelist Alexandre Dumas, and King Ludwig 1 of Bavaria. When Ludwig lost the throne he lost Lola and she was forced to return to the stage where her notorious Spider Dance, scandalised polite society and delighted the goldfields diggers. The dance involved much wriggling to dislodge spiders attached to her dress (right) and all too often revealed all of La Lola.

No Medals for Our Fighting Boys of '45

*A*ustralians like ironic nicknames. Redheads get 'Bluey', quiet blokes, 'Rowdy'. Ken Hands, a Carlton footballer, renowned for his ability to jog away from a seemingly innocuous encounter leaving his flattened opponent and 30 000 spectators wondering what hit him, was affectionately known as 'Solvol' – a brand of gritty industrial soap used for cleaning very dirty hands.

Solvol's was an ironic, if laboured, nickname. There was no irony in Jack 'Basher' Williams's nickname. The South Melbourne big man was fond of a stoush and used to take time off from work to fight in Jimmy Sharman's famous travelling boxing tent. Bob Chitty didn't have a nickname. The surname was enough. Chitty was a word that would give opposition players ... suffice to say that half a century after he called it quits some still remember Bob Chitty with a shudder.

Put 'Solvol', 'Basher' and Chitty together in an Australian Football grand final and you had the makings of one of the most violent games in more than 100 years, the 1945 grand final – the 'Bloodbath', as it is nostalgically remembered today. Of course, not everyone saw it that way at the time. *Truth* newspaper, a scandal sheet that, each week, put shocking stories and photographs on its front page (*'More shocking pictures inside'*) was outraged. 'The game's greatest blot and the most repugnant spectacle the game has ever known,' *Truth* frothed, '... a loathsome brawl in which players from both teams resorted to the vilest and most cowardly breaches, obscene language and blatant disregard for football rules.' *Truth* headed its horror story: *Bloodbath marks war's end*, referring to the recent – on 2 September – surrender of the Japanese that was the end of World War Two. On 26 September, however, the fighting men of Carlton and South Melbourne carried on the carnage.

Basher Williams, in a 1997 interview with The *Australian's* Michael Davies, remembered that 'Carlton's Ron Savage started it all. He was such a quiet bloke, too. If you were at a function he'd be the type of bloke sitting in the corner reading a book.' But the records clearly show that the Carlton captain, Bob Chitty, put some ginger in the game when he ironed out South's dashing centre half forward, Ron 'Smokey' Clegg. (A Turf cigarette was seldom far from Smokey's lips.) Chitty, who off the field was soon to play Ned Kelly in a movie, was on something of a roll on the field. The week before, in a vicious preliminary final against Collingwood, he had collided with Des Fothergill, scattering several teeth belonging to the Magpie champion. Carlton's ironman didn't lose sleep over that. Just a few days before, in an accident at the sawmill where he worked, Chitty had sliced the top off one of his fingers. When Saturday came, he simply pulled on a finger guard and led the team out against the hated Magpies.

Until midway through the second quarter of the grand final, the crowd of 63 000 packed into Carlton's home ground, Princes Oval, had enjoyed a fast, even contest. But, from the moment when Chitty floored Smokey Clegg, it was on. Carlton's Mclean somersaulted the Swans' Danckert to the ground. Basher Williams' opponent, Ken Hands, was knocked to the ground unconscious. Basher always maintained Solvol fainted, but he had few takers. Fists and boots and bottles were flying – and that was just among the spectators – when the half-time siren sounded and Hands, his lights out, was carried from the ground.

All of the above was just a rehearsal, however, for the show's finale. In the last quarter, it was Chitty's turn to go down, a signal for some of the most tempestuous scenes in Australian Football history. The violence seemed to envelope everyone: players, umpires, ambulance men, trainers, spectators and police. At one point, as beer bottles rained, an 'unidentified' man ran on to the field to be grabbed and thrown back by two policemen. The man was fiery Fred Fitzgibbon, the Carlton winger who was serving suspension for his misdemeanours the previous week against the Magpies.

When the dust and the debris had settled, Carlton had won by 28 points and the umpires left the field to spend two hours writing reports. Nine players, six from the Swans and three from Carlton along with Fred Fitzgibbon, appeared before the Tribunal the following Tuesday. South Melbourne's Ted Whitfield was rubbed out for the entire 1946 season, and Bob Chitty got eight weeks and retired. South's 'Gentleman' Jim Cleary – not an ironic nickname – also got eight, for punching Solvol Hands, and was so incensed by the injustice of it that he, too, quit the VFL. Ron Savage, whose surname cried out in vain for a nickname, got eight weeks.

It was worth it to Carlton. The Blues had won their seventh premiership, and they would go on to play in many more and win another nine. South Melbourne never again appeared in a grand final until, as the Sydney Swans, they appeared against North Melbourne, 51 years on.

They lost that one, too.

Sixty-five years before the Bloodbath grand final, Carlton was involved in a match that appalled the journalist Julian Thomas. Writing in the *Vagabond Papers* in 1879, he had this to say of the Carlton–Melbourne match:

> Football, as now carried on here, is not only rough and brutal between the combatants, but seems to have a decided moral lowering and brutalising effect upon the spectators.
>
> The records of the past season show that several promising young men have been crippled for life in this "manly" sport, others have received serious temporary injuries, and laid the foundations for future ill-health, the luckiest of them getting off with scars which they will bear with them to the grave.
>
> Towards the end of the game one man fainted: several must be lame for weeks, and every man must have been bleeding or scarred.

The gentleman who played in spectacles was plucky, but I would advise him to relinquish the game before he receives further injuries.

The victory of the Melbourne Club proved unpopular with the larrikins, who commenced stoning the players outside the gate. One offender, however, received a thrashing for his pains.

I consider that football, as played in this match, is a disgrace to our civilisation.

The *Sportsman* was disturbed by the language: '... something fearful to listen to, and they do not whisper their profanities and curses, it is difficult to find a spot where respectable people can witness the popular pastime.'

The *Argus*, too, was concerned. 'Everybody knows that in the football season the game becomes an obsession with many thousands of young men. It amounts to a sort of fever. They talk of nothing else in the railway trains and tramcars but chances of the Saints beating South and so on. These young men do not play football, they talk football, read about football, and go to football matches; but they derive neither physical nor intellectual advantage from the game.'

Edward Dyson attended just such a St Kilda versus South Melbourne game in 1905, and in *Benno and Some of the Push,* he gave this fascinating account of the language that so shocked the *Sportsman*, and the intellectual deprivation that had the *Argus* wringing its hands:

"Wade into 'em Saints!" he yelled. "Swing him on his ear, Cumby. Snatch th' air off him! Bring 'em down you boshters! Jump 'em in the mud. Good man, Barwick, tat shifted 'im. Give 'im another for his mother!"

Benno's 'appiest moments was when an S'melbin' player got busted, or took the boot in er tender place, 'n' curled up on the field, wriggling; like a lamed worm. These affectin' incidents stirred th' clerk deeply. "Oh, a bonzer, a bonzer, a boshter, a bontoshter!" screamed our Christian brother. "Fair in the balloon, 'n' good enough for him! That's the way to tease 'em, the blighters! They're lookin' fer it, so let 'em have it wet 'n' heavy! Lay 'em out! Stiffen' 'em. You can get better players fer old bottles anywhere!"

The Day They Tried to Kill the Legend

Nielsen told me to keep Phar Lap on the move until he returned with assistance. On no account must I allow him to stop, but when Phar Lap had swollen to half his size again and was groaning in pain, I took him to the barn.

He whinnied, he groaned, dementedly, I rushed about to make him more comfortable. Coming toward me he nosed affectionately under my arm. Then something inside him burst, he drenched me in blood and fell dead at my feet.

*T*ommy Woodcock's account of the last moments of Phar Lap remains, seven decades on, deeply moving. Imagine, then, the feeling when Australia heard the news. Far away, in California, Phar Lap, who only two weeks before had set the racing world ablaze, was dead.

The great horse's death left a nation sharing the stunned disbelief that is seen only once or twice in a lifetime. When John F. Kennedy was assassinated and when Princess Diana died, the moment we heard the news remains in our memories. And hardly has the news broken than the conspiracy theorists get to work. Kennedy was shot by the mob, they say; the Kennedy brothers had Marilyn poisoned; the British Royal Family arranged Princess Di's 'accident'. And the theories endure and proliferate with time. The theories never die.

Yet it is undeniable that Phar Lap's sudden death has never been satisfactorily explained – and now never will be. Officially, colic was to blame, but Bert Wolfe, 'Cardigan' of the Melbourne *Herald*, the most respected racing writer of the time, always insisted that Phar Lap was poisoned deliberately. Wolfe was at Agua Caliente when Phar Lap streeted the best horses America could offer. He was at the California stables soon after Phar Lap's death and tried to smuggle out clay balls he believed held the poison. They were taken from him. Bert Wolfe refused to subscribe to the theory that the horse had eaten alfalfa spayed with a zinc concentrate, enough to kill. 'If Phar Lap had eaten this,' he said, 'why hadn't every other horse on the place also died?'

Many Australians still incline to the patriotic view that 'it was the Americans that killed Phar Lap.' But few today remember that it was Australians who attempted to kill the champion. They gave it their best shot – or the best they could, thanks to Phar Lap's devoted attendant, Tommy Woodcock.

Seventeen months before Phar Lap fell dead at Tommy Woodcock's feet, 'Big Red' had been walking on the road back to his stables after a workout at Melbourne's Caulfield racecourse. He was to race that afternoon and again three days later, on the first Tuesday in November 1930 – Melbourne Cup Day. Tommy was riding a grey stable pony and had Phar Lap on a lead when he noticed two men, newspapers to their faces, sitting in a parked car. Odd. The engine of the big blue sedan rumbled into life and the car pulled out from the kerb. As it came alongside, a double-barrelled shotgun poked out the window. Woodock acted immediately, digging his heels into the pony's flanks to get them between the gun and Phar Lap. The shotgun fired. Phar Lap reared in fright. For some miraculous reason, the big horse was not hit. Woodcock, too, was unscathed, but in the confusion the car sped off before he could get a good look.

Racecourse gangs flourished in Melbourne in the decade after the end of World War One. The soldiers who had come back from the trenches of Ypres, the Somme and Gallipoli were hardened, tough men, and some turned to crime, joining gangs that introduced a new level of violence with the garrotte, the razor and the gun. There was a new generation of home-grown toughs, too, cunning and ruthless men for whom the racing game, with its illegal book-making, crooked trainers and jockeys, was fertile ground for deception, race fixing and subtle or downright violent ways of relieving punters of their winnings.

The two men in the car have never been identified, but their purpose, to kill or injure Phar Lap, has never been in doubt. The gangsters may have intended to put him out of the running that afternoon. The mighty horse was at prohibitive odds on to win the ten-furlong Melbourne Stakes, and he did so with his accustomed ease. Much more likely is the surmise that the gangsters wanted to stop Phar Lap winning the Cup. At 11 to eight on, Big Red was the shortest priced Cup favourite in history. Nuns in quiet cloisters, grey-faced government clerks, the girls at the Cross and the mugs who bought them for a quick time – the whole country was putting a few bob on Big Red. It was the Depression and a few shillings on Phar Lap would put a chook on the table and a half dozen bottles of ale in the icebox. The bookies – and there were thousands of them, from the flamboyant and famous names in the betting ring to the illegal, small-time operators – stood to lose millions. Phar Lap was worth a lot more dead than alive, and he spent the next three days hidden. The newspapers were thrilled. An attempted killing of the nation's idol, a mystery hideaway, the hottest Cup tip of all time: it was heaven for the circulation managers.

Big Red came out of hiding – he had been under armed guard in a stable 40 kilometres from Melbourne – on Tuesday morning. And, that afternoon, with his jockey, Jim Pike, duly won the Melbourne Cup on the bit from Second Wind and Shadow King.

The following year, Phar Lap was given an impossibly heavy weight in the Cup. Some conspiracy theorists say that, for reasons of its own, the Victorian Racing Club simply didn't want him to win. If so, the crushing weight ensured that Pike went easy on the champion and rode him home eighth.

Then Phar Lap went to the United States of America. In training for his first race, at Caliente in Mexico, Phar Lap split a hoof – you can see the split to this day at the Melbourne Museum on the remarkable taxidermist triumph that is Phar Lap's body. He raced, nonetheless, and won the Agua Caliente handicap from a field that was considered the best in North America. The prizemoney was immense – $50 505.

Phar Lap's superiority over this elite field astonished all who saw it. George Schilling, a leading racing steward in America, said, 'To me Phar Lap is still the incomparable horse … Over the back stretch at Agua Caliente Phar Lap started to run and it was a sight to see. The big horse was galloping and cutting down the other horses as though they were on merry-go-round replicas.' The great jockey Eddie Arcaro, who began his career at Agua Caliente on that memorable day, stated 30 years later that Phar Lap was one of the four greatest horses he had seen.

Back home in Australia millions cheered. Then, just two weeks later, they were in mourning. On the morning of 5 April, Phar Lap developed what the vet Bill Nielsen diagnosed as colic. By early afternoon, in great pain, he was taken to his stalls and died in Tommy Woodcock's embrace.

Phar Lap's death traumatised Australia and shocked America. Newspapers throughout the United States editorialised along the lines of the *New York Times*: 'Great horses come and go … but few attain such a hold on the imagination that their names and fame penetrate to the general public. Phar Lap was rapidly gaining such distinction in this country.' The *New York Sun* – like the Melbourne *Sun News-Pictorial* and many other newspapers – resorted to verse:

In the thoroughbred Valhalla,
Where the bravest horses go … There's a pawing and a neighing
Where the lion hearted roam,
And a whinnying of welcome
Phar Lap – 'Big Red – has come home!

But perhaps the now famous Australian poet Peter Porter put it best:

A horse with a nation's soul upon his back
Australia's Ark of the Covenant, set
before the people, perfect, loved like God.

The Last of the Bareknuckle Men

*J*eff Fenech the greatest of all Australian boxers? When the news came out that the Americans had enshrined Fenech among boxing's immortals, there might have been a stirring six feet down where the father of Australian boxing has lain since 1911.

Larry Foley trained some of the greatest boxers of all time. Bob Fitzsimmons, Peter Jackson, Paddy Slavin and Young Griffo all went through his Australian Boxing Academy in Sydney. He himself would go the full nine yards, as the Americans have it, in a fight. And he'd walk, as he once demonstrated, 15 miles in rain and through swamps to get there.

In March 1871, Larry Foley, just five feet eight inches and ten stone seven pounds, had fought a famous draw at George's River, outside Sydney. The police interrupted the illegal bout after two and a half hours, just when, Foley's supporters insisted, their man was about to flatten Sandy Ross, a Scot. The fight created tremendous interest because of the enmity that then existed between Irish Catholics and the Scottish Orangemen, the legacy of which continues today. The Catholics were exultant and the Scots determined on a re-match. Each fighter was to put up 100 pounds and the winner would take all. This time, to ensure that the police would not stop the bout, both parties agreed to get there by circumspect ways.

At dawn on the bitterly cold and wet morning of the fight, Foley's team set out by boat from the Sir Joseph Banks Hotel and rowed four miles, as directed, in a straight line across Botany Bay to George's River. Then they walked inland to get to the site – a George Hill residence. They couldn't find it. There was no sign of any prize-fight ring, and no one but an old man in a bush humpy who was able to direct them to George Hill ... 15 miles away.

Larry Foley and the boys began walking. They had about five hours to get there before 11 a.m., when Larry's bond of 100 pounds would be forfeit to the Scot. They made it, stumbling along in the wet, through swamps and long grass just in time for Larry and Sandy to put 'em up and hop into each other. It was a short fight, as they went then. A mere 30 minutes. And it ended when Larry knocked the Scot unconscious. The victory was almost immediately immortalised in a folk song sung to *The Wearing of the Green*.

John Davies hears with great regret the news that's going round
That Sandy Ross has lost the fight at George's River ground.
No more his crowing will be heard, no more his colours seen,
For I think he's had enough this time of Foley and the green.

Oh, the green the colour of the brave we'll raise high in the air
And to our enemies we'll show the colour that we'll wear.
For the orange flag has been pulled down, the battle fought out keen,
And Sandy Ross has lost the fight at George's River green.

Larry Foley had an even greater triumph in 1879, at Echuca, when he beat a presumptuous fighter who came to Australia with an impressive record in England and America. Abe Hicken was a brawler who reckoned he could take the championship of Australia from Foley and do it in style. 'I want a fight, not a pillow fight or gallop around the ring,' he said, referring to the new Marquess of Queensberry Rules. 'I'll cut this fancy dancer to pieces if only he'll stand up and fight like a man.' When it was over, Foley, the master boxer, had Hicken, the brawler, on his knees, his eyes almost closed, his lips cut and bleeding, his nose smashed out of all shape.

Foley said he was congratulated after the fight by the champion boxer of north-east Victoria, Edward 'Ned' Kelly, who had won his title in a 22-round bareknuckle fight with Isaiah 'Wild' Wright at Beechworth. Ned was certainly in the vicinity. Five weeks before, the Kelly Gang had held up the town of Jerilderie and robbed the Bank of New South Wales of 2000 pounds, an immense amount in those days. Larry Foley earned just a quarter of that for his troubles. But it was, nonetheless, a handsome purse, and when jubilant admirers took up a testimonial for him back in Sydney and raised 1000 pounds, it was enough for Foley to retire from the prize ring. He opened a hotel in the Rocks area of Sydney, his Australian Boxing Academy and, later, a stadium known affectionately as The Iron Pot.

Foley fought at a time when men stripped to the waist, soaked their bare fists in brine, and went at it, often for three or four hours. A round lasted until one man was knocked off his feet. Some rounds lasted two or more hours. One, a bout between Jim Kelly and Jonathan Smith near Daylesford in Victoria in 1854, went for six and a quarter hours until Smith threw in the towel. That fight went for 17 rounds, but some, like the fight between Matt Hardy and Alf McLaren at Lal Lal in Victoria in 1863, went for an extraordinary number of rounds – anything up to 180. The Lal Lal fight was over in 82 rounds and just under five hours. The sporting journal *Bell's Life* recorded that Hardy's face 'was literally chiselled all over; there was not a square inch that was not cut up and carved.' Reassuringly, however, 'Matt's face next day looked a very pretty picture, highly coloured like a coconut, beautifully carved. Constant fomentation had got Alf's head back into shape.'

Larry Foley's record of 22 undefeated bareknuckle bouts defies all modern comparisons. Can you see Jeff Fenech walking 15 miles to fight bareknuckle? Easier to see Larry Foley spinning in his grave.

The Sweet Science's Fabulous Freak

*H*e's Australia's forgotten world champion. The kid they couldn't lay a glove on. A lowbrow boxer with quicksilver reflexes who loved booze and brothels, who died in New York in 1927 and who, today, is remembered and revered only by true connoisseurs of The Sweet Science. In their opinion, Young Griffo was the greatest boxer Australia has produced and one of the world's greatest.

Albert Griffiths was an astonishing athlete. He was a freak who never trained, but who could pluck a fly from the air and would stand on a handkerchief, hands by his side, and challenge anyone to hit him in the face. Griffo would bet 'drinks for the bar' if he were hit. He never was. That sort of training regimen would have disappointed the boxing writer from the Sydney newspaper *Bell's Life* who was of the opinion that:

> It is recommended that the fighter should drink a pint of beer a day, no more. He should avoid drinking beer from two different breweries in one day – different ingredients will derange his bowels ... Pure old port, at two or three sips in the intervals of his eating will make blood, increase its quantity and good quality ... All young meat are good for nothing. They contain no nourishment for the muscle. Soups, fish, pies, puddings, must be left to the clubhouse gourmands; they are poison to the boxer.

Young Griffo would make his celebrated bar bet when he was in the money – as he often was, and when he was broke – as he often was: money meant very little to him. Once, in Chicago, the promoter of one of his fights was peeling off Griffo's take, a formidable $1500. The promoter began counting it, dollar bill by dollar bill. When the man got to $500, Griffo's patience was at an end. 'Enough sir, enough! Wot yer think hi h'am, a bloomink truck. Carry all that with me? Not on yer life! Gimme that stuff. H'it's h'all hi want!'

Needless to say, Young Griffo died in poverty, but not penniless. After his death, it was discovered that he had $2700 in a Broadway bank. He hadn't needed the money because friends and admirers looked after him as he descended into the abyss of alcoholism. For the last 12 years of his life he lived in a rent-free room, courtesy of the widow of an old boxing mate. A vaudeville star ensured that he had a standing order of free breakfast and supper at a restaurant in Seventh Avenue. And, in the side entrance of the Republic Theatre on 42nd Street, a theatre owner allowed him to sit while those who remembered how much pleasure he had given in the ring threw dimes into his cap.

Albert Griffiths, born in Bathurst, New South Wales, in 1871, was outrageously gifted. As a kid he was a gang leader, head of his own 'push' in Sydney's notorious Rocks area. By the time he was 19 he had done enough to win the featherweight championship of the world. At Larry Foley's Iron Pot in Sydney, he beat the defending champion, 'Torpedo' Billy Murphy. The Torpedo sank in round 14, taking off his gloves and advising the referee that they had been tampered with and he would not continue. Beaten, in short.

Two years later, Griffo staked his world title in a bout against Jerry Marshall at Darlinghurst and neglected to enter the ring sober. After 12 rounds, he called for more drink. Apparently, as he told his corner, he hadn't 'seen the other blighter most of the fight', and he was about to call it quits when the police intervened, saying enough rounds had been fought, and the referee awarded the fight to Young Griffo. It was a home-town decision, almost certainly, but the only one that ever went his way.

American authorities have never recognised Young Griffo as world champion. As Les Darcy – born five years later – was to learn, the Americans were reluctant to let their world titles go outside the country.

Still, Young Griffo was clearly good enough to mix it with the best, and the best were waiting – with bulging purses – in the United States. In America, he had been told, were rivers of dollars and pubs and whorehouses to make the Rocks look like Adelaide on a damp Sunday night. The following year, he set sail on the steamship *Alameda*. Parting from the 'push' was such sweet sorrow that the master of The Sweet Science took a dive – the only one he was ever known to take – and plunged over the *Alameda's* rails to swim back to the throng of friends and hangers on waving goodbye on the docks.

Some 15 weeks later, freshly arrived in New York, Young Griffo was once again overcome by the warm sentiments he detected from his fellow man. He noticed a prominent billboard advertising Grotto's Café. He stopped and stared at the sign. Young Griffo was illiterate, but there was something about it that he recognised. Clearly, it was some sort of welcome mat. 'My word,' he said to his companion, 'they 'aven't bin long finding out I'm 'ere!'

Within a year Young Griffo was fighting for the title that he had in fact won from Torpedo Billy Murphy. But the Americans argued that although the 1890 fight had been billed as a bout for the championship, Murphy had no authority to take the title from its rightful home – America, of course – and that Jack McAuliffe was the true titleholder. The two were billed to fight for the world lightweight title, and at 68 kilograms McAuliffe weighed in 6.5 kilograms heavier than Griffo. It wouldn't be the last time the Australian went up against champions, like Joe Gans, George Dixon and Jack Everhardt, conceding six kilograms or more.

Griffo won the fight easily – but lost the decision – his first loss in 115 fights. Afterwards, the referee discovered that he had incorrectly added the points and that it was Griffo's arm he should have raised in victory. For the next eight years, Griffo fought in and out of the ring. In 1896, he did a six-month stretch for disturbing the peace, and his drinking and whoring was reducing him to a shadow of the Young Griffo of the turn of the century. He grew fat – up to 89 kilograms, and in his last years he could barely scratch himself, let alone flick out a fist and snap a fly from the air.

Griffo was 58 when he died in New York on 27 December 1927. Young Griffo fought 166 bouts and was beaten nine times.

This Sporting Strife

*T*he intense sporting rivalry between Australia and England reached its peak in 1932 and 1933 during two bitter confrontations ... in the dressing rooms.

In Adelaide, during cricket's infamous Third Test of the 'Bodyline series', the manager of the English team, Pelham Warner, visited the Australians in their dressing room. The Australian captain and opener, Bill Woodfull, had been hit on the head by a ball from Larwood and reeled to the ground. In the days when there was just a baggy green cap between the batsman and a ferociously fast bowler like Larwood, bodyline bowling was life threatening.

Warner came to offer his sympathy to Woodfull. The opener cut him off, saying: 'I don't want to see you, Mr Warner. There are two teams out there. One is trying to play cricket and the other is not.' Bill Woodfull had been set a precedent. The year before, England's Rugby League team had come to Australia, as its cricket counterpart was to do, with a new tactic. And, like bodyline bowling, the Australians saw it as dangerous and underhand. The stiff arm tackle, 'an extended, stiffened arm swung simultaneously with a high tackle and making contact with the force of a baseball bat', was every bit as dangerous as bodyline bowling. There was a further new element. The English close-up defence, the Australians felt, was frequently off-side without being penalised.

Harry Sunderland made the feelings of the Australians plain when he visited the English dressing rooms just before play got underway in the Second Test in Brisbane. Sunderland, the manager of the Australian team, walked up to his counterpart, Bob Anderton, fished in his pocket and produced a pile of coins. From it he arranged 13 two-shilling pieces and 13 pennies, all in field positions. 'We are the two bobs [shillings], you are the pennies,' he said, and moved them to show how he felt the

English were cheating. Then he picked up his two-shilling pieces and left, telling Anderton, 'Keep the pennies.'

The stage was set for the 'Battle of Brisbane'.

The First Test between the two countries had been bitter. Played before a crowd of 70 204, a record that was not surpassed for four decades, it was a nail biter, with the English winning 8–6. Now Harry Sunderland's visit to the rooms ignited the bad feeling between the teams, and the Englishmen, one of the toughest teams ever to tour Australia, were breathing fire when they ran out. What followed is still remembered as one of the most torrid yet triumphant days of Australian sport. It was a brutal, unrelenting war, with fighting from the start. Players faced up and flailed away, face to face, boots and all. There was savagery – Hec Gee, the Australian half-back, had a large part of his lip ripped out. And there was extraordinary courage.

Dan Dempsey, the formidable Queensland forward, had his arm broken. He went off, had it set, and tore back onto the field, pulling off the splint and begging to be allowed to be play. He was sent off, trailing bandages and splint. The lock, Frank O'Connor, refused to stay on the stretcher when he was being taken from the war zone, and five-eighth Ernie Norman was three times carried unconscious from the field.

The decisive try came, typically, from two of the walking wounded. Five-eighth Eric Weissel was playing with a suspected broken ankle, but when Joe Pearce sent him a pass, Weissel ran through the pain and tackle after tackle until, just five metres from the line, he was brought down. Weissel struggled to his feet, Hec Gee took the ball and dotted it down between the posts. Australia won 15–6. But England won the Third Test and the series – as they had, with one exception, 1920, every Anglo-Australian series played in Australia. For the first half of the last century, England dominated League the way Australia does today.

In 1948, hopes were high when five-eighth Wally O'Connell led the Kangaroos to England. The Australian cricketers under Donald Bradman had gone through their tour earlier that year undefeated, and the flamboyant Kangaroos, with the 'Little Master', Clive Churchill, at full-back, felt ready to match the cricket team's lustre. They got a rude awakening in the very first match. Against rough, tough Huddersfield, Australian second-rower Fred de Belin broke his leg and 'Whacker' Graves lived up to his name when he stiff-armed a fellow Australian, Johnny Hunter, who played for and was adored by Huddersfield. After the fiery game, some were demanding that the team be sent home on the next available ship.

At Castleford, in the neighbouring county of Yorkshire, the Kangaroos faced hard men who came up from the coal face to play, and the game degenerated into running brawls. Seasoned journalists said it was the most vicious game of Rugby League they had ever seen. The *Yorkshire Post* said it 'bore no more resemblance to a game of Rugby League football than street corner brawling does to friendly sparring with the gloves.' Years later, in his autobiography, Clive Churchill wrote, 'Nothing will ever efface the foulness of that Castleford game.'

The Australians had three days to lick their wounds and ready themselves for the First Test. It promised to be the most savage ever played. Instead both teams turned on a match that will always be remembered for the spirit in which it was played and the brilliance of both sides. There were 36 529 at Headingly and the *Yorkshire Post* got it right when it said: 'Fifty years hence the recital of its story will be a sore trial to bored grandchildren.' The game ebbed and flowed, with Australia always behind but refusing to admit it. In the last seconds, Clive Churchill came so close: 'I only had to breathe to score the winning try,' he said. But he was flattened just short of the line. England won 23–21. The Ashes stayed at home and the series was won 3–0.

Then, in 1950, the tide turned. In the Third Test in Sydney, with both teams at one win apiece, winger Ron Roberts touched down in the quagmire of the Sydney Cricket Ground and Australia had won 5–2 and with it the Ashes for the first time in three decades. The game has seen nothing like the emotions Roberts' try triggered. The crowd wanted to souvenir anything that was not bolted down: corner posts, goal posts, line flags, towels and buckets and benches, the ankle-deep mud itself. They invaded the sanctity of the members' reserve and demanded that the Australian captain, Clive Churchill, come out to be feted. The first official to congratulate the players, tears streaming down his crumpled face, was John Quinlan, co-manager of the 1911–12 Australasian team that took its England series 2–0, with one game drawn. That team is considered by some the greatest in League history. But it never knew a moment of exultation to match the Third Test of 1950.

It was too good to last, of course, and in 1952 things were back on course when the players went at each other, toe to toe, in the Third Test, the Battle of Odsal, at Odsal Stadium in Bradford. Australia won the game but lost the series and all the goodwill of 1950. England's vice-captain refused to shake hands with Clive Churchill, Australia's captain, and the team returned labelled by Fleet Street 'The Kicking Kangaroos'.

Two years later, England was back at the Sydney Cricket Ground, this time for a game against New South Wales, which was so violent that the referee, Aub Oxford, called it off 16 minutes into the second half. The *Sydney Morning Herald* had this to say:

> George Orwell said that the surest way to foment ill will among nations was to arrange a series of football matches before 100 000 spectators. But the players on the Sydney Cricket Ground showed that good progress can be made towards the same objective when the crowd numbered only 27 000. A few of these may have enjoyed watching the mauling and brawling in the mud, but thousands who came to see a game of football and saw only a brutal display of animosity must have felt shocked and depressed as they left the ground. Their feelings will be shared by the mass of Australians who believe that both England and this country will lose much if they allow their common sporting traditions to be damaged by such shameless exhibitions.

It was a valiant editorial and nobody took the slightest bit of notice.

6 | The Lady Killers

More Tea, Dear?

*B*obby Lulham was a 26-year-old Balmain Rugby League star. He had dinkum Aussie good looks, blond hair swept back, a thick neck, broad shoulders, blistering pace and a ripper sidestep. Against Manly at Leichhardt Oval on 4 July 1953, Bobby, a winger, played a blinder, racking up the Tigers' entire winning score. Two weeks later against Canterbury, and back at Balmain's home ground, Bobby didn't dazzle. Tiger fans booed him. His chest ached, he had pins and needles in his toes and his legs were heavy. He wasn't worth a cracker. A few days later – in hospital – Bobby Lulham was in a bad way, he was in real pain, his hair falling out in handfuls.

That was a pretty good sign, in 1953, that someone was poisoning you.

Poisons come in and out of favour. Around 400 BC, Socrates ended it all with a draught of hemlock. A millennium later, Lucrezia Borgia liked the toxic cocktail of copper, arsenic and crude phosphorus. In Shakespeare's time, it was more poetic: mandrake. Later, cyanide was popular with the James Bond crowd. And, arsenic, of course, is hard to beat, the all-time favourite.

But, whatever your poison, it's mostly women who administer it (men are more inclined to the bloody and the brutal, the blunt instrument, the knife or the gun). In the early 1950s, Australian women practitioners of the art led the way with a new and very deadly poison. It was odourless, tasteless and easy to get. For some years, this mysterious poison sent any number of men to their graves. How many we'll never know because, as well as being a poison that appealed to women, it was also a poison that baffled doctors. Its victims died in agony. Post-mortems failed to reveal anything incriminating. And the bodies were buried or – better – cremated. Perfect!

It came in a little brown bottle, it could be bought over the counter at the corner store – the milk bar had it on its shelves side by side with Lux soap ('The choice of nine out of ten movie stars'); Brylcreem ('A little dab'll do you'); Saxa salt ('See how it pours!') and Mortein, the scourge of Louey the Fly. A one-ounce (28-gram) bottle cost just two shillings and six pence (25 cents) and it was a killer … it slowly did away with whoever was unlucky enough to imbibe it.

Its symptoms were slow to emerge. Once swallowed it would take days to manifest itself. At first it would announce itself in the form of pins and needles. But, that tingling, mildly ticklish affliction, disturbingly, would be followed by hair loss, then agonising joint pains and nausea. In its final stages, it put its victims through delirium, blindness and total organ failure. Ironically, its very popularity doomed the wonder poison. Once its symptoms gained notoriety, it was no longer any use popping a drop or two into hubby's cuppa. At the first sign of pins and needles, he was likely to say: 'Hang on! You've been putting something into my Horlicks!', and shortly a policeman would be talking to you. Then, when the New South Wales Government hastily changed the *Poisons Act* to prohibit its sale over the counter, it was all up for … thallium.

Thallium was a poison that killed rats. It reached Australia in the mid-1940s, just in time to combat the near plague proportions of rodents along the east coast of the country. New South Wales, alone among the states, allowed a thallium-based rat poison to be sold over the counter, and a bottle of Thrall-rat was in hundreds of thousands of homes in Sydney. In addition, most councils had rat catchers on the payroll and private pest control companies prospered.

In 1952, one of these rat catchers died in suspicious circumstances. His death unravelled a series of murders and attempted murders that sent a thrill – a vicarious mix of horror and humour – through the suburbs of Sydney. The crimes shared a certain stealthy symmetry. All were caused by Thrall-rat. All were the handiwork of Sydney women.

Yvonne Gladys Fletcher did away with two husbands in short order. Caroline Grills – 'Aunt Thally' – the chirpy granny from Gladesville, murdered four friends and relatives and was working on another three when they came for her. Beryl Hague, the housewife from Leichhardt, gave her husband too much thallium-laced tea and – in the nick of time – sympathy. And Veronica Mabel Monty poisoned her lover – her son-in-law, Bobby Lulham.

All four women faced court on thallium poisoning charges. All but Veronica Mabel Monty went to gaol.

Bertram Henry Fletcher, a rat catcher for a private company in Newtown, an inner-Sydney suburb, was the catalyst for the series of arrests that followed his death on 23 March 1952. Friends of Bert were struck by the similarity between his demise and that of his predecessor in the affections of his wife of five months, Yvonne. She had been married to Desmond Butler, a 30-year-old department store cleaner, who died after nine awful months, in 1948. When his suffering began, and his hair started falling out, Yvonne – 'Vonnie' as friends called the auburn haired 25-year-old – had him admitted to hospital. He was in excruciating pain, but after many months he recovered and came home to Newtown where Vonnie was waiting.

A doctor who was finally called to the Butler house discovered Desmond 'a protoplasmic mass, like a jelly', and he died within hours. Astonishingly, a post-mortem found that he died of natural causes.

Bertram Fletcher went much the same way four years later, but, this time, when police were alerted, a post-mortem showed he died of thallium poisoning. As a rat catcher, Bert had plenty of thallium-based rat poison at his home, and when Desmond Butler's remains were disinterred, there were three grains of thallium, enough for police to charge Mrs Fletcher with the murder of both husbands.

At Yvonne Fletcher's trial at the Sydney Central Criminal Court in August 1952, the jury heard how Vonnie had remained seemingly unaffected by her first husband's death. Desmond never gave her a fair go, she had told the doctor, and she didn't see why she should be shackled to him for the rest of her life. On the other hand, when Bert was drunk, he brutally bashed her, often. She was sentenced to life imprisonment.

The case created a sensation. Housewives queued to get into court. Newspaper sales soared. The case was compulsive reading, and among those who followed the trial in *The Mirror, Truth* and *The Daily Telegraph* were John and Christine Downey of Redfern. The couple had been suffering nausea and hair loss. Christine Downey's mother, Eveline Lundberg, lived across the road in Great Buckingham Street and she was even worse. Like the Downeys, she had suffered nausea and hair loss, but in her case she had also lost her vision, suffered excruciating agony and sunk into deep depression. The Downeys, like the friends of Bertram Fletcher, had their suspicions raised when they realised that they shared the well-publicised symptoms of thallium poisoning.

Once again, the police were called in, and on 20 April 1953, with the Downeys' complicity, they sprung a trap for Mrs Caroline Grills, a chipper 62-year-old who played bridge regularly with the Downeys and Eveline Lundberg. Once again, bodies were exhumed and found to have traces of thallium. Caroline Grills was charged with four counts of murder and three counts of attempted murder. After she was convicted, Grills was sentenced to death, later commuted to life imprisonment. (The full story of Caroline Grills, the serial killer granny, is told in 'Killing Them With Kindness', page 155.)

A month before Caroline Grills was charged, Beryl Hague, 35, of Leichhardt, was sent to trial for administering thallium to her husband, Alan. The mother of three admitted that she had poisoned Alan after an argument during which he brandished a carving knife to 'quieten her down'. She popped a small drop or two of thallium into his cup of tea, but, remorseful, quickly told him what she had done. 'Alan can be very aggravating and I am quick tempered,' she later explained when she was released from prison.

A week after Caroline Grills was charged came the titillating case of the football star Bobby Lulham and his mother-in-law lover, Veronica Mabel Monty.

Mrs Monty shared a house in Ryde with Bobby and her daughter, Judith, and had begun an affair with the Balmain winger around the middle of 1953. Bobby and Judith had been married only two years. In court, on charges of attempted murder and malicious wounding, Mrs Monty denied trying to kill Bobby.

True, Monty had been in Nock and Kirby's hardware store when she saw a bottle of Thrall-rat. 'I don't know what subconscious urge made me buy thallium,' she said. 'At no time had thallium ever been discussed in our household. I dare say I had read about it. I must have. My mind was in torment and I seemed to be losing control.' True, she had poured half a bottle of Thrall-rat into a steaming cup of Milo – the health food of a nation – which she took to Bobby one night as he lay in bed with Judith. But, it was not true that she intended the poison for him, she claimed. She couldn't bear the guilt of her illicit affair and the betrayal of her daughter, and had decided to kill herself. She simply got the Milo cups confused. The old poisoned cup switch, gone wrong.

'I have never borne any ill-feelings towards Bobby in my life,' Mrs Monty maintained. Her daughter believed her, and so did the jury. She was acquitted, and a few days later Judith Lulham filed for divorce. Bobby Lulham's marriage was over – and so was his career with Balmain. A few months later, he moved back to his home town in the north of the state and settled into obscurity. Veronica Monty killed herself two years later – she put a gun to her head in a hotel room. And, within six months of Veronica Mabel Monty's acquittal, the State Government brought in laws changing the *Poisons Act* to restrict the sale of thallium.

Throughout Sydney and New South Wales, many men slept easier.

Killing Them with Kindness

*C*aroline Grills looked like everyone's idea of what a granny should be. Think of the late Queen Mother. Tiny – 122 centimetres in her bare feet – butterball round and sweet, she was fond of brooches pinned to her bosom, Minnie Mouse open-toed high heels, and frothy veiled hats. Under the veils, granny spectacles framed twinkling little eyes, and below them a warm, dimpled smile beamed above a generous number of chins. Kindness itself, Aunt Carrie, as her relatives called her, was forever visiting folk, taking them lollies and cakes made with her own plump little hands. Her home-cooked pikelets were particularly popular.

Caroline Grills wouldn't hurt a fly. In her prison cell, humming hymns, she would shoo the flies out of the bars rather than swat them with the handkerchiefs she embroidered to pass the time. She was doing time – life – for attempting to murder a relative, one of a number of relatives and friends she had disposed of. She was a poisoner, of course, but her motives were not the usual. As Frank Hidden, the Defence Counsel, pointed out at her trial: 'If she has committed these crimes there can be a no more treacherous or violent poisoner in history.' (Mr Hidden was clearly not familiar with such notable and cold-blooded practitioners of the art as Lucrezia Borgia or the little old ladies of the then popular movie, *Arsenic and Old Lace*.)

'All the historic cases of murder and attempted murder are prompted by motives of revenge, lust or gain,' Mr Hidden went on. 'In these cases there is no question of revenge, of sexual motive, or of gain.'

And Aunt Carrie herself supported this contention. 'Why on earth would I want to do such a thing as that?' she said, turning wide-eyes at the jury in Sydney's Central Criminal Court. She was in the dock because she poisoned – first – for gain. Why she went on poisoning will never be precisely known, but most likely she did it because of the sheer thrill of it. It was delicious fun to be the only one in on the joke: jovial Aunt Carrie was killing them with kindness and the cakes she baked.

Caroline Grills was 57 when, in 1947, she killed her stepmother with the deadly metallic toxic, thallium. Months later, in January 1948, she killed a family friend. And, later that year, her husband's brother-in-law. Twelve months later, it was her sister-in-law's turn. Two years after that, in 1951, she set about poisoning – simultaneously – three other relatives. What began as envy had become a very bad habit for Aunt Thally, as she would be known a few years later.

There was no inkling of that, however, when, in 1907, Caroline Mickleson, 17, wed Richard William Grills and began a long and happy marriage that lasted 53 years. They had four sons, and Caroline was Granny to numerous grandchildren. Her father died 20 years later and left his new wife, Caroline's stepmother Christina, the family home in the desirable Sydney suburb of Gladesville. Caroline was living in a less than desirable inner-city house in Goulburn Street, an area infested at the time with very large rats. Mrs Christina Louisa Adelaide Mickleson was living in luxury, while Mrs Caroline Grills was living with giant rats. The rats or Mrs Mickleson: one of them had to go.

The local council endorsed the rat poison Thrall-rat as the most effective way to rid houses of rodents, and Richard Grills laid it around the family house. The thallium-based toxin could be bought over the counter at small cost and had a rapid and impressive effect. It killed big rats very quickly. Watching it work set Mrs Grills's mind in motion. Her father's will had ceded the big, comfortable family house to his widow … for as long as she lived. Then it would pass to her, his daughter, Caroline.

One afternoon, in 1947, Caroline popped over to Gladesville to visit her stepmother. Over a chinwag, Caroline quietly slipped a deadly dose of Thrall-rat into Mrs Mickleson's tea and the old lady went into convulsions. The family doctor was called, the old lady was taken to bed, and she died that night. Mrs Mickelson was 87, and in light of the circumstances – an old woman having a fit over a convivial cuppa with her stepdaughter – no autopsy was held. A few days later, Mrs Mickleson's remains were cremated and Mrs Grills moved into the Gladesville house.

No more rats now. But there was another house. It belonged to a friend of her husband. Mrs Angelina Thomas was 84 and had known Richard Grills since he had lived with her as a child, at Leura in the Blue Mountains. She was very fond of Richard, considered him her foster son and had written him into her will, as she often reminded Richard and Caroline. They would inherit the house when she eventually passed on. Angelina Thomas was fond of Caroline, too, and the women shared many cosy hours over tea and home-made cakes, taken to Mrs Thomas by Caroline.

On 17 January 1948, after afternoon tea with Caroline, Mrs Thomas fell ill and died.

Now Caroline Grills had two very nice houses. But, the thrill of killing took over, and almost immediately she selected a fresh target. This time, the luckless victim was a man, a robust and athletic ex-seaman, her husband's brother-in-law, John Lundberg. He was holidaying with the Grills when he was struck by a mystery ailment. Doctors were baffled. The man's hair was falling out, his eyesight was affected, but they were at a loss to know what ailed him. Caroline made it her business to give John all the care needed to get him back to good health, but by the time he lapsed into a fatal coma, on 17 October 1948, he was bald and blind and his mind was wandering. Once again, doctors failed to order an autopsy and Lundberg was cremated.

A year later, almost to the day, Caroline Grills's sister-in-law, Mary-Anne Mickelson, died after a long illness. She, too, lost her hair and her sight, and she had also been given tender loving care by Aunt Carrie.

Then Caroline's attention turned to her surviving sister-in-law, Mrs

Eveline Lundberg, the widow of John Lundberg. Once again, the symptoms manifested themselves: hair loss, blurred vision, agonising cramps, depression. Once again, doctors were at a loss. And, once again, Aunt Carrie was a frequent visitor. This time, however, Caroline Grills was thwarted. Eveline Lundberg's daughter, Christine Downey, and her husband, John, lived across the road from her at their Redfern home in inner-Sydney, and they decided that the bedridden and almost completely blind Eveline had to be admitted to hospital. There, she began to recover rapidly.

The Downeys knew doting and dependable old Aunt Carrie as a distant relative and close friend. Each week, they played bridge with her and Eveline Lundberg at their home. Aunt Carrie could always be relied upon to put on the kettle for another round of tea, and she always turned up with cakes and tempting little sweets. With Eveline beyond reach under the watchful eye of the hospital staff, Caroline Grills took out her frustration on the Downeys. The weekly card games continued, but suddenly the Downeys, Christine and John, were having problems with agonising cramps in their arms and legs. They suffered nausea, their hair was falling out, their vision was failing. Aunt Carrie was feeding them just enough thallium to make their life a misery, but not enough to kill them.

And, still, the Downeys didn't suspect Aunt Carrie.

The Downeys might have been headed for a slow, miserable and extremely painful death but for an extraordinary coincidence that emerged in September 1952 when Yvonne Gladys Fletcher was arrested for the murder of her two husbands. The trial of Yvonne Fletcher the following month in the Sydney Central Criminal Court created a sensation in Sydney. The court heard that Mrs Fletcher's second husband, Bert, treated Yvonne brutally, repeatedly getting drunk and bashing her. Bert, a rat catcher by profession, kept plenty of thallium in the house. When he died in agony, the gossip started. Mrs Fletcher's first husband, Desmond Butler, a cleaner, had died four years before, suffering the same symptoms as Bert. Friends of Bert went to the police. Police exhumed the husbands' bodies and found thallium in both, and in August 1952 Yvonne Fletcher was sentenced to life imprisonment.

Christina and John Downey read the reports of the case with morbid fascination. They learned that Desmond Butler and Bertram Fletcher had both died after a long and mysterious illness and from the same symptoms that afflicted them and Christina's mother, Eveline. These were the same symptoms that had preceded the deaths of Mary-Anne Mickleson and John Lundberg. It was time to talk to the police, who laid a trap for this jovial old rat.

The police told the Downeys to carry on as usual when Aunt Carrie called, but to avoid eating or drinking, without rousing her suspicion, and to keep samples of the food and tea she prepared. At first, the samples showed no trace of thallium, and it wasn't until months later – in April of the following year – that the trap was sprung. Eveline Downey, blind but now out of hospital, was sitting on the Redfern veranda soaking up the sun. Aunt Carrie was bustling about, making cuppas and passing around plates of home-made pikelets and delicious strawberry jam. As she came out of the kitchen with a cup of tea for Eveline, she dipped her hand into her pocket, sprinkled something into the cup and gave it a good stir with the teaspoon. John Downey saw it all. He alerted his wife, who diverted Aunt Carrie's attention long enough for him to switch the cups.

Inevitably, thallium was found in the cup meant for Eveline, and in the pikelets Aunt Carrie had made. When she was arrested, police found thallium in the pocket of the dress she had been wearing that day. When the bodies of Mary-Anne Mickleson and Angelina Thomas were exhumed, they contained traces of thallium too. Aunt Carrie was charged with four counts of murder and three counts of attempted murder, but because the Crown Prosecutor believed the evidence of the attempted murder of Eveline Lundberg was overwhelming, she was called to answer that charge at Sydney's Central Criminal Court on 7 October 1953.

The courthouse was packed. When Mr Justice Le Gay Brereton ruled that the prosecution could use evidence from the other six cases that had led to charges, the public gallery thrilled with anticipation. When Eveline Lundberg entered the court, tapping a white walking stick before her, the public gallery held its breath. And the star, Mrs Grills herself, did not disappoint. She played the role of the chirpy little old granny, indomitably cheerful, always smiling and sometimes laughing. Outside the court, she was given to giggling and flirting with the press. 'It's the fun of the world!' she trilled, skipping away on her little legs as photographers' bulbs flashed.

Richard, her husband, explained that his wife was really just a dear old granny who had no idea of the gravity of the situation and who was clearly incapable of so much as crossing the road against the lights. Her counsel, however, was forced to demand that she stop laughing in court. Mrs Grills's chirpy demeanour was unfazed in court as well. She admitted that she was accustomed to using Thrall-rat, but only to kill rats, she assured the jury. As for lacing someone's tea with it, she was almost at a loss for words: 'Why would I do such a thing?'

Mr Hidden, her lawyer, was equally at a loss. What was the motive, what did his client have to gain by attempting to murder Mrs Eveline Lundberg? The Crown's response was that Mrs Grills murdered 'for the thrill she got from watching the effect of the poison and knowing that she alone in the world knew what was causing the symptoms and suffering.' The jury was unmoved by the mystery of the motive. It took just 12 minutes for them to return with a guilty verdict. When she heard it, Caroline Grills dropped the pose. Grim-faced, she drummed her fingers on the dock rail and rapped, 'I helped to live, not to kill.' Mr Justice Brereton summed up: 'The jury has found you guilty and I agree with the verdict. The evidence disclosed that under the guise of friendship and loving kindness, but with apparently motiveless malignity, you administered poison to Mrs Lundberg, condemning her at least to a life of blindness and possible death. You are hereby sentenced to death.'

with two smaller islands, little more than outcrops of rock, beside it. The islands were their only chance, and that morning Pelsaert ordered the women and children put ashore while the crew struggled to salvage all possible food and supplies. Foolishly, the crew ignored the fresh water on board, presuming there would be plenty on the islands, and took the opportunity to break into the grog.

As the storm raged, 180 people were safely landed on the main island and 40 on the smallest – among them the warring commander and the captain. Also landed were food and a few barrels of water. On the second day more crew and passengers, merchandise and some of the silver coins and jewels were taken off.

On the third day it was decided to take off Cornelisz and 70 others who were still on the *Batavia*. Heavy seas beat the crew back four times. With a heavy heart, Pelsaert later said, he left 'with the utmost grief, my lieutenant and seventy men on the very point of perishing on board the vessel.' Sink or swim. As conditions worsened 30 of them sank. Tragically, Cornelisz was not among them. Eventually, ten days later, he swam and survived – to be greeted as a hero when he at last made it to land.

In the meantime the castaways on the islands began to explore their new habitat. There were birds and fish but no fresh water, and Pelsaert knew the group would quickly die unless water was found. For the next three days he oversaw the hurried construction of two skiffs with covering decks built from timbers from the wreck of the *Batavia*. Intending to find water on the mainland, he set sail on 8 June with 47 others, among them Jacobsz, Zwaantie Hendrix and Jan Evertsz, the Bosun.

The rocky, barren west coast of the 'great south' mainland was guarded by high cliffs and treacherous breakers and the little ships sailed and were blown further and further north looking vainly for a safe landing. With just enough water to keep them going, and 1000 kilometres from the wreck, Pelsaert decided the best course was to keep

And They Call Women the Weaker Sex!

*T*he call from Mrs May Howard to the Carlton police station was a new twist on an old tale. She wanted to report that a noisy party had suddenly gone quiet. Where there was laughter, now there was silence. And it was only eight in the evening. Had the noise from the party continued past Mrs Howard's early bedtime, Jean Lee may well have gone on to live another 20 or so increasingly dissolute years. Instead, 15 months later, on 19 February 1951, Jean Lee's life ended. Heavily sedated and propped in a chair, she was hanged in Pentridge Prison.

Jean Lee, like her prostitute peers Nellie Cameron and Dulcie Markham, was from a respectable North Sydney family. Popular at school, with red hair and big golden brown eyes, she was athletic and intelligent and her future seemed assured. But, in 1933, aged 14, Jean left school, married five years later against her parent's wishes, had a child, and by the time she was 23 had left her baby with her mother and was working in Brisbane as a drinks waitress at Lennon's hotel.

Jean was a girl who liked the high life and low life. Inevitably, she drifted into prostitution. Then, like Nellie Cameron and Dulcie Markham, she became an underworld moll, a prostitute 'protected' by criminals who took most of the considerable money she earned servicing American and Australian troops during World War Two. She was attractive, slender with a creamy complexion and a come-hither smile, but she was not stunning in the ways of Nellie and the Angel of Death and she had none of their macabre style. But Jean Lee will be remembered long after Nellie and Dulcie are forgotten. Jean Lee was the first and last woman hanged in Australia in the 20th century. Did Jean Lee deserve to die? There are those who believe her death was a government-sanctioned warning to other women not to stray from the approved path of femininity, motherhood and domesticity. And there are others who have no sympathy for a woman who took part in the fatal torture of an old man.

In 1949, Jean and her current lover and pimp, Bobby Clayton, headed for fresh fields. In Sydney, the pair had successfully worked an ancient swindle. Lee, with a client in bed or partially unclothed in the back seat of a car, would be 'discovered' by her 'husband' Bobby Clayton. In a fury, Clayton would threaten to beat the mug senseless but would then calm down and demand money as compensation for the seduction of his wife and the hurt to his sensibilities. Melbourne offered a new venue for this long-running theatrical production, and a new start for Bobby, who had just come out from 40 months' hard labour for sexual assault and various counts of larceny.

The couple headed south in November, not long after Cup Day with nasty Norman Andrews who sometimes played the role of Jean's aggrieved and enraged brother. At other times, Jean would simply lure a drunken or lonely man into a back lane where Norman, a big brutal man, and Clayton, a despicable bully, would 'roll' the easy target for his money. Easy targets such as Bill Kent. Around 5.00 p.m. on 7 November, in the University Hotel then in Lygon Street, Carlton, the three were down to their last few bob and drinking in the lounge bar when they noticed 'Pop' Kent drinking by himself. A big, overweight SP bookie of 73, he was an easy mark. What's more, they reckoned, after they'd got chatting with 'Pop' and learned he was an illegal bookie, they realised it was the end of the Melbourne Cup Carnival and it followed that an illegal bookie was bound to have big dough stashed somewhere.

Jean and the two men suggested to Pop that they all go back to the boarding house the old man owned in nearby Dorritt Street. An hour later, a tenant who went to the landlord's room for a newspaper surprised Jean sitting on Pop's knee while he and the other two men shared a bottle of wine. 'Mr Kent was rather partial to the young ladies,' the tenant later told the jury. It was all very well making an old man happy, but when Jean tried to help herself to the money in his fob pocket, Kent resisted. When Clayton and Andrews joined the pair and the old man continued to put up a fight, someone – the police said it was Lee – smashed a beer bottle on his head and then hit him with a piece of wood. They tied the bookie with strips of a sheet and told him they needed to know where he hid his cash.

At 9.00 p.m., Mrs Hayward, who lived in the next room, saw the three leave Kent's room. 'Goodnight, Bill, I'll see you tomorrow,' one of them called as they switched off the light and closed the door behind them. Then quiet. Mrs Hayward got on the phone. At 10.30 p.m., the CIB found William Kent dead on the floor of his room – strangled by a powerful right hand – and within five hours they were knocking on the door of the Great Southern Hotel in Spencer Street, the hotel of choice of transients. The police met the trio in the hotel lobby. It was 3.00 a.m., and the merrymakers were coming back from celebrating at Sammy Lee's Copacabana night club. In Jean Lee's handbag, they found three airline tickets for a flight to Adelaide later that morning.

Bobby Clayton was the first to crack. He claimed that he had left the room when Norman 'gave me the drum that he was going to "do" Pop, but I told him I would not be in it and I left, leaving Norman and Jean in the room ... I am not going to take the rap for what others do.'

Jean Lee proved harder to crack. 'You can say what you like, Bobby won't make a statement and I'm not saying anything.' Then the detectives brought in Bobby and read his statement. 'So you made a four-page statement, did you?' Lee asked scornfully. Clayton snivelled. 'Yes.'

'And they call women the weaker sex!'

Clayton was taken out, and Lee, although she had shown her contempt for Bobby, decided to confess to hitting the old man with a beer bottle and a lump of wood. 'I knew he was dead when we left him,' she explained.

'Who do you mean by "we"?' asked Detective Cyril Currer.

Lee paused and then blurted, 'There was only me. I'm not saying any more!' That confession was patently a lie. She was trying to shield her lover. Jean Lee was not strong enough to strangle Kent, a big man, and in any case she soon reneged on it. Yet her confession was allowed as evidence.

On 25 March 1950, after a trial lasting five days, Jean Lee, Robert Clayton and Norman Andrews were sentenced to hang for the murder of William Kent. Lee was aghast. She broke down, cried out her innocence and had to be supported from the court. Clayton turned to the jury and snarled, 'May your next feed choke you, you swine!' Andrews said he had nothing to say. 'Not at this juncture, no,' he told the judge.

On appeal, a new trial was ordered, but the High Court reversed that decision and the Privy Council in London turned down a further appeal. Jean Lee was convinced that they would never hang a woman. But she was seen as hard, brittle and unrepentant, the torture of the old man, rare in those days, repulsed many, and the State Government appeared determined that all three must go to the scaffold.

On Monday, 19 February 1951, Lee was the first of the three to hang. In the days before her death, she had been violent, screaming hysterically that she hadn't committed the murder. On the night before her execution, she was heavily sedated, and the following morning, still faint, she was carried to the scaffold, seated on a chair and died of a broken neck seconds after the hangman stepped off the trapdoor and signalled for the bolt to be pulled. Clayton and Norman followed two hours later.

At the time of Jean Lee's death, a newspaper summed up people's feelings about her:

> From school tomboy to playful young teenager, from easy soldiers' girl to candid young harlot, from underworld moll to simpering decoy for bashers, from restless crooks' urger to callous killer – spirited redhead, Jean Lee, made that flaring transition from the classroom to the gallows in just 15 years.

But did she do it?

Mrs Scott's Sad Mistake

*J*ean Lee was the last murderer to stake her life on the belief that no Australian government would hang a woman. She was wrong. But she was not the first to make this mistake. Mrs Elizabeth Scott firmly believed that being a woman would save her from the gallows. She, too, was wrong. Both women made history, one as the first and the other as the last of their sex to be hanged in Victoria.

Mrs Scott was 23, a pretty Englishwoman who had been married to 37-year-old Robert Scott for nine years when, in 1863, she decided to end the marriage. She had come to Australia with her parents, drawn by the lure of gold, and within a year, aged just 14, had been wed to Scott.

That was her first mistake. Scott was an unprepossessing man, coarse and vulgar and too fond of the bottle, but he had made some money on the diggings and Elizabeth's parents thought he was something of a catch.

Together, Robert Scott and his young wife ran a shanty pub for miners at Devil's River in north-east Victoria, and in the first six years of their marriage, she had borne him four children. Only two of them survived, and by the time she was 23 the marriage itself was long dead.

Bob Scott was an alcoholic who was often drunker than his customers, and Elizabeth began to look for a way out of the marriage and Devil's River. She found it in a customer, a 19-year-old customer, at the pub. David Gedge was shy and sensitive, and the two began a passionate affair.

At the same time, Elizabeth had another young man devoted to her. Julian Cross, a Eurasian labourer who worked at the pub, may not have been her lover, but he was under Elizabeth's spell, and on the night of 13 April 1863, she put her two young men's devotion to the ultimate test.

Julian Cross's and David Gedge's differing accounts of the end of Bob Scott converge at one point: Elizabeth Scott. Both told the police that she desired the murder of her husband.

Gedge claimed that he had been sitting by the kitchen fire when Cross walked past him, carrying a pistol, into Scott's room. There was a shot, and Cross had reappeared, pointed the pistol at him and threatened to kill him if he 'split'.

Cross said that Gedge had tried to shoot Scott in his bed, but the gun had misfired. Gedge had said it was now his turn. Cross had said, 'No, perhaps missus don't want me to do so.'

But, in the kitchen, missus had confirmed, 'Yes, I do want you to shoot him.'

She had poured Cross a large brandy, and according to Cross, 'I took up the gun and went into the bedroom and shot Scott.'

Mrs Scott thought to present the death as suicide, but the police quickly realised that it was murder. By early morning, they had a confession out of Julian Cross implicating the other two.

On 11 November 1863, at the Melbourne Gaol, 17 years to the day when Ned Kelly would stand on the same spot, the three were hanged simultaneously.

To the end, like Jean Lee, Elizabeth Scott had believed she would be reprieved. After all, she had not pulled the trigger, and she was a woman. A beautiful woman.

When she appeared from the condemned cell, the spectators below the platform gasped at her beauty. She was dressed in a long black coat, with her dark hair carefully braided.

As she was placed between the two young men who were to die for her love, she carefully adjusted the noose so that it didn't spoil the folds of her cloak.

Then, at the very last minute, she asked her lover, 'David, will you not clear me?'

She never heard his answer, not in this life.

7 | The Ghosts and the Ghouls

Condemned by the Ghost on the Post

*F*isher's ghost is perhaps our most celebrated spectre. There are those who say – and who said at the time, in so many words – that the apparition of the murdered Fisher was nothing but an urban myth. But then there's the problem of explaining the bloodstains …

Frederick George Fisher came to Sydney, a convict on the *Atlas,* in 1814, and as a ticket-of-leave man he settled down as a farmer on a small property at Campbelltown. He made a comfortable enough living and kept to himself, never marrying. But, when he ran into debt, Fisher went to prison rather than settle with his creditors. On the neighbouring property was another ex-convict, George Worrall, a man whom Fisher trusted. To hide his assets, he transferred his property to Worrall and gave him full power of attorney in all his business matters.

Fisher came out of gaol and suddenly disappeared. One June night in 1826, he was getting solidly sozzled at a local inn and the next morning he was gone. Worrall told neighbours and his ticket-of-leave mates down at the inn that, on an impulse, Fisher had sailed for England on the *Lady Saint Vincent*. Worrall was vague about the reasons for Fisher's going, but the town tongues quickly supplied them. It was all to do with a girl Fisher was trying to avoid marrying, some know-alls said; he was skipping from a debt, said others; and there were those who believed he was running from a charge of forgery, Fisher's reason for being in the colony. Worrall had often urged Fisher to go home to the 'Old Country', the boys at the inn knew, and they had no reason to doubt that, this time, probably in the grip of the grog, he had decided to up and go.

Worrall took over the Fisher farm on the basis of his power of attorney.

When he began trying to sell some of Fisher's belongings, however, the authorities grew suspicious. Documents allegedly drawn up and signed by Fisher looked decidedly dodgy, and when someone checked and found that the *Lady Saint Vincent* was not in Sydney Cove when Fisher was supposed to have boarded her, police posted a 20-pound reward for information as to his whereabouts. Then, they sat down to put some awkward questions to Worrall.

Under questioning, Worrall cracked. He agreed that Fisher had been murdered, and claimed that he had seen the murder: it was done by four men with whom Fisher had been living. This story didn't hold up. The men were questioned and released, but Worrall was held in custody while the search for Fisher, or more probably his body, went on. Without a corpse, Worrall would go free.

James Farley was a prosperous farmer, highly respected in the Campbelltown district. He was out one night four months after Fisher's mysterious disappearance when he saw, 1000 metres from Fisher's home, the missing man. Or rather, Farley said when he had gathered his wits, the outline of Fisher sitting on a fence railing by the creek. Farley fled in terror and was delirious with shock for some days. When he finally told of his sighting, Campbelltown's Constable George Newland and an Aboriginal tracker named Gilbert went to the paddock and the fence near the creek. The fence had been set on fire, possibly to destroy evidence of the murder. But the ruse had failed. There were bloodstains on the fence rail precisely where Farley had said the ghost was sitting.

Gilbert now used his skills, peering closely at the ground and following a path only he could see that took the pair to a nearby waterhole. Gilbert threw a leaf into the water, skimmed it out, and sniffed it. The leaf smelled of 'white man's fat' he said, and he pointed to where, he said, a body lay. Gilbert was right. The body was found and brought to the surface. A doctor who had come to Sydney on the same ship as Fred Fisher identified it as the missing man. It wasn't easy.

Tom Robinson, a local farmer, was also there to identify the body when it was laid out on the bank of the creek. It was a gruesome sight. The jacket, the braces and the configuration of the body were Fisher's, Robinson was sure, but 'on my removing it [the right hand] to get a sight of his brass buckles [sic] the palm was gone and the flesh stuck to my fingers and came of [sic] the bone ... At the bottom of the back of the head between the ears there was a gash in the skull that a man might have put his hand into – another on the crown, and a blow as if with a blunt instrument had carved away the bottom of the face.'

Worrall confessed that he had killed Fisher but claimed it was an accident. The jury didn't agree with him, and on 5 February 1827, he was hanged for the murder of Frederick Fisher.

Today, Fisher's body lies in the old pioneers' cemetery behind Campbelltown's beautiful Georgian church, St Peter's, built three years before his death. But his ghost lives on prosaically in the name of the creek where Gilbert skimmed the water for his body: Fisher's Ghost Creek.

The Phantom of the Princess

*T*he longest running show on the Australian stage, *The Phantom of the Opera*, ran for seven years, two and a half of them at the glorious Princess Theatre in Melbourne. But the longest running performance on the Australian stage is that of the Italian basso baritone, Federici. On and off, Federici has been playing at The Princess for more than 115 years.

On Federici's opening night in March 1888, Gounod's opera, *Faust,* was also having its premiere. It was a dazzling occasion. Three years before, the great journalist George Augustus Sala of *The Times*, London, had visited the city and dubbed it 'Marvellous Melbourne'. Now, the audience at the Princess epitomised the wealth and elegance of the city at its very peak. (The brilliance and confidence would last only another year, when the land boom went bust and Melbourne took a century to recover).

The Princess Theatre, like the Paris Opera built a decade before, was ornate and elaborate, with grand marble stairs, stained glass, arches, a vast ventilating roof that slid back in hot weather, and topping it all a gilded angel trumpeting over its portal. The mood of Melbourne's opera goers was high that glittering opening night. In the audience, the luvvies were basking in the bliss. On stage, the opera was coming to its tremendous finale. The urbane Mephistopheles, the satanic figure in scarlet tights and twin pointed cap, was going about his evil business with Doctor Faust. In the role of Mephistophles was the famous Federici. Now, as the opera reached its climax, he swirled his scarlet cape around him and vanished to the nether regions – through a hidden trapdoor on stage – in a cloud of sulphurous smoke.

Almost exactly a century later, in the same theatre, Anthony Warlow did the same thing on the opening night of *The Phantom of the Opera*. At the high point of the musical, Warlow, as the Phantom, appeared in a red death's head mask on the Grand Staircase and then – in a swirl of his great cloak – disappeared down the trapdoor.

At both events, the audience thrilled at the effect. There would be bravos for this spectacular exit alone. Warlow took his triumphant bows in *Phantom*. But Federici was missing when the curtain came down on *Faust*. As he went down the trapdoor, Federici may have hit his head. But, whatever the cause, he was certainly dead by the time he was hurried to his dressing room and lowered on to a couch.

Federici was next seen at the Princess during a season of *Macbeth*. Late at night, a fire-fighter discovered a man in a top hat and long black cloak standing in the dress circle. When the fire-fighter called to the man, there was no answer and, as his hair stood on end, the fire-fighter watched the figure dissolve into the darkness. He had no doubt that the wraith was Federici, a man he knew well.

Since then, there have been dozens of sightings of Federici. Elaine Marriner, the wife of the theatre's owner, David Marriner, who is writing a history of the Princess Theatre, says that the phantom of the Princess makes his appearance mostly when the theatre is empty and late at night. Rob Guest, who played the role of the Phantom in *The Phantom of the Opera* for six of its seven years, has a letter from a woman who says she saw Federici standing beside Guest during a performance. Rob Guest also played the lead in *Les Miserables*, the musical that preceded *The Phantom of the Opera* at the Princess. He and other cast members of *Les Mis* believe they have glimpsed the ghost of Federici.

Federici now has a bar in the Princess Theatre named after him. Pop in if you're passing and enjoy a nip of spirits!

Carnage at the Ice-cream Cart

*F*our months before the fatal Sunday, 25 April 1915, when the Anzacs landed at Gallipoli, the first Australians to fall from Turkish enemy fire were Oddfellows and members of their families – civilians on a Broken Hill picnic train. Until recently just a hazy memory, the Battle of Broken Hill has poignant echoes today.

It began on New Year's Day, 1915, and by the end of the day Australia had changed. Until then, Australia had never known guerrilla warfare. Australia had never considered interning aliens. But these things were about to change when, on that sunny New Year's Day, the good people of Broken Hill's Manchester Unity Order of Oddfellows and their families – 1200 men, women and children – crammed happily into the open ore trucks of a train steaming to the picnic grounds at Silverton, four kilometres east of the town. Short of the picnic grounds, however, the train unexpectedly groaned to a halt.

The engine driver had braked at the curious sight of an unattended ice-cream cart by the side of the track. Attached to it was a pole, and from the pole hung a flag – a Turkish flag, although no one recognised it as such. The happy babble on the open train died down as the passengers pondered the meaning of the deserted cart and the forlorn flag.

Then a shot cracked the silence. And another. They were being shot at! Almost at once, a boy, a girl, an old man and three women were hit. It was unbelievable, but now through the screaming and the tumult, some on the train could see that they were under fire from two men in a trench dug in a nearby sand dune.

The two men firing at them – dropping men, women and children –

were the town's ice-cream vendor and part-time camel driver, Gool Mahommed, and the butcher for the Afghan camel drivers and the leader of their Islamic community, the elderly Mullah Abdullah. It was astonishing, but true, and while the people on the train were absorbing these facts, a man riding by was toppled from his horse, shot dead. Soon, others were dropping, screaming in pain and fear. Five hundred metres away, a man who went on chopping wood, ignoring his daughter's pleas to take cover, was killed by a ricochet.

The train started up again, taking the picnickers safely out of range where news of the attack was telegraphed back to the town police and militia. At the same time, Gool Mahommed and Mullah Abdullah made a run for a new vantage point, back to the town's west. On the way, the two stopped to deal with a man who had barricaded himself inside his hut. They shot him through the door and hurried on.

Near the Cable Hotel, the pair ran into a group of police. When the police saw they had rifles, two constables were ordered to approach them to ascertain their identity. The strangers identified themselves by shooting, and one of the constables went down, hit by two bullets. The police decided to retire and wait for reinforcements. The killers ran for cover to a rocky white quartz outcrop a few hundred metres away that gave them good protection, and from here, for the next hour and a half, they shot it out with police. Then the militia and enthusiastic civilians with rifles joined in.

'The general operations were under the direction of Inspector Miller and Lieutenant Resch,' the *Barrier Miner* reported. 'The attacking party spread out on the adjoining hills, and there was a hot fire poured into the enemy's position, the Turks returning the fire with spirit but without effect, which is rather surprising, as the range was short and the attacking parties in some cases exposed themselves rather rashly to get a shot.'

One of the reasons for the ineffectual fire from the pair was – probably – that the old man, Mullah Abdullah, had been shot dead earlier in the battle. At any rate, the two were doomed. At the climax of the battle, one of the men, a witness said, stood up with something white tied to his rifle. It may have been the Turkish flag – or a white flag of surrender. Whatever, it did him no good. 'He was cut down in the white heat of the town.'

The *Barrier Miner* picks up the story:

> In the battle there was a desperate determination to leave no work for the hangman or to run the risk of the murderers of peaceful citizens being allowed to escape.
>
> It was not a long battle. The attacking party was constantly being reinforced by eager men who arrived in any vehicle they could obtain or on foot. At just about one o'clock a rush took place to the Turks' stronghold and they were found lying on the ground behind their shelter. Both had many wounds. One was dead, the other expired later in hospital. They were in the dress of their people, with turbans on their heads. The police took charge of the bodies.

The battle had probably been sparked by three factors: patriotism, as Turkey was officially at war with Australia; resentment, as the two had been treated rudely by some; and dope – Gool Mahommed had made several journeys to Turkey and was a pedlar of the drug.

The Battle of Broken Hill left six dead and seven others wounded. It led to the then Attorney-General, Billy Hughes, agitating successfully for the internment of all enemy nationals. The ghosts of the battle are still with us.

Line Up, Line Up, for the Girl in the Bottle

*T*hese days we do it differently. When the police want to identify a body, they arrange for the media to publish and screen images of the victim as he or she would have looked in life and the images are usually less frightening than the *Who Weekly* spread of Hollywood stars caught popping out to the supermarket. In 1898, they were more down to earth. When the Victoria Police discovered a corpse floating in a box in the Yarra River, they decapitated and then exhibited the head of the victim.

The victim was a teenage girl, that was clear. But the face she presented – floating in embalming fluid inside a large spirit jar – was not. Blackened, grotesquely swollen and distorted, it was the stuff of nightmares. If a decapitated head were – unthinkably – exhibited today, would people queue to see it? In 1898, more than 1000 people a day thought viewing the girl in the bottle would be a good way to fill in time, and despite today's counter attractions – Internet porn, SMS messaging, reality TV and Russell Crowe movies – there is no reason to suppose that human nature is very different.

What has changed is the abortion law. In the late 19th century, unmarried teenage girls were not supposed to get pregnant, and when they did, the consequences were almost always sad and often very unpleasant. In some cases, girls died during 'backstreet' abortions. That was how the girl came to be in the bottle.

Less than a month after the head went on show at the City Morgue, a young man appeared at police headquarters and said he knew who the girl was. He wouldn't give her name, he said, but his friend, Miss Thekla Dubberke, a domestic servant on whose behalf he had gone to the police, could help there. Miss Dubberke was certainly helpful. She worked for Madame Olga Radalyski, who read palms and peered into crystals in Osborne Street, South Yarra. Madame Olga was also an abortionist, and one of her clients in this murky business was a Chapel Street real estate agent called Travice Tod, who had made his 18-year-old girlfriend, Mabel Ambrose, pregnant.

Thekla Dubberke, like her mistress, had a sideline. In addition to her house duties, she was also a prostitute, and was in the Osborne Street house when Madame Olga botched the abortion. She told police she had heard screaming and rushed into the room to find Mabel Ambrose on the floor, foaming at the mouth. Madame Olga had told Thekla to rush to the nearest pub for brandy, but when she came back with a bottle the girl was dead.

Madame Olga then sent Thekla to fetch Travice Tod. This gentleman, Thekla said, came up with the idea of getting rid of the problem by consigning his girlfriend's body to the bottom of the Yarra. At hand was a box 83 centimetres long, 45 centimetres wide and 38 centimetres deep. It belonged to Thekla. It was her 'glory box' in which she kept items in readiness for her forthcoming wedding to a Mr Atkins. Thekla had lined the box – a carton in reality, used to carry shoe boxes – with wallpaper, and had inscribed it with her fiancé's name, T. R. Atkins.

At one o'clock on the morning of 14 December, Thekla and Travice Tod took the naked body – doubled up and crammed into the glory box – down to the river, tied a stone to it, and saw it slide into the depths. There, inevitably, the box popped up to the surface where, five days later on Saturday afternoon, three boys punting along the river spotted it. When they eagerly pulled it to their punt, they found themselves looking, through a gap in the box, at a woman's feet.

The trial of Travice Tod and Madame Olga – Thekla had turned Queen's Evidence – was enjoyed by packed galleries. Madame Olga screamed and collapsed when, through an ear trumpet, she heard that she had been sentenced to hang. Tod, who had affected a certain arrogance, fainted before he heard the verdict. He, too, was to hang. Public petitions caused the Executive Council to reconsider the sentences of the pair, and Tod's was commuted to six years while Madame Olga was to serve ten years. Her crystal ball should have told her to have nothing to do with the man from the real estate agency.

The Hand in the Grisly Glove

*C*riminals talk about being 'fitted' – framed – by police. It happens and it has always happened, but no criminal has ever been fitted in such macabre fashion as in the investigation that followed the Murrumbidgee mystery, in 1933.

It was Christmas Day in Wagga when a corpse was fished from the Murrumbidgee. The bloated body of a middle-aged man, it had been in the water for several weeks. Badly decomposed though it was, it was clear that the dead man had come to a grisly and violent end during the season of peace on Earth and goodwill to all men. His head had been caved in by an axe or a tomahawk. But, other than that, it was hard to take the investigation much further. The body could furnish no clues and fingerprints of the putrid hands were out of the question.

Then, trawling the river for clues, Detective Joe Ramos saw, snagged near the muddy bank, a flimsy shred of something. Ramos waded in and had a close look. It was, he decided, the skin of a human hand complete with five fingers and a thumb. A human glove. Police deduced that the skin had peeled from the hand when the man's woollen shirt had shrunk in the water and, after some weeks, floated downriver, filled with water. The question the police now wanted answered was: could they get fingerprints from the 'glove'?

The skin was rushed to Sydney where, in a classic piece of forensic science, it was treated with a special ink. Then, a doughty policeman volunteered to fit the 'glove' over his own hand to get a set of prints. The prints, in turn, revealed that the skin glove came from the hand of a bushman, Percy Smith, who lived upriver with another bushie, Ted Morey. Police found an axe in Morey's hut and charged him with the murder of Smith. Apart from the bizarre discovery of the human glove, a routine murder trial followed until a key witness for the prosecution was shot dead.

Moncrieff Anderson, was shot dead from behind, and his wife Lillian was charged with his murder. She admitted the crime but said she did it because her husband had killed Percy Smith. The Riverina flew with rumours. It was said Lillian loved Morey and shot Anderson in an attempt to claim that he, and not Morey, had murdered Smith. It was true that she wrote letters to an unnamed lover, but Morey was an illiterate rabbit trapper and the identity of Lillian Anderson's lover was never established. It made no difference, however. Morey was found guilty and sentenced to death, although the sentence was never carried out. He was given a life term and released after 20 years, suffering from tuberculosis. Mrs Anderson was convicted of manslaughter, sent to gaol for 20 years, and released after 12 years.

8 | The Gruesome

Norah, My Dear, Who Murdered You?

*T*he Bogle–Chandler mystery of 1963 and the Murphy family murders of 1898 are perhaps the two most intriguing whodunits in Australian crime. In both cases bodies were neatly laid out after sexual activity, both ignited the gossip of a nation, and both gave birth to an army of amateur detectives exploring endless avenues of conjecture.

Above all, both cases seem to mirror the mores and the morals of their time. The Bogle–Chandler case was spiced with the ingredients that were soon to mark the Swinging Sixties – free-ranging casual sex and the drug culture. The Murphy mystery, on the other hand, is redolent of the rough but sunny bush culture: of sliprails and sulkies and bush dances, of Banjo Paterson and *Around the Boree Log* – along, too, with dark sex, suppressed and forbidden, which was so much a part of the Victorian era.

Three siblings, young, intelligent adults from one of the most respected families in the district, were found dead in a secluded paddock up a shadowy bush track: the women sexually assaulted, their hands bound. What were they doing there? Did they go willingly? There was the puzzle of the newspaper clipping, an In Memoriam notice found at the scene of the crime; there were shots in the night, screams and cries; the 'incomprehensible' apathy of the five remaining Murphy brothers; the two suspects the police couldn't get excited about; the disappearance of one of them; and a succession of disturbing questions that remain unsolved a century later. Put simply, the Murphy murders, to this day, don't add up.

The Murphy tragedy began to unfold on the night of Boxing Day, 1898, in the back-blocks farming town of Gatton, in the Lockyer Valley,

98 kilometres west of Brisbane. Michael Murphy, the eldest of the ten Murphy children and two of his four sisters, Norah, 27, and Ellen, 18, were going home. They had been to the races at Mount Sylvia that afternoon and were in town at the Boxing Night Ball at Gatton's Divisional Hall. It was only 9.00 p.m., but they found the doors closed. Too few women turned up, so the dance was cancelled, and while Michael might have enjoyed a beer with the blokes at Charley Gilbert's hotel, he couldn't leave the girls.

The sulky turned around in the almost deserted main street and the horse perked up: it was headed for home, the Murphy farm at Blackfriars Creek. A few moments later, outside the town, the three met young Patrick, one of the six Murphy boys, a student at the newly opened Gatton agricultural college where he lived during terms. He was home for Christmas, riding in to Gatton, and in the mood to celebrate. When they told him the dance had been called off, he went on in to town anyway. Michael flicked the reins, gave a 'Gee up!' and the horse started the sulky down Tent Hill Road to home.

They never got there, the horse and the three in the sulky. Early the next morning, the patriarch of the Murphy family, old Dan Murphy, full-whiskered and beetle-browed, was up and about. But three of his children hadn't arrived home. Where on earth were they? His son-in-law, Bill McNeil, a butcher married to Polly, was having a cuppa over breakfast and wondering too: they had gone off the night before in his sulky. It had a crook wheel. Maybe they had been out late, had a good time and were coming back at a good old pace when the wheel fell off. Michael was able to take care of himself – he used to be a Mounted Policeman, but if the horse had bolted or something … Bill finished his tea and announced he was going for a ride down the track, to see what he could see.

Five kilometres along the Tent Hill Road, Bill reined in his horse. There were track marks of a sulky coming from Gatton, but instead of continuing on towards Blackfriars Creek, they turned off, under a sliprail, to another rougher track that led off into the scrub to Moran's paddock. No sulky or dray ever went up that track. But there it was. The tracks were wobbly, as if a wheel was loose. McNeil was sure it was his. McNeil lowered the sliprail, walked his horse through, replaced the rail and rode on. He was really puzzled now, but about 400 metres on, up and over a ridge, he got some answers. There they were. The brother, the sisters, the horse – dead, in a dell.

All three had been murdered. Bill McNeil saw this at once because of the way the bodies lay. They were not sprawled across the grass as they would have been in an accident. Instead, they appeared to gave been laid out – facing west. Bill went closer, close enough to see the ants busy on the face of Norah. The body was on a blanket, her jacket was pulled up to her shoulders, her skirt undone at the back. Tight around her neck was a harness strap, brutally buckled. Her hands were tied behind her back.

Ten metres away, back to back, were 'Ellie' and Michael. She, too, had her hands tied behind her back and her underwear ripped and bloodied. Michael was on his side, also bound and clenching an empty purse. Whoever killed him had taken his gold-handled riding crop, a present he had got the day before, but his pockets appeared not to have been rifled. There was a bloodied lump of wood nearby, and all three had been bludgeoned, hit on the head with tremendous violence. Yet around the bodies was no sign of a struggle. The horse, shot dead, sprawled across the sulky's shafts.

Bill McNeil rode for help. When the local policeman, Sergeant William Arrell arrived, he was accompanied by six men from Charlie Gilbert's Gatton pub. He ordered two of them to keep sightseers away and rode back to Gatton to send telegrams to his superior at Ipswich police station and to the Commissioner of Police in Brisbane. He returned to find dozens more at the scene, standing over the bodies, gaping, walking around the paddock, trampling underfoot any clues there may have been. McNeill had ridden off to Blackfriars Creek to break the awful news.

When Bill arrived back at the farm, he was met by Mrs Murphy. 'Did you see them?'

McNeil told her that her children were dead. Their bodies were about five kilometres away, lying in a secluded paddock down the track. She listened in silence. Dan Murphy was away, somewhere on the 60-hectare property and – astonishingly – McNeil and Mrs Murphy went to the scene without him. When she got there, Mrs Murphy got down from the sulky and walked through a crowd that had now grown to about around 40. Some began weeping when they saw the mother. Mrs Murphy held her feelings in tight check. She walked up to Norah's body lying under the big gum tree, looked down and said: 'Norah, my dear, who murdered you?' And then she sagged to her knees and prayed. She prayed over each of her children's bodies while the crowd bowed their heads in silence.

The Government Medical Officer arrived from Ipswich in good time and held a post-mortem at Charley Gilbert's pub later that day. It showed that, although there had been no signs of a struggle around the paddock, the girls had fought ferociously for their lives. There were scratches on their lower limbs, and both had been sexually assaulted.

All three had died from a blow to the skull, and Norah and Michael – along with the horse – had also been shot. (Michael's bullet wound was discovered only weeks later, when he was exhumed for a second post-mortem.)

Two days later, 300 horsemen followed the cortege and flags flew at half-mast as the funeral closed Gatton. The Murphy clan was held in the highest regard, and the Queensland premier's condolences were among dozens of telegrams read to the congregation. Then the police investigation began.

Two witnesses told of a shadowy figure in a 'soft hat' they saw at the sliprail on the night of the murders. Mrs Margaret Carroll and her 13-year-old son saw the man in the shadows facing the sliprail as they returned from the race meeting.

'That's Clarke's man,' the boy said, meaning Thomas Day, a young man who had arrived in town only 11 days ago and was working for Arthur Clarke the butcher. It was, they reckoned, 8.30 p.m.

Forty-five minutes later, Florence Lowe rode past the sliprail and a man in dark clothes and a soft hat stepped out to speak, but she spurred her horse and galloped on.

Louise Theuerkauf, Arthur Clarke's domestic servant, heard screams. She was putting the cat out, the clock had struck ten o'clock and she first heard gun shots coming from the direction of Moran's paddock. Minutes later, she heard a woman scream twice. She also said that each time she heard the word 'Father!' both times. Louise stood frozen for about ten minutes, listening intently, but there was silence and she went to bed.

Catherine Byrne was outside her home, too, about a kilometre from the sliprail when she heard one shot and screams that faded in the night. Just young people fooling around on the Tent Hill Road, she thought. Two men heard a shot about 9.30 p.m.

So the murders could be fixed at between 9.30 and 10.00 p.m. That much was clear, but nothing much else was. The investigation got off to a bad start. The police from Brisbane took a day to get to Gatton, and by that time, the area round the bodies had been well trampled.

But there were clues: the bloody lump of wood; the incongruous laying out of the bodies, Norah's on a blanket; and a newspaper clipping found nearby. It was an In Memoriam notice, commemorating the death of an 18-year-old girl who died in Gatton on Christmas Eve 1896 – almost two years ago to the day. The notice had been inserted in the paper the following year. The girl was known to the Murphy girls, and Norah had suggested to her sister Kate, 13, that she cut it out of the paper and keep it. Kate told police she did so, but about six months ago she had noticed it was missing from the box in her room where she kept it. Someone had taken the cutting and had it at the scene of the murders.

The police investigation now became thorough. The Governor, Lord

Lamington, had issued notice of a reward of 1000 pounds for information leading to the arrest of the killer – or killers.

The head of the CIB took personal charge of the case. The best black trackers in the state were called in, and parties of mounted police searched the area thoroughly. The first man police questioned was William McNeill. He was in bed with her at the time, his wife, Polly, said, and his mother-in-law confirmed it: she heard him talking to Polly and their children.

The Murphy family itself was little help. The Police Magistrate later said that the boys' behaviour had been 'beyond all comprehension' and that evidence 'had to be dragged out of them'. The police wanted to hire horses for the search, and although the Murphy paddocks held a couple of dozen horses, they declined to give them to the police.

When Old Man Murphy was asked whether he had told police everything he knew, he replied: 'Yes.'

'You have concealed nothing?'

'I only wish to God that I knew the parties that did it.'

Parties? Could there have been more than one killer? The killer or killers had to contend with three able bodies, one of them a former policeman. Perhaps they were forced off the track at gunpoint, to be bound, robbed and violated.

But, if so, why was the horse shot? Why were the victims attacked so ferociously? Why was Norah, in particular, singled out to be so brutally treated? She had been bludgeoned after she was shot. And the harness strap, tightly buckled around her neck, spoke of hatred literally beyond understanding.

So much violence, yet around the bodies there was no sign of a struggle. If they were not forced off the road, who could have persuaded them to go down a little used track at around 9.30 at night into the darkness of the bush? Only someone they knew well. What, then, was the motive? Robbery was unlikely. Not even a maniac bothers to hold up three people coming back from a dance and kill them for the little money or valuables they might have had on them. Was it lust? Or was the sexual assault part of the insane frenzy that caused even the horse to be killed?

On 6 January 1899, police arrested a swaggie on a vagrancy charges, and while he was held, they investigated any connection he might have had with what an agog nation now knew as 'The Gatton Tragedy'. The man had a history of petty violence and of half-hearted sexual assaults, and years later he used to boast that he was the Gatton murderer. But he was a blowhard, a nobody who enjoyed his moment in the limelight, and few took him seriously then or at the time he was brought in.

Their next suspect was far more promising. Thomas Day, 21, had turned up in the district a short time ago and worked in the butcher's slaughter yard. He was strong, a loner who read books, and liked to go for walks in the bush. His hut was close to the scene of the crime, and he was the man Johnny Carroll believed he saw standing by the sliprail.

Day told police he had been in bed a couple of hours before that time. It was an early time to go to bed – seven o'clock, and no one saw him at the Boxing Day bonfire that Arthur Clarke held on the property where Day put up. When police searched his room, they found a blue jumper with a blood stain and a soft, slouch hat. Still, slouch hats were common in the bush, and working in the slaughter yards meant a man was bound to get blood on his clothing. Arthur Clarke himself remembered seeing Day in a blood-stained jumper just a couple of days before the murder.

The police investigation of Day was, many believed, inadequate. The men at the top held the view that he was a beardless boy incapable of a triple murder of such complexity and violence. Some of the police and some of the Murphy family disagreed and held strong feelings that it was Day who did it. Yet, on 10 January, just two week after the killings, the itinerate labourer said he didn't like Clarke's food, packed his swag, and walked out of the district.

And there the case remains. The poet John Manifold summed it up:

Whether it was a madman's work
Or that of a fiend from Hell
Only the stark white ringbarked gums
And the silent moon can tell.

Perhaps. But you may have a theory.

The Day Despicable Deeming Was Lost for Words

*F*rederick Bayley Deeming's counsel, Alfred Deakin, the brilliant young barrister destined to become the second prime minister of Australia, had failed in his bid to have his client declared insane. When the jury came back with its guilty verdict Deakin must have wondered why there could be any doubt about Deeming's insanity. Having insulted the jury – the ugliest people he'd ever seen, Deeming said – the multiple murderer turned to the judge and said: 'I hope in passing sentence Your Honour will make it as short as possible. I have been here for four days and I have been here since ten o'clock this morning and it is time I was released from it.'

His Honour obliged. 'It is not my intention to say one word beyond passing upon you the sentence of the law,' he said, and donned the black cap, telling Deeming that he would be taken to the place from whence he came 'and thence on a day appointed by the Executive Council to a place of execution, and there you will be hanged by the neck until you are dead. May the Lord have mercy on your soul.'

On a grey May day in 1892, the irritable man who had urged the judge to keep it short stood under the same hanging beam Ned Kelly had seen in his final moments 12 years before. Asked if he had any last words, Deeming's insouciance failed him. Shaking with fright, he could manage only a choked, incomprehensible response. He threw down a large brandy, and they pinioned his arms and led him the few steps to the noose. The hangman, wearing a false beard to disguise himself, stepped forward, dropped a white cap over Deeming's face and quickly slipped and tightened the noose around his neck. Then the trap sprang open and he dropped. Outside the Melbourne Gaol, a crowd of 12 000, many of them fashionably dressed women, waited and cheered when the news was delivered. Deeming the monster was dead.

Like Ned Kelly, Frederick Deeming was the talk of the English-speaking world. But where Kelly was and is admired by many, Deeming was universally loathed. And, unlike Kelly, his name has long faded, remembered today only by those who delve into the history of serial killers, where Deeming and Jack the Ripper were contemporaries. The Ripper is the most notorious of all serial killers, incontestably. But, of the two, Deeming was incomparably the more loathsome. Unlike the Ripper, he was sane, if stupid. Deeming cut the throat of his wife, strangled his eldest daughter, and cut the throats of his other three children, cut the throat of his second 'wife', and was set to make it three in a row but for an astute bit of detective work by a Melbourne newspaper reporter.

Deeming probably murdered more during a stay in South Africa when he had to leave Sydney to avoid arrest for insurance fraud, and he might have gone on muderering but for his inability to keep his mouth shut. People remembered Frederick Deeming long after he had left the room. He was a congenital liar, a man given to outlandish boasts and tall tales of his derring-do in the far corners of the globe. He was that frightening and unforgettable thing: a crushing bore.

Frederick Deeming's abominable crimes came to light in the Melbourne inner-city suburb of Windsor early in March 1892 when the owner of the rental house at number 57 Andrew Street investigated a revolting smell coming from one of the bedrooms. It wasn't hard to trace its source. Under the fireplace, set in cement, was the putrefying body of a woman. She was aged about 30 and her throat had been cut. Police were soon conducting investigations into the whereabouts of the last tenant, a Mr Druin, whom they had reason to believe could help them in their inquiries.

Tradespeople gave police a good description of Mr Druin. He talked a lot. He was tall, in his mid-30s, with a large moustache and a North Country accent, and from one of them he had bought cement, a spade and a trowel. In the fireplace grate, there was a torn luggage ticket that led them to the shipping records of the previous year when an Albert Williams and his wife, Emily, arrived in Melbourne from the United Kingdom.

Her throat slashed, Melbourne police dug up 'Mrs Druin' under the hearth in this bedroom. In England, 13 days later, police dug up another five bodies beneath another hearth.

Albert Williams, police believed, was the missing Mr Druin and the decomposed body, Emily, his wife. What's more they learned that a man answering his description, and now calling himself Baron Swanston, had taken a late booking on the steamship *Albany* in January. Perth police got on the job, and within 24 hours a mounted policeman arrested the Baron in Southern Cross, a mining town 380 kilometres west of Perth.

The news of the arrest of Baron Swanston, alias Mr Druin, alias Mr Williams, alias, as the police quickly discovered, Mr Frederick Bayley Deeming, caused a sensation. The 'Windsor Tragedy', as the *Age* sombrely called the murder, had gripped the city. But no one was more riveted by the news than attractive 19-year-old Kate Rounsefell, who was on her way to marry the Baron. The two had met on a ship from Melbourne to Sydney, and by the time it berthed at Circular Quay, the smooth-talking Baron – he had changed his name on the voyage – had the teenager in his sights. He went to Bathurst with her and was introduced to her sister, Elizabeth, and when he proposed, on a buggy ride, Kate readily agreed to be his wife. The Baron gave her a diamond and sapphire ring that had last been on the finger of Mrs Emily Druin. Soon after, the Baron left for the West, where he wrote to 'Dearest Kitty', asking her to join him in Southern Cross, where, he said, he had got a job as an engineer. He sent 20 pounds for the fare.

Kate left Bathurst at 5.25 p.m. on the train to Melbourne, and just hours later, police were knocking on Elizabeth Rounsefell's Bathurst door. When Kate alighted from the train in Melbourne, she was handed a telegram, one of four her sister had sent in desperation. 'For God's sake, go no further,' it read. The front page of that evening's *Herald* newspaper explained the telegram. 'Windsor Murderer arrested,' it said, and Kate read it and fainted.

Now, the many Sydney people who had known Deeming and his wife, Marie, came forward. He and Marie had arrived there from England in 1881, 11 years earlier, and had lived in Rowntree Street, Balmain. They had one child and then a second when they left Balmain for Surry Hills and Petersham, and wherever they went, Deeming left bad debts and dubious insurance claims. Yes, people had no trouble remembering Mr Frederick Deeming. But Mrs Deeming was another matter. She was older, dark and stout, not at all like the woman Melbourne people knew as the late Mrs Emily Druin.

The perplexity of Sydney people was understandable. The Mrs Deeming they had known had in fact returned to England with her husband and two children and there had two more children by him, as police were to learn when, once again, a discarded piece of paper at Andrews Street, Windsor, took them to the next stage of their investigation. The scrap was a memento: a ten-year-old invitation to a dinner hosted by an Albert Williams at the Commercial Hotel, Rainhill, a village outside Liverpool, England.

When the editor of the Melbourne *Argus* heard of the paper trail, he wired his Fleet Street correspondent and told him to hop on the first train to Rainhill and see what he could learn. There, the reporter discovered the mother of the murdered woman in Windsor – Emily Mather – who told him that her daughter had been swept off her feet by the debonair and dashing 'Albert Williams'. They had married on 22 September 1891, and sailed for Australia, Deeming, as always, leaving a trail of bad debts from Rainhill to London.

Mr Williams, Mrs Mather told the *Argus* editor, had leased a house, Dineham Villa, on behalf of a Colonel Brooks who had never materialised. Williams himself had put up at the Commercial. Liverpool police decided to pay Dineham Villa a visit. On 16 March 1892, less than a fortnight after the discovery of the second Mrs Deeming's body, they dug up five bodies. Neatly laid out, side by side under the hearthstone, were Marie Deeming and their four children. All but one had their throats cut. Deeming had strangled his nine-year-old daughter, probably because she came across him as he was killing the others.

On April Fools' Day 1892, Deeming was brought to Melbourne to stand trial for the murder of Emily Mather, the only murder charge he could be arraigned on in Australia. As his ship, the *Ballarat*, sailed into Hobson's Bay, thousands crowded the beach hoping to see the mass murderer. Deeming did not disappoint them. He stood on the deck, surveying the scene, smoking a cigar and seemingly in control of the situation.

In the coroner's court, Deeming was suave and charming, particularly to the women who filled the courtroom. *The Bulletin* called him 'that expert in the female nature of the middle and lower classes ... ogling the women, arousing all manner of base desire in the breasts.' And, it is true that, in his caddish way, Deeming, a fluent conversationalist and an habitual liar, did have a way with some women. After his arrest, many from around the world claimed to have been married, or almost married, to him.

Alfred Deakin led the defence for Frederick Deeming when he went on trial. Deakin argued that, at the time of committing the murder, Deeming was insane. Dr Shield, the government medical officer, would have none of it. He had questioned Deeming at some length and found him to be a pathological liar, and he brushed aside Deeming's story that his dead mother visited him each night urging him to kill.

Deeming, who had been withdrawn and subdued throughout the trial, suddenly announced that he wished to address the jury. He attacked the press for its prejudice and finished with a flourish: 'If I had been a guilty man I would gladly give a full statement of it rather than have submitted myself in this court for four days to the gaze of the most ugly race of people I had ever to face in my life.'

Chastened, the jury retired to consider its verdict. While they were out Deeming asked his solicitor what would happen if he were found not guilty, and was told he would be sent to England to be tried for the Rainhill murders. 'In that case I'd better get it over and done with here,' Deeming said. Three weeks later, at the Melbourne Gaol, it was over and done with.

The Girl Who Spent Ten Years in the Bath

*B*arry Humphries, among his other talents, has a gift for plumbing the shallows of the Australian psyche, the minutiae of shared experience, the triggers that set off common reactions. The Pyjama Girl is one of those triggers. Six decades on, people who were born in the days of Skyhooks and *Star Wars* still think, 'Pyjama Girl' when the subject of famous Australian murders is broached – although they may not have the faintest idea of who or what the Pyjama Girl was.

The Pyjama Girl holds a special place in Barry Humphries' more esoteric affections. He once proposed that Melbourne should make her killer the King of Moomba, Melbourne's annual answer to Rio's Mardi Gras and New York's Macy's Parade. The City Fathers, he proposed, should fly the wretched man to Melbourne to lead the Moomba Parade. There, in his Moomba monarch's crown and cloak, he would sit atop a giant float ringed by a crowd of slim young platinum blondes wearing yellow pyjamas.

The case of the Pyjama Girl opened on Saturday, 1 September 1934, with the discovery of a body, clad in yellow crepe pyjamas with a green dragon motif. A farmer, Tom Griffith, walking his prize bull home from Albury, saw, just off the road and half inside a storm-water culvert, the body of a woman. A sack covered the head. When the sack was lifted, police saw the face of a young woman in her mid-twenties with grey-blue eyes and brown hair dyed platinum, in the style the then screen queen Jean Harlow had made fashionable. She had once been quite attractive.

She was petite, 155 centimetres tall, and slim, but there was one odd feature: she had virtually no ear lobes. And below the peroxide-blonde hair, her head was smashed on one side and had a 0.25 calibre bullet hole in the other.

Police had no idea of the identity of the Pyjama Girl, as the tabloids soon dubbed her. All they had was the corpse, the distinctive oriental-style pyjamas, the sack, and a white, bloodied towel that had been wrapped around the battered head. There was no way of knowing who she was, how she came to be several kilometres outside Albury or where she had come from. But they knew where she was going. Straight into an ice pack, and then, a few weeks later, into a zinc-lined bath filled with formalin, the preserving fluid. There, for the next nine years, the Pyjama Girl lay while thousands of Australians came to look at the body in the bath.

Ostensibly, the spectators were there – first at Albury Hospital where she lay in the ice pack and then in the bath at Sydney University – to help police in their investigations. The police needed all the help they could get. The few leads, the sack, the bullet, the towel, all petered out. The police hoped that someone would recognise the corpse and, in particular, her distinguishing feature – the absence of ear lobes. This peculiarity and the dead girl's colouring and physique led a number of people to identify the Pyjama Girl as Anna Morgan, a woman who had disappeared a year before the discovery of the corpse in the culvert. Others thought the body was that of Linda Platt, who had married an Italian, Tony Agostini, and moved with him from Sydney to Melbourne in 1932.

Detectives who investigated the Anna Morgan clues drew a blank. And the Linda Plant lead was little better. They had no trouble finding Mr Agostini – he was living and working in Carlton, the first place you would look for an Italian in the 1930s. But, when shown a photograph of the Pyjama Girl, Tony Agostini shook his head. No, that was not his wife. She had upped and left about a year ago, he said, and he hadn't heard from her since.

Despite the fact that Linda Platt's leaving ten months before coincided almost exactly with the discovery of the Pyjama Girl, the detectives thanked him for his time and said goodbye to him. And, for four more years, the mystery body remained in the bath. All the while, thousands of ghouls made the trip to have a free peep at Sydney's medical school.

The Pyjama Girl had been ten years in the bath when the New South Wales Police Commissioner, William Mackay, made a telephone call to his favourite restaurant, Romano's, one of Sydney's most exclusive. When he was appointed to the top job in 1935, Mackay had decided that the file on the Pyjama Girl should be looked at afresh and assigned two detectives to the case. The name Linda Agostini – or Linda Platt as she was before she married Tony – kept cropping up.

Mackay ordered that the corpse be taken from its preservative bath, dried, and given a macabre make-over with the use of cosmetics and a hairdresser. The body was to be made to look as normal and presentable as possible. Then 16 people who had known Linda were invited to view the body. Seven were positive that it was the corpse of Linda.

Now Mackay thought it was time to make that call to Romano's. He asked to speak to one of the waiters. Tony Agostini, the quiet, polite, Italian waiter who always attended to Mr Mackay on his regular visits, came to the telephone. He had left Melbourne and gone back to Sydney in 1944 and got a job once again at Romano's where he had worked in the late 1920s. There, he got to know Bill Mackay, the tough young copper from Belfast who was making a name for himself cracking down on the razor gangs. Bill Mackay was an innovative and outstanding policeman. He was also gregarious and enjoyed a drink, and he and Antonio had enjoyed a genial relationship.

This time, however, Mr Mackay was talking as a policeman. He told Agostini that seven people had identified the body as Linda's, and said, 'You don't seem to be the same smiling Tony that I used to know.' That was enough to tip Tony Agostini into the quickest and easiest murder confession Mackay had ever known.

'I've been through hell for ten years,' he told the Commissioner, 'and no matter what happens I'm going to tell you the truth.'

The truth, Agostini said, was that his marriage was rocky, his wife liked to hit the bottle, she was given to black depression and jealous rages. There were frequent splits and tearful reconciliations. It came to a head one night when he woke to find her bending over him, a revolver to his head. He grabbed her wrist, they wrestled, and the gun went off. Linda was dead. He panicked, put the body in the back of his car, and drove north through the night up the Sydney Road, past Pentridge Prison and on to the Hume Highway. Outside Albury, he pushed the body into a culvert, sloshed petrol over it and threw a lighted match on to it. It began to rain, and he got back in his car and drove home to Melbourne.

The trial lasted nine days, but the jury was out for just 90 minutes before they returned to announce that they found Antonio Agostini not guilty of murder, but guilty of manslaughter. He was sentenced to six years' hard labour and deported after serving almost four years. Tony Agostini died in Italy.

But the Pyjama Girl lives on.

The Grim Reaper's Groundhog Day

*T*he last tragic passage of John Lynch's life seemed to be one gruesome Groundhog Day.

Get up in the morning, meet new people, kill them.

Get up in the morning, meet new people, kill them.

Get up in the morning ... it went on and on in much the same way, day after day. So much so that, a century and a half after he was hanged, the sanctimonious John Lynch remains one of Australia's most prolific serial killers. He killed at least five men, three boys, one woman and one girl.

Lynch may have been mad – he constantly consulted with God, he claimed, and God encouraged his killings – and he murdered with a methodical callousness that clearly caused him not the slightest twinge. But, in the end, he was just a cunning, cowardly little rat who would kill for the pennies in your pocket.

Sir James Dowling, the judge who, at Berrima in April 1842, passed sentence on Lynch for the murder of a farmhand, put it floridly but fairly:

> John Lynch, the trade in blood which has so long marked your career is at last terminated, not by any sense of remorse, or the sating of any appetite for slaughter on your part, but by the energy of a few zealous spirits, roused into activity by the frightful picture of atrocity which the last tragic passage of your worthless life exhibits.
>
> It is now credibly believed, if not actually ascertained, that no less than nine other individuals have fallen by your hands. How many more have been violently ushered into another world remains undiscovered, save in the dark pages of your own memory? By your

own confession it is admitted that as late as 1835 justice was invoked on your head for a frightful murder committed in this neighbourhood.

Your unlucky escape on that occasion has, it would seem, whetted your tigrine relish for human gore, but at length you have fallen into toils from which you cannot escape.

The immediate neighbourhood the judge referred to was Berrima, 150 kilometres south of Sydney, then a prosperous centre on the old Hume Highway in the southern highlands of New South Wales. And his unlucky escape referred to his acquittal for the first of the killings he confessed to.

Born in 1813 in County Caven, Ireland, John Lynch was 19 when, transported for 'false pretences', he arrived in Australia on the convict ship *Dunvegon Castle*. Brown-haired, with hazel eyes and quite harmless looking, he was a stumpy 160 centimetres. He had been sentenced to seven years and was put to work in a road gang before being released as an assigned servant. In 1835, three years after his arrival, Lynch was charged with stealing a saddle from his master, and although he was acquitted he took to the bush – he 'bolted'. Not long after, the battered body of Thomas Smith, a witness to a highway robbery, was found dead. Several bushrangers, among them Lynch, were arrested on suspicion of the murder. Police believed Smith had been lured from his hut and his brains beaten out of his skull as a warning to others.

Lynch and two others were charged with the murder of Thomas Smith, and brought to trial. But, while his companions hanged for the crime, Lynch once again went free – the trigger, perhaps, for his belief that God was firmly in his camp and should be consulted whenever he was planning a murder.

Later, Lynch spent a year in gaol for harbouring bushrangers. And, in 1840, after he resumed his criminal ways, he had what proved to be a fatal run-in with John Mulligan. Lynch came to Mulligan, a receiver of bushrangers' stolen property, and asked him for payment, but Mulligan told him he wasn't prepared to pay anything like the 30 pounds Lynch wanted. Eight, maybe. The pair had a blistering row, and Lynch left, swearing he'd be back with a vengeance. It took him a fortnight and the lives of two men and two boys, but Lynch was true to his word.

At first, however, Lynch decided to try the honest life: to steal a team of bullocks and start afresh. He went to T. B. Humphrey's farm at Oldbury where he had once worked and drove off a team of eight bullocks. 'I'd broken them myself. I took them because I wanted to start out again honest. I intended taking the bullocks to Sydney and selling them,' he confessed to the goal chaplain Mr Sumner and police on the day before his execution. He continued: 'At Razorback Mountain I met a cove named Ireland and fell in with him.' Ireland and an Aboriginal boy were also in charge of a team of bullocks, a full team pulling a load of wheat, bacon and other farm produce to Sydney for its owner, Thomas Cowper.

Lynch immediately saw a commercial opportunity. 'It seemed to me that it would pay me better to kill Ireland and take possession of the dray and its load of saleable produce than to drive Mr Humphrey's bullocks to Sydney.' So began John Lynch's Groundhog Day.

Lynch camped with the pair that night, accepted Ireland's hospitality – dinner and a cigar – and went to sleep after consulting with God about what he would do to the pair in the morning. It was simple enough. Lynch got up early and asked the Aboriginal lad to help him round up his stray bullocks. The two were well away from the camp when Lynch took a hatchet from under his coat and hit him in the back of the head. 'Just one tap with the tomahawk,' the little feller reminisced in his lilting brogue. 'He dropped like a log of wood.'

It was time for breakfast. Lynch told Ireland the boy was still looking for the bullocks, and while he was about to be handed a hearty breakfast to start the day, he pointed to something in the scrub. Ireland looked around and Lynch stove his head in with the hatchet. Lynch finished his breakfast. Then he dragged the bodies to a rock cleft and covered them with undergrowth and rocks, turned the stolen team of bullocks and the dray in the direction of Berrima and set them on their way home. With any luck – and Lynch was a lucky man – they would be found and returned without any bother.

Lynch relaxed another two days at the camp, the bodies close by, until he was joined by two men in charge of a team of horses. Lagge and Lee were the men's names. Lagge and Lee – their names sounded like a vaudeville duo – and they gave Lynch, by his account, a splendid night's entertainment, drinking, singing and even dancing an Irish jig for him. He was so pleased he didn't kill them for their horses while they slept.

The next morning, the trio set out for Sydney. At Liverpool, on the outskirts of the city, a stranger rode up, reined his horse alongside the dray and asked Lynch what did he think he was doing driving his, the stranger's, team? Lynch almost lost his composure, he confessed: 'I nearly died of shock,' but recovered quickly with his rat cunning: 'I'm glad I've seen you,' he told Thomas Cowper, 'I was just wondering whether I'd knock into you. The fact is that your man Ireland was taken ill back there and begged me to take the load to Sydney for you. He said I'd probably meet you somewhere along the way.'

Tom Cowper was a gullible man. And a kindly one. Instead of taking over the team, he happily agreed to Lynch's offer to continue to Sydney while he went back down the trail in search of his stricken farmhand. He would find him, Lynch told him, being cared for by the Aboriginal boy around the campfire. They'd all meet in Sydney in a few days' time.

Lynch parted with Lagge and Lee and hurried on to Sydney, driving the team all day and throughout the night. He had to move smartly to sell it before Cowper either found the bodies of Ireland and the boy – or, almost as bad, couldn't find them and went for the troopers. Lynch found a drunk and got him to sell Cowper's farm produce so that if he was ever questioned he could claim it was stolen from the dray. Then he got out of town as quickly as he could with the bullock team pulling the empty dray.

Then came another shock. Lynch recalled:

> As I neared the George River I saw Chief Constable McAlister of Campbelltown and, fearing he'd recognise me, I turned into a cross track leading towards the Berrima Road. This close shave frightened the living daylights out of me and I decided that I would get rid of Cowper's team at the first opportunity, as it would only get me into trouble.

Lynch may have been shaken, but he was not sufficiently stirred to mend his ways. He had had no sooner scuttled from the Chief Constable than he met another man and boy – the Frazers, father and son – who were making their way with a team towards Berrima. Once again it occurred to Lynch that this was a fine time to swap teams. All he had to do was to kill the father and his son and claim their team as his own. The teams made their slow way to the Bargo Brush where others were camping. Lynch remembered:

> We all had supper, then I crawled under my dray with the intention of sleeping. No sooner had I got there than I saw a trooper ride into the camp. He asked Frazer if he had seen the dray I had stolen from Cowper and Frazer shook his head and said he didn't know anything about it.

The trooper, amazingly, took no notice of the dray that was under his nose – or the little Irishman under the dray. He rode off, and that night Lynch thanked God. In turn God gave him this advice: he must kill the Frazers in gratitude for his deliverance and take their team. As the first step Lynch set free his team of bullocks.

The following morning, Lynch used the stray bullocks strategy once again. This time, however, he said he needed to go home to get another team. The Frazers lent a hand concealing the dray, and the three of them left the Bargo Brush and travelled all day until they reached Cordeux Flat and made camp for the night.

Next morning it was Groundhog Day. 'In the morning young Frazer and I went in search of the horses. I put on my coat as to hide the tomahawk. I let the youngster go ahead. Then, when we were in the bush, I thought to myself, there's no difficulty settling him. So I crept up behind him and hit him with one blow.'

Lynch hid the dead boy and came back with one horse. He told Frazer his son was looking for the other horse and then 'discovered' the boy coming out of the scrub behind his father. He pointed, Frazer turned and Lynch hit him, 'a nice one on the back of his head and he dropped like a log of wood.' Lynch, sanctimonious as ever, gave thanks to the Lord, buried the bodies in a shallow grave and, taking the horse and the dray, went to fulfil the promise he had made two weeks ago. He was going back to the Mulligan's with a vengeance.

Lynch rode up to the farmhouse where Mrs Mulligan, seated in a rocking chair on the veranda, asked: 'What do you want?'

'The 30 pounds your husband owes me.'

'What 30 pounds?'

'You know very well what – for the articles which I got from burglaries and highway robberies I did at the risk of my life and which your old man was supposed to be holding for me!'

Mrs Mulligan told Lynch that there was only nine pounds in the house. So he decided to walk to the Black Horse Hotel about five kilometres down the road at Berrima and buy two bottles of rum to get Mulligan of a mind to pay him the 30 pounds. Mr and Mrs Mulligan were waiting and greeted him warmly when he returned. Glasses were produced and after an amicable chat the conversation turned to the 30 pounds, Mr Mulligan asking for Mr Lynch to be reasonable.

Lynch was now morose. He gave Mulligan a bottle but drank little himself. He went outside and sat on a log and brooded: 'This man passed me by as if he didn't know me when I was in the iron gang in Berrima. He never offered me a shilling though he made pounds out of me, and I risked my life to obtain it … Oh, Almighty God, assist me and direct me what to do.' He returned to the hut where Mrs Mulligan told him she had dreamed that she had a baby and that Lynch had taken it and killed it. 'It was all covered with blood and looked horrible.' Lynch believed that Mrs Mulligan could foretell things and he had another consultation with God.

Groundhog Day.

Mulligan went off into the paddocks and his wife into the house. That left Lynch with Johnny, their 16-year-old son. He suggested that he and Johnny cut some wood for the fire. Once out of sight, Lynch killed the boy and covered his body with brush, just as he'd done with the other boys. He came back to the farmhouse where Mrs Mulligan had an awful premonition. 'Where's the boy?' she asked.

'Gone to the paddock with the horses.'

Mrs Mulligan, Lynch knew, suspected that the worst had happened to Johnny and began to get hysterical. She told Lynch to fire his gun as a signal for the boy to come home.

'What's all the urgency?,' Lynch said, 'I only saw him few minutes ago.' If he fired the gun, 'it would alert the police' and he didn't want them to see 'that dray'. Mulligan appeared and wanted to know what was going on. He summed up the situation while he paced up and down, and then, while his wife ran back into the house, he ran for the scrub to find his son.

Once again, Lynch used the ruse of pointing out something and while Mulligan looked that way, was on to him, swinging the hatchet and felling Mulligan dead before he hit the ground. He dragged the body into the bush and followed Mrs Mulligan, who was running, shrieking in terror, and he tripped her up and killed her with one hatchet blow to the head.

There was one remaining Mulligan. He found their 14-year-old daughter in the kitchen. 'I saw her standing behind a table with a butcher's knife. She was sobbing with fear and trembling violently. I hadn't prepared for this so I just stood there staring at her. Then I yelled, "Put that knife down!" but she didn't move, so I yelled again, "Put that knife down!"

The girl was frozen with fear. 'Put that knife down,' he told her a third time. She put it down. He went round the table, took her hand and told her: 'I don't want to kill you but if I let you live you'll only put me away.' He gave her 10 minutes to pray and then took her into the bedroom and raped her. 'I then brought her back out into the kitchen and tried to comfort her, saying that life was full of trouble and that she'd be better off dead. Then I mercifully distracted her attention and, as she turned away, I struck her with the axe and she fell without a murmur.'

Lynch built a bonfire and threw the bodies of the Mulligans on it. 'I've never seen anything like it. They burned as if they were bags of fat,' he recalled.

Now Lynch called his cunning into play. He stayed at the farm all the next day, 'making things right' by burning all clothing and personal items of the Mulligans, and then he went to Sydney. There, he put an advertisement in the *Sydney Gazette* notifying the public that because Mrs Mulligan had deserted the family home he would not be responsible for any debts she might incur. The classified insertion was signed 'John Mulligan'. Then he wrote to Mulligan's creditors telling them that he, Mulligan, had sold the farm, Wombat Brush, to a John Dunleavy for 700 pounds and that Dunleavy took responsibility for any outstanding debts. And he forged a deed to the farm and all its affects to John Dunleavy.

Lynch then returned to the farm and employed a couple to work it while he stayed there for six months, the Lord of the Manor. No one seemed to be concerned about the missing Mulligans and all was going swimmingly for 'John Dunleavy' before, driving on the road, he met a big Irish labourer, Kearns Landregan, looking for work. 'Dunleavy' agreed to engage him to do some fencing and Kearns got into his cart and they drove on until they passed Crisps' Inn.

Here Landregan crouched down and tried to hide because, he admitted, he didn't want a row with Crisp about some clothes Crisp claimed he had stolen. This was enough for the wee small killer. 'After I heard that I was determined to get rid of him.' It was the final Groundhog Day. While Landregan sat by the campfire, Lynch crept up behind him, as always, and struck him with the hatchet.

This time, however, Lynch departed from the routine. Because Landregan was so big and burly – he had boasted that he'd never been bested in wrestling – Lynch gave him not one, but two and still more blows to the back of the skull. The first blow knocked him unconscious and he went down with a grin still on his face – Lynch had been telling him a joke. It took more to finish him off. As usual he covered the body with freshly cut scrub.

Landregan's body was discovered on the 20 February 1841 after Hugh Tinney and his bullock dray camped for the night at Ironstone Bridge. Mr Tinney alerted the Berrima Chief Constable. The body was identified, and Chief Constable Chapman followed a long and incontrovertible trail of evidence, beginning with grey horses' hair at the campfire near the body and ending with the identification of 'John Dunleavy' as John Lynch, a prisoner at large.

Lynch confessed all at the end, although for two months he vigorously protested his innocence. He was hanged at Berrima on 22 April 1842. John Lynch was 29. In his short life he set a grisly record that is still unsurpassed – to our knowledge.

The Shark That Coughed up a Killer

*F*rom this distance in time, the Shark Arm in the Coogee Aquarium has almost become an urban myth. Like the Pyjama Girl, its contemporary murder mystery – and like the limb in question – the Shark Arm has lodged itself deep in the belly of the nation's shared memory. Now and again, like the limb, it gets coughed up in memory's murky waters.

After that the tribal memory tends to get hazy. People have a vague idea that the arm belonged to a criminal – there was a tattoo, wasn't there? – and they like to think that the arm belonged to a crook who had been fitted with concrete shoes and deposited in Botany Bay, where the shark took him, in the tabloid parlance.

The real story is far more complex and sinister – even far bloodier. But like many criminal cases in the days before drugs drove the underworld environment, the Shark Arm mystery had a touch of amateur theatricals. To begin with, the arm wasn't in the Coogee Aquarium's shark. Strictly speaking, it was in a smaller shark ... which was in the Aquarium shark. This smaller shark had been worrying bait left out by the owner of the Coogee Aquarium in Sydney when a tiger shark twice its size slammed into it and devoured his smaller cousin in half a dozen ferocious bites. In its frenzy the big, four-metre tiger became hooked and entangled by the baited line and the Aquarium owners delightedly towed it to its new home. There, a week later, the shark was clearly ill. On Anzac Day 1935, the prize exhibit was looking seedy when, to the mingled horror and delight of the handful of spectators, all of whom would retail the story with relish for the rest of their lives, the shark vomited and up came the arm.

211

Sydney sharks and Sydney crims: tabloid heaven. Mrs Smith got it right. Her husband had gone fishin' – but never came back. By now he was fish food.

The following day experts examined the arm. They agreed that the arm had not been in the stomach of the tiger, but in the stomach of the smaller shark and that it had not been torn from the body by that shark, but severed by a knife wielded by an amateur surgeon. The arm sported a primitive tattoo of a pugilist, as boxers were then glorified, and there was a length of rope still tied to the wrist. There was no problem tracing the owner of the arm. His brother saw its photograph in the *Truth* newspaper and recognised it, and when Sydney CIB took fingerprints, they confirmed that the arm was that of a 40-year-old small-time crook called James Smith.

The detectives went to Smith's home, where Mrs Smith told them that a few weeks before, on 7 April, Jim had left home, ironically, to go fishing. That was the last his missus saw of him. Mrs Smith suggested that police should have a word with Patrick Brady. An old mate of Jim's, Brady was a forger. He and Smith cooked up get-rich-quick schemes, and their names regularly appeared on police station blotters.

When the detectives went looking for Brady, a barman at the Cronulla local near where Brady rented a cottage told them he had seen him driving a man who looked like Jimmy Smith. The local real estate agent filled them in further. Brady had left the cottage in immaculate condition – but there were two or three items missing: a large tin storage case, an anchor and two lead window weights.

A third local, a taxi driver, gave another interesting piece of information. He remembered taking Brady to the Sydney Harbour home of a well-known boat builder, Reginald Holmes. Smith had been associated in some way with a luxury boat that Holmes had built and which later sank. An insurance claim had gone in, but then it was cancelled. The insurance company had awkward questions that it wanted answered. The detectives talked to Holmes who couldn't help them. He didn't know Brady, he said. But when the detectives caught up with Brady, he said yes, Jimmy Smith had come to the Cronulla cottage on 9 April the day his wife last saw him, and he had left the cottage with two men, one of whom was Reginald Holmes.

The detectives went back to McMahon's Point, Sydney Harbour. Holmes had done a bunk. The game was up, so he decided to go out in appropriate style: blow out his brains in one of his stylish speedboats on the Harbour. Holmes didn't bother to cut the engine when the time came. He put a .32 calibre automatic to his head, squeezed the trigger and … blew himself, practically unharmed, out of the speeding boat. Holmes had been getting Dutch courage from a bottle of whisky, and when he squeezed the trigger, his hand was trembling so much that the bullet merely grazed his temple. The impact was enough, however, to catapult him out of the boat before, befuddled, he clambered back in and sped off.

What followed was worthy of a Keystone Cops comedy. Two police launches set out after Holmes, alerted by astonished boaties who saw a man with blood streaming from his face at the wheel of a speeding motor boat that seemed to be going nowhere very fast. Holmes was too hot for them. For two hours, he led the launches through a hair-raising course between boats and buoys, jetties and wharves. Finally, exhausted, he stopped at Watson's Bay. He told the police he had run because he thought he was being chased by someone else. Then, after four days under guard in hospital, he told police that Smith's killer was Pat Brady. What's more, Brady had promised to kill him – or have him killed, he said, if he talked to the police. 'If I'm not able to get you, one of me cobbers will.'

Brady had already been charged with the murder of Smith and was being held in custody. The inquest was set for 12 June, and Holmes would be the key to it. But, on the morning of the inquest, someone did to Holmes what he had tried to do to himself on Sydney Harbour a few weeks before. He was shot dead in his car just below the Harbour Bridge.

Patrick Brady was released. Smith's body was never found, and due to lack of evidence, two men were acquitted of charges of murdering Holmes.

The Shark Arm began its journey into the Australian collective memory.

9 | Three Odds and a Sod

Awful Arthur Orton, the Man Who Hoodwinked Two Nations

*H*e was a grossly unattractive man. Obese, near illiterate, unabashedly belching and farting at will, afflicted with a twitch and with a tendency to drool, the butcher from Wagga Wagga was the type you find yourself next to on a very long plane flight in a very long nightmare.

She was the head of one of England's most illustrious families, one that had been prominent for a millennium, and the ninth richest in the land. The two had never met. Yet when Arthur Orton, the oafish butcher from Back o' Burke, arrived in Paris in 1867 to meet Lady Tichborne, the immensely wealthy dowager widow of the Baronet Sir Roger Tichborne, she 'recognised' him as her long lost son, Roger, and settled an annual allowance on him of 1000 pounds.

This was all very well. One thousand pounds a year was then a handy sum. At the time, labourers in Britain received around 30 pound a year. But it was just a fraction of the wealth that came with the family hereditary title. And Arthur Orton wanted to get his hands on that hereditary title.

The legal battle Orton instigated became one of the most controversial and comical in British legal history. It had half the population of the British Isles and Australia – 'the lower class' – fervently convinced that this fat, uncouth man was indeed the aristocratic Roger Tichborne. And it had the other half outraged at the idea that a member of the aristocracy could so much as conceive of being a butcher in Wagga Wagga, Australia. (His counsel put it down to 'uninterrupted sunshine in Australia ... the kind of place that could seduce a man, make him forget his family and everything that was proper ... a vagabond life, pleasant but wrong.'

All that was debatable. The real question was not whether Arthur Orton was Roger Tichborne, but how on earth did he manage to convince even one solitary soul that he was? In the annals of confidence trickery, there is nothing to touch the monumental audacity of the butcher from Wagga Wagga.

The trial to determine the truth about the Tichborne Claimant was one of the first 'celebrity trials', and until the 1997 McLibel case fought by McDonalds, the longest running legal action in British history. The cost was colossal. Around the world it was followed with intense interest. An army of witnesses for both sides was cross-examined by the finest jurists of the time. Outside the court on some days, more than 10 000 people milled. Yet the whole matter could have been resolved in an instant. Roger Tichborne had tattoos on both arms. Arthur Orton had none. Yet nobody – inexplicably – thought to ask the Tichborne Claimant to bare his arms.

Roger Tichborne was born in Paris in 1829, the eldest son of an English baronet. Arthur Orton was born in 1834, the son of an English butcher. Apart from that, they had nothing in common. Roger was educated in Paris and grew up speaking French as his first language. Arthur was educated in inner London's Wapping, and grew up speaking Cockney as his first language.

At 15, Roger was sent to England to study at the famous Jesuit school, Stonyhurst. At 19, he obtained his commission in the renowned 6th Dragoon Guards, the Carabineers, and fell in love with his cousin, Catherine Doughty, and she with him. At around the same time, young Arthur Orton was apprenticed at sea in the hope of curing him of the curious nervous condition, St Vitus's Dance. His family thought that a return sea voyage to South America might cause it to disappear. Instead, Arthur disappeared. At Valparaiso, in Chile, he jumped ship – life at sea for a boy was brutal – and lived anonymously and out of touch with his family in the little town of Melipilla where a family called Castro befriended the young gringo. Then, after 18 months, he sailed home.

Meanwhile, Roger had resigned his commission – his men made fun of him – and fallen out with his family over Catherine. His parents, who were at odds with each other, were united in their opposition to the marriage, and in 1853, Roger left for South America in something of a huff. In June, he arrived in Valparaiso, Arthur's old stamping ground. A month earlier, Arthur Orton had stepped off a ship at Hobart Town in Van Diemen's Land. Arthur, too, had gone to sea again after his parents opposed his wishes to marry a Mary Ann Loder.

From Chile, Roger travelled to Peru, Buenos Aires and Rio de Janeiro, all the while sending his mother and other relatives letters and travel souvenirs, stuffed birds, animal skins and the like. In 1854, a year after he had said goodbye to the family seat in Hampshire, Roger sailed in the *Bella*, bound for Kingston, Jamaica. He never arrived. The *Bella* was lost at sea with all hands; only an upturned longboat and debris were ever found.

Lady Tichborne, however, would not accept that her firstborn child was gone. (Around this time, Charles Dickens created the character of Miss Havisham, the spurned bride who could never accept that she had been left waiting at the church. Miss Havisham would have applauded Lady Tichborne's stubborn refusal to face the facts.) She resolutely forbade any talk that her boy was dead and kept a lamp light burning – metaphorically and literally – for his return.

To this light, burning through the night in the entrance at Tichborne Park, came vagabond sailors, rogues and down-on-their-luck wanderers who had heard that Lady Tichborne wanted to believe that her son was alive. They would regale her with stories of shipwrecked survivors and leave with a shilling or two in their pocket. Her husband, Sir James Tichborne, was intensely irritated by her blind optimism, but this may have only strengthened her. Lady Tichborne and Sir James were constantly fighting and she loathed his family. When he died in 1862, and when Roger's only brother, Alfred, followed four years later, she stepped things up. She began to advertise for news of Roger. The personal section of classified advertisements columns in newspaper around the world carried insertions such as this:

A HANDSOME REWARD will be given to any person who can furnish such information as will discover the fate of ROGER CHARLES TICHBOURNE. He sailed from the port of Rio Janeiro on the 20th of April, 1854, in the ship La Bella, and has never been heard of since, but a report reached England to the effect that a portion of the crew and passengers of vessel of that name was picked up by a vessel bound to Australia – Melbourne it is believed – it is not known whether the said ROGER CHARLES TICHBORNE was amongst the drowned or saved. He would at the present time be about 32 years of age; is of a delicate constitution, rather tall, with very light brown hair and blue eyes.

The description of Roger Tichborne was not wholly accurate. He would have been 36, not 32, he wasn't tall, and his hair was black, not very light brown. (Arthur Orton's hair was brown with a reddish hue.) But the hint of a fragile soul is echoed in a daguerreotype photograph taken around the time he set sail from England. It shows a twerp. A limp, wistful gentleman who gives every appearance of being, perhaps, an enthusiastic collector of railway timetables.

Arthur Orton, on the other hand, tipped the scale at way over 124 kilograms, and at his peak weighed in at an enormous 171 kilograms. Where Roger Tichborne had, it was said, 'walked like a Frenchman', Arthur Orton was stooped and shambling. And where Roger had been mocked by his men in the Carabineers, Arthur was a gent who had been around. After his arrival in Hobart Town, Arthur spent the next 13 years living, sometimes on the wrong side of the law, in various places around Australia. In 1859, he was digging for gold at Reedy Creek, New South Wales, when he heard there was a warrant for his arrest for horse stealing. Orton disappeared once more and reappeared in Wagga Wagga, New South Wales, working as a butcher and calling himself Tom Castro – the surname of the family who looked after him in Melipilla, Chile.

Wagga Wagga was a town of around 1000 inhabitants, one of them a solicitor named Gibbes. Among his clients was Orton, who had gone bankrupt, but who was in the habit of telling people that he was from a famous titled family back in England and that his name was not really Castro. Gibbes used to drink with Orton, and his interest in Orton's alleged links with English aristocracy was fired when Orton asked if property in England to which he was entitled would have to be included in the bankruptcy. It was fuelled further when Orton casually dropped a titbit of intriguing information – he had been shipwrecked at sea, he claimed.

When the solicitor got home and told Mrs Gibbes what Orton had told him, her feminine intuition put two and two together: Tom Castro must be the missing heir she had read about in advertisements in the *Sydney Morning Herald*. When the question was put to him, Orton would not confirm or deny that he was the man. That was enough for Gibbes to write to Arthur Cubbit, the proprietor of the Missing Friends Agency, who had placed the advertisement. The Tichborne Claimant juggernaut was underway.

Arthur Orton, at the suggestion of Gibbes, wrote a letter to Lady Tichborne in which he claimed he had arrived in Melbourne on 24 July 1854, after being rescued from the *Bella* by a ship named *Osprey* and had since lived under the name of Castro. He apologised for 'the trubl and anxsity [sic]' his long absence had caused. (The real Roger, like Orton, had also been no great shakes with the English language.)

Orton intended, he confessed years later, simply to get enough money to see him and his wife and child out of the country. 'The reason I wrote the letter was because I was hard pressed for money at the time, and I thought that if she was fool enough to send me money so much the better. I could go to Sydney and take the steamer to Panama where I could join my brother and nobody would ever hear anything from me.'

But Lady Tichborne declined to send money. She wrote to Mr Cubitt: 'You do not give any details whatever about the person you believe to be my son, you do not name even the town where he is, and you do not say anything about the way he was saved from the shipwreck.' Her interest, however, was roused. One of the stories she had been told about the loss of the *Bella* was that it had not been sunk at all, but stolen by a mutinous crew who re-named it, re-painted it and sailed it to Australia. Lady Tichborne offered 200 pounds to cover the voyage to England if Cubitt and Gibbes could provide some proof. She herself accelerated matters by recommending that Gibbes and Cubitt get in touch with an old former servant of the Tichbornes', Andrew Bogle, a West Indian who had been rescued from slavery by Roger's uncle. Bogle had been given an annuity by the family and retired to Sydney. Tichborne Park's former head gardener, Michael Guilfoyle, was also in Sydney. Both had known Roger – now the baronet, Sir Roger, if indeed he were alive.

At this stage, the game should have been up for the Wagga Wagga butcher. Instead he and his harridan wife and child went to Sydney – he had little to lose after all – and found to his amazement and intense delight that he and his wife were treated like royalty. Then Bogle arrived. It took him only a few minutes to pronounce that the large fat man before him was indeed the slim young man he had known. After all, Bogle reasoned, Sir Roger had at once recognised him and he had such knowledge of Sir Roger's family and background that he must be the missing baronet. Guilfoyle the gardener came to the same conclusion. And both of them wrote to Lady Tichborne telling her so.

Andrew Bogle was no fool. He could not possibly have believed that the man Castro was Roger Tichborne. Almost certainly he did a deal with Castro. He would teach Castro the social skills a gentleman such as Roger would have, and he would brief him on all possible details of the Tichborne family and the events surrounding Roger's disappearance. In return he would be employed, once more as a valet, at Tichborne

Park, a life far more luxurious than that he knew in Sydney.

Arthur Orton, too, was no fool. Near illiterate, yes, coarse and uncouth, yes, but he was intelligent and quick. He had a real talent for rhetoric and a vivid imagination, possibly aided by the nervous condition, St Vitus' Dance, which left its physical legacy in his twitch. And he had just enough knowledge, from letters Lady Tichborne had sent, from *Burke's Peerage* and from newspaper articles, to start a conversation and then get the other person talking. He retained what he was told and repeated it to the next person, in turn gathering more information.

Years later, in a confession he wrote for publication in *The People*, Orton claimed that Andrew Bogle was genuine in his belief. Awful though he appeared on the surface, Arthur Orton was a decent bloke deep down.

Bogle thoroughly believed I was Sir Roger, he used to converse very freely with me about the family, giving me the whole history of it … I was pumping him all the time as to names and habits and customs of various members of the family. I have always been a good listener and by listening quietly and patiently for hours, to statements which have been made to me by, I suppose, many hundreds of people, all of whom gave information concerning the Tichborne family, I learned such facts that really induced me to prosecute my claim. I found by listening to others the story built itself and grew so large I really couldn't get out of it.

With the assurance of Bogle, the faithful old servant, Lady Tichborne now threw aside all caution and wrote to Castro urging him to hurry to England. To Gibbes, she confided: 'I think my poor, dear Roger confuses everything in his mind, and I believe him to be my son, though his statements differ from mine.'

On Christmas Day 1866, the Tichborne Claimant arrived in England. Almost his first action had been to visit the Globe Inn, Wapping, where he made inquiries 'on behalf of an old friend – Arthur Orton – back in Australia.' His father, George, had been a butcher on High Street,

Wapping, and had 12 children, and Arthur needed to buy their silence.

Next Orton and his party travelled to Paris where his 'mother' – Lady Tichbourne – had summoned him. In a darkened room in the Place de la Madeleine, he lay fully dressed on a bed, too unwell to see his 'mamma'. She came anyway. She bent down and kissed him. 'He looks like his father and his ears are like his uncle's,' she said, like a proud mother looking at her newborn child for the first time. The claimant was sick with worry that he was about to be denounced. Instead Lady Tichborne declared, in the presence of a doctor, that the man in the bed was her firstborn son.

The dowager was delighted. The servants hadn't seen her laugh in years. She and Castro were inseparable, and for weeks they walked and talked. Arthur Orton, when making a will before setting out for England, had got Lady Tichborne's name completely wrong, but the dowager was unfussed by any mistakes he made or questions he was at a loss to answer. He could remember nothing of his childhood: the names of his friends, his favourite dogs, books he had read – even the fact that he couldn't speak French, his native tongue, didn't faze her. A head injury in the shipwreck, illness, alcoholism and the passage of time, all accounted for these lapses, she insisted.

Then Lady Tichborne died. The Tichborne estates now belonged to the infant son of Roger's brother, Arthur. This left Orton in a pickle. Either he had to drop the pretence and seek anonymity – perhaps, as he was later to reveal, in Panama – or he had to fight to establish that he was Roger, the heir to the Tichborne estates. Naturally, he chose to go for broke. In his published confession, Arthur Orton gives a plausible glimpse into this thought process.

> I could not get away from those who were infatuated with me and firmly believed I was the Real Sir Roger ... Of course I knew perfectly well I was not, but they made so much of me, and persisted in addressing me as Sir Roger, that I forgot who I was and by degree

I began to believe I was really the rightful owner of the estates. If it had not been that I was feted and made so much of the by the colonists of Sydney I should have taken the boat and gone the rest of my days to Panama with my brother.

The trial of the century that followed Arthur Orton's decision to legally establish he was Sir Roger involved the most eminent jurists of the day in what was, until the 1990s, the longest running legal action in British history. It remains the most expensive. It was watched with fascination around the world. Gilbert and Sullivan based *Trial by Jury* on the case. Mark Twain was so inspired by Orton that he used him as a model for some characters in *Huckleberry Finn*. It was the best show in town – far funnier and with more twists and dramatic developments than anything on in the West End. Before each session, the streets outside the court were crowded with people trying to get a seat in the public galleries. European royalty took their turn in the ticket queue.

The court case was, at times, pure *Monty Python*. Here is the exchange between the Solicitor-General, Sir John Coleridge, and Orton regarding his claim to have studied Latin, Greek and Hebrew (a course not on the curriculum at Stonyhurst).

Coleridge: 'Can you read Hebrew now?'

Orton (triumphantly): 'Not a word!'

'Have you studied Greek?'

'Yes.'

'Did your studies in Greek go as far as the alphabet?'

'I don't know.'

'You surely remember that?'

'I went there unprepared.'

'Could you make out Greek at that time?'

'Perhaps a sentence.'

'Could you read the first chapter of St John?'

'No.'

'Does any of it linger in your mind now?'

'Not a bit of it.'

'Could you give us the Greek for "and"?'

'No, and I'm not going to do anything of the kind.'

'Did you get on better with Latin?'

'I believe I got further in Latin.'

'Was Caesar a Latin writer or a Greek writer?'

'I can't say. I suppose it was Greek.'

Laughter in court. There was often laughter in court – and often it was led by the Claimant. No one laughed more loudly or seemed less agitated about the outcome than the man in the dock – this 'great body of evidence' as one counsel sneered. (Orton had by this time blown to elephantine girth.)

The game seemed up. But then the claimant's solicitors played their ace: a sailor from the *Osprey* named Jean Luie. He told the court that he had helped rescue the claimant from the sinking ship and nursed him back to health. The claimant, he said, had told him his name was Sir Roger Tichborne.

Jean Luie, the Good Samaritan of the sea, was, however, better known to the police as a confidence trickster named Sorensen, and, exposed after two days cross-examination, made a run for it. Sorensen was gaoled for perjury – seven years in his case. Goaled too, were others who were found to have perjured themselves for the claimant.

Arthur Orton's brother Charles, like his two sisters, at first denied that the claimant was known to him. (Orton was bribing all three). But in court he identified the claimant as his brother.

A Dr Lipscombe, described as Sir Roger's personal physician, gave evidence of a rare physical defect that, he said, distinguished Sir Roger. The young aristocrat, he said, had an abnormal penis. It regressed, like a horse's, into his body. The claimant, Thomas Castro, had that same abnormality.

Was there to be no end to the sensations in court? Suddenly there was. Under cross-examination Dr Lipscombe admitted that he had seen Sir Roger only twice, and that he had failed to disclose his association with friends of the claimant. And when Arthur Orton's sweetheart of years ago, Mary Anne Loder was called, she drove another nail into the case that was now a coffin.

Not only did Mary Anne identify the man in the dock as her old flame Arthur, the Wapping butcher boy, she also gave evidence that in the course of the courtship she had become acquainted with Arthur Orton's penis – at times it regressed into his body, she recalled. A pocketbook belonging to Tom Castro was tendered in evidence. Among the addresses in the book was Mary Anne Loder's.

It had always been inevitable that the Tichborne Claimant would lose the case, and it followed inevitably that he was charged with perjury. Orton's trial began in 1873, and ten months later, he was sentenced to 14 years' penal servitude. He was released from prison in 1884, a changed man. He wrote and had published his confession, but to the delight of students of the case and many authors who were later to make money from the confidence trick of the century, he later retracted it. Naturally, he took to the boards; as 'The Tichborne Claimant' he performed a wretched parody of himself for music hall audiences who delighted in pelting him with rotten fruit. The same people throwing tomatoes had wanted to rescue him from gaol and carry him to freedom when he was convicted. And, to this day, there are those who still believe Arthur Orton was the missing baronet. There was something about Arthur that attracted admiration and belief.

Orton died on April Fools' Day 1898. At the end, Arthur Orton had finally come clean. He had revealed himself as a likeable man.

Hats Off to Mr Whippy!

*M*rs Rose Grainger, the widow of the distinguished architect and the mother of the world-renowned pianist, stepped out of the window of the artists' management agency. Eighteen storeys below was the Manhattan street. She had been ill for years, but the letter she left behind to her son, Percy – one of thousands she wrote to him and he to her – showed that the reason she had taken her life lay in the dark rumours that had begun to circulate: that mother and son were lovers.

The letter read:

> My dear son,
>
> …You must tell the truth, that in spite of everything I said – I have never for one moment loved you wrongly – or you me – not for one moment or thought of doing so. The whole thing has driven me insane and I have accused myself of something I have never thought of. You and I have never loved one another anything but purely and right. No one will believe me – but it is the real truth as you know.
>
> Every day gets worse. I am an idiot and no one seems to realize it. I am so sorry – I have loved you and so many others so dearly.
>
> Your poor insane mother
>
> You have tried so hard to be all that is noble – but your mad side has ruined us, dear. God knows the truth – man will not believe the truth I am writing.

Percy Grainger's 'mad side' is one of the most striking examples of the axiom that genius is just a hair's breadth from insanity. Born out of his time, he is nonetheless Australia's most eminent composer, and one of our greatest pianists. His composition *Country Gardens* is one of the few tunes that almost everyone knows and can hum. In 1918, it was a hit around the world and broke all records. For more than 20 years, it sold 35 000 copies a year, and it should have ensured Percy Grainger's name would be remembered long after his death, aged 79, in his house in White Plains, New York, on 20 February 1961.

Yet today, although *Country Gardens* is seemingly immortal, outside music circles Percy Grainer himself is largely forgotten. He did his best to be remembered – no one could have asked more of him – and in today's society he would be enormously successful, hailed as one of the most original, eccentric and attractive personalities Australia has known. Russell Crowe, Germaine Greer, Peter Carey, Nicole Kidman – the contemporary Australian artistic figures who are internationally known – are puny and pale before Percy. Only Barry Humphries (who met Percy), with his own genius, candour and love of creating unexpected sensations, comes close.

Everything about Percy Grainger was, most right-thinking folk agreed, distinctly odd. There was his appearance. He was short, only 160 centimetres. But, to add to that was his vivid orange hair. Percy wore it brushed high to the heavens so that from tip to toe he measured around 180 centimetres. In the 1920s and 1930s, when Percy was at the peak of his fame, men wore hats. It was, by unspoken agreement, compulsory. Look at a photograph of a crowd of men at the time and you won't see one hatless individual. Unless Percy was there. In that case, you would see a handsome man with a face sensitive and strong, and a lithe body that advertised power and energy. He might be dressed in a tweed jacket, white linen trousers – or, often, shorts – and tan military boots of the type favoured today by skinheads.

Percy was well aware of the impression his clothing caused. In America, where he was a celebrity, he was sometimes mistaken for a vagrant. When this happened, he would immediately notify his publicist. He once wrote to Police Officer Harry Anklam:

> I see in tonight's *Wausau Daily Record* that Police Officer Harry Anklam is mentioned as the patrolman who spoke to me this morning

in the streets about my trousers … I wish to report this incident to my Press Agent, but do not wish to report it incorrectly. Unfortunately I have not got a very good memory for dialogue – for the exact words spoken in conversation, Thinking it over, I believe I was wrong in attributing to you the words "What business have you got walking about in those thin pants?" I think what you said was "What do you mean by walking about in those thin pants?" I would like to report the incident to my Press Agent quickly as possible.

This letter can be seen in the Percy Grainger Museum at Melbourne University. Percy himself designed the Museum, paid for it and even had a hand in its construction. The contents of the Museum are extraordinary. There is nothing like it. It is Percy's personal Smithsonian. He wanted it to contain all manner of things to show what can inspire a composer. The exterior is immensely disappointing: a squat red brick building that appears to be a genuine 1930s public lavatory. Inside there is as eclectic a collection as can be imagined. There's the 'Model yacht bought for me by my mother at the boat house at the NE end of Albert Park Lagoon in 1894 or 1895 when I was eleven or twelve years old. It went to each new country, to Germany, England and America and has always been one of my cherished possessions, none the less dear to me because I never after leaving Australia in 1895 had a chance to sail it.'

There are the clothes of his lifelong friends, the composers Scott, Quilter and Balfour Gardiner. There are his mother's clothes, locks of his hair, pubic hair and thousands of letters, books, tapes, recordings and sheet music. There are pianos, an early Edison phonograph and his unique free-form music machines, devices made from found objects like brown paper rolls, valves, pulleys, oscillators. Percy's wish for his skeleton to be exhibited in the Grainger Museum was not granted, but there are other skeletons from a closet he kept closed until after his death: his large collection of whips. Narrow, bamboo-handled whips with a variety of lashes in different sizes and weights according to which part of the body Percy wanted to whip or be whipped are on display alongside a brown paper envelope on which Percy had scrawled: 'Not to be opened until 10 years after my death,' and in which he described his love of the whip.

Percy's obsession with flagellation probably began around 1895 when his mother's health began collapsing with the onset of syphilis. She had contracted the disease from her husband, John, a brilliant Adelaide architect who designed many fine public buildings around Australia. John and Rose Grainger came to Melbourne for him to supervise the building of Princes Bridge, which he designed, and George Percy Grainger was born, at the couple's upper class seaside home in Brighton, in 1882.

The marriage was unhappy, and by the time Percy was five or six, Rose had contracted syphilis from her husband. When her husband came home amorously inclined, Rose would take to him with a whip and this may be the root of Percy's fascination with whipping. The couple separated in 1890, and John Grainger became an alcoholic, supported for many years, like his wife and half a dozen others, by Percy. The need to support up to nine people kept Percy on the concert hall circuit when he should have been free to compose.

Whatever the trigger for Percy's love of flagelantism, as he called it, he was an enthusiastic and unabashed advocate. 'I attach enormous importance to flagelantism (like boxing, football and other sports) it is a means of turning the hostile, harsh and destructive elements in a man into *harmless channels*. Much of civilisation consists of turning hostility into playfulness,' he wrote in the sealed letter he instructed was not to be opened until ten years after his death.

The fact that I have enjoyed whipping myself, or having myself whipped by a woman does not (as far as I can see) arise out of the wish to humiliate or dominate the woman. The photographs of myself whipped by myself in Kansas City and various photographs taken of my wife whipped by me show that my flagelantism was not make believe or puerile and my flagelantsim was never inhuman or uncontrolled. And the fact that neither my wife or my sweethearts resented my flagelantism suggests that it was not unduly harsh.

... I have always been potent sexually and never had any interest in homosexuality. My flagelantic orgies by myself were always followed by self help (onanism) and flagelantic orgies with my wife and sweethearts were almost always followed by coitus ... I have always disliked pornographic or indecent pictures, photos and literature [but] ... I consider pornographic literature (for those that like it) flagelantic literature etc. most important for the future of mankind – as a means of releasing the sexual fury proper in a vigorous male. I have had more pleasure from badly written flagelantic books than from the world's best literature. Sex is better than art – goes deeper.

Percy Grainger was that rare thing, an honest and candid man, but he was not without vanity. He knew the effect he made when he appeared at concerts with only seconds to spare. Often he would have hiked many kilometres to the concert hall, in khaki and with a rucksack on his back. He didn't care for the starched shirts and tails of the concert pianist. He never ironed his shirts and washed all his clothes in the hotel bedroom basin. 'It's quicker that way. Don't even have to iron the shirts – they don't show from the stage you know.'

Percy was understandably disappointed that, in Australia and in England, his fame was far less than it was in America, where he lived from 1914 and where he was lionised. He became an American citizen, reluctantly, 'I am bitterly ashamed of having to change my nationality,' and above all he wanted to be acknowledged as an Australian composer.

It was never my intention that the Australianism of my music should be overlooked. Yet this is what happened. British musicians who welcomed my settings of British tunes suddenly became deaf when I set out to develop an Australian theme or an Australian mood ... The most Australian mooded of all my compositions *The Marching*

Song of Democracy has been shunned like the plague.

One of these Australian-inspired compositions, *The Warriors*, an Aboriginal ballet, was written for three grand pianos, and a full symphony orchestra and performed in the Chicago Civic Opera House in 1930 with no fewer than 19 pianos.

Percy liked innovation in music. 'Audiences only like music they know. How can they get a thrill out of it when they know what's coming up all the time?' And, in the same spirit, he told The *Christian Science Monitor* that he never went to concerts because he couldn't abide the solemn silence during the performance. He got no pleasure from something that he couldn't discuss while it was going on, he said. And, most shocking of all, he pronounced Duke Ellington one of the three greatest composers who ever lived. (The other two were Bach and Delius.)

Percy Grainger was a close friend of Delius and Grieg. Of Percy, the great Norwegian composer said: 'If I had his technique my conception of the nature of piano playing would have been exactly the same. Like a God he is lifted above all suffering, all struggle. But one feels they have been there, but are overcome. It is a man, a great and distinguished man who plays. May life go well for him.'

Life did go well for Percy. Rose had made Percy the centre of her life. She arranged his education at home (Frederick McCubbin gave him art lessons), and before he was ten, she had launched him as a child prodigy, taking him to London and then to Frankfurt, where she supported them by giving English lessons. There she began suffering the manifestations of syphilis. Its shadow, and her fear of poverty, preoccupied her, but her emotional health was linked to the relationship she had with her son. In turn, he was bound to her. Rose's death was a traumatic blow that was softened five years later when he met a poet, the beautiful Ella Strom. 'After the death of my mother ... it is an unspeakable boon to me to have this soul satisfying comrade ... as lovely as the morning to look upon, and a regular Amazon to walk, run, swim and dance, and play games.'

In his last year, Percy wrote to Ella, 'My own heart's dearest Ella ... I think both you and I are unusually gentle and subtle, and therefore I consider it a miracle of good luck that we met and wedded. I am so endlessly thankful to my darling wife.'

I Say, Christie, That Drunken Sailor Was You, Old Man!

*H*e came to be called the Sherlock Holmes of the Antipodes, a detective who stalked the streets of 19th century Melbourne, a city where Holmes would feel, well, at home. In the latter decades of the century, in the aftermath of the Gold Boom, Melbourne was lavish, grand, big, booming and, very often, bad.

Despite the impressive parks, boulevards and buildings, Melbourne was perhaps most distinguished for its nightlife: there were said to be 10 000 whores known to the police, and many of them were to be found in the block bordered by Lonsdale, Spring, Latrobe and Exhibition Streets. (In one of those whore houses, Madame Brussel's, it was said, the five-foot gilded Parliamentary Mace from the nearby State Parliament was involved in revelry with the ladies and pollies and has never been seen again.)

Just a block away was Little Bourke Street, today's Chinatown, where one could wile away the days in an opium haze, or plan a garrotting or two to make ends meet. Little Bourke Street, wrote the Reverend John Cole, a contemporary observer, 'was a perfect "pandemonium". A viler hell on earth, reeking with every description of abomination, could scarcely be found. The horrible scenes that I witnessed appalled me. Unless I had seen what I did, I could never have believed that human nature could have sunk so low – lower by far than the beast of the field …'

John Cole, whose Methodist ministry was just around the corner in Lonsdale Street, shuddered: '19 December 1875 – From ten to one o'clock, I visited amongst brothels and thieves' rendezvous. I have been in the lowest parts of London, but it would be well-nigh impossible to witness more horrible scenes of moral delinquency and degradation. It was disgusting and loathsome.'

Down by the river, where the warehouses stood darkly, there was all manner of skulduggery to be found. Into this world of pleasure-bent politicians, brothel keepers, garrotters and larrikin gangs came Australia's Sherlock Holmes – two decades ahead of his time. Sir Arthur Conan Doyle created the 'real' Sherlock Holmes 20 years later, in 1890. A new type of hero, an amateur detective with extraordinary powers of deduction, he fought a never-ending battle against evil wherever it was found. From misty Yorkshire moors to sunny stately homes, the man in the Deerstalker puffing on his Meerschaum as he discovered telltale signs in a thread, a flak of cigar ash or a mite of dust enthralled millions.

Evil tended to find Holmes. There would be a knock on the door of his Baker Street apartment, and Doctor Watson would usher in someone with a dark and mysterious tale to tell. And if evil didn't find Holmes, he would go looking for it: put down his violin, doff his Deerstalker and don quite a different hat. A Chinese coolie straw hat, say. Some pancake make-up, a little judicious glue for the drooping S moustache and something to slant the eyes, and Sherlock, transformed beyond all recognition, would venture to the opium dens of old Limehouse (he was partial to prohibited substances) to unravel yet another Curious Case. Then back to Baker Street to change into a smoking jacket while he regaled an agog Watson with details of his escapade: 'I say, Holmes! That was you, sir, all dressed up like a Chinaman!'

Holmes was a revelation. Fiction had seen nothing like him. Yet, in fact, the prototype of Sherlock Holmes had been going about much the same business decades before the superhero made his bow. As his case papers in the Victorian State Library reveal, Detective Inspector John Christie of Melbourne had the same fascination with solving crime through deduction and the use of disguise. But, in his case, his fame stayed local and has long been forgotten.

Christie, like thousands of young men in the wake of the Gold Rush, came to Melbourne to join a relative who, the Christie family believed, might make him heir to a fortune. When that failed to eventuate, young John turned to crime fighting. As a member of the Victoria Police, he soon established a reputation for intelligent, resourceful work, marked by his fondness for solving crimes in unorthodox ways.

Today, Christie would be an undercover cop, a Stinger. Or he might be treading the boards in a Cameron Mackintosh musical. Christie enjoyed dressing up and acting a part: male or – despite a splendid moustache – female. He specialised in your common drunk or swagman (usually also drunk), but he had a large repertoire of characters. Here he is, in 1868, as a seaman at the scene of a warehouse about to be broken and entered.

I jumped into the cab and returned home. On the way I gave cabby his coat &c. and on arrival at home I put on an old fore-cabin stewards' rig-out, with plenty of bright buttons on it, and the cap. I then tied a handkerchief round my head over one eye, and put some spots of a red liquid which I had on my nose and mouth to resemble blood. I then put my ordinary clothes in a bag in the cab, and started back to Elizabeth Street, where I got out (gammoning to be very drunk) opposite the Duke of Rothsay Hotel. I staggered down Flinders Lane to where Detective Hannan was. Finding all right, I told him to keep me in sight at a distance. I then lay down in a store doorway commanding the entrance to the right-of-way where the ladder was laying.

I was pretending to be asleep when the constable on the beat came along, turned his bullseye on me and shaking me said, "What ship do you belong to?"

I stammered out, "The steamer *Aldinga*."

He said, "Well you get out of here or I'll lock you up."

I rolled down the street in front of him. When he got to Elizabeth

Street, as his time was up, he went off up to meet the relief.

As soon as he was gone I went back pretending drunkenness (as Briely might be watching in the vicinity) and dropped down in the same doorway, and almost immediately Briely came along and seeing me came over to me and had a look at me. He caught hold of me and shook me saying, "Hallo, mate. What's up?"

I replied in a drunken state, "Is this the Model Lodging House?" and dropping my head on my knees rolled over.

(Christie had deduced that the warehouse would be broken into by a criminal named Briely, an old lag whom he caught in the act, wrestled into submission – Christie had begun his career in the colony as a pugilist – and saw him sent down for five years' hard labour.)

Here Christie is again, this time bringing Chinaman Jack to justice.

In March 1873 a contractor named John Pigdon was stuck up and robbed of a valuable gold watch with chain and seal attached. Also several sovereigns … amongst some silver there were two rupees, one of which had a small round hole in it.

As there had been several similar robberies about the time, I determined to disguise myself and have a look through the various drinking dens.

So I blacked up a la Christy minstrel [with] black skull cap, and when I got on my plantation clothes and old battered white belltopper, I looked the character. I got this rig-out in a present from George Arnott, an old nigger minstrel. I got my banjo, which was one of Frank Weston's worn-out instruments. This completed my make up.

I got a cab and on getting to the corner of Stephen and Little Bourke Streets, I instructed my batman to go down [to] the Golden Fleece and wait for me.

I walked down Little Bourke Street and into the Morning Star Hotel. The bar was full of speelers, mapmen, thieves and prostitutes. They hailed me with 'Good then, Bones, give us a tune.'

I played and sang 'Ten Thousand Miles Away' to a rousing chorus of thieves – I was taking stock all the time.

After the song I made a collection which amounted to about 2/6. They insisted on another song so I gave them 'The Old Log Cabin in the Lane', after which I left and started down to the Star of the East, kept by an ex-sergeant of police named Andrews who had got very low in the world, and his house was the resort of notorious burglars and highway robbers.

There was only a few prostitutes in the bar with a drunken bushman, so I went round into the back parlour which was pretty full of thieves. They were having a barney about changing a coin. The barney was between the landlord and a desperate character named John Wallace, alias Chinaman Jack.

On seeing me, Jack said, 'I say, Darkie, can you change a florin?' I replied yes.

He handed me what I saw at once was a rupee, but pretended not to notice it. I gave him 2/- and they all, including Jack, heartily laughed at me, thinking I had been gulled. I played them a tune and sang 'Ten Thousand Miles Away' and went round and collected somewhere about 1/6, after which I had a clue to Pigdon's robbery through the rupee.

I left the hotel and went quietly down to my cab and told him to drive me to the detective office where I picked up Detective Hartney and we called at my hotel close by, where in less than five minutes I was dressed in my ordinary clothes (and the black face turned white). Rejoining Hartney we proceeded to Little Bourke Street. On the way we examined the rupee and found it had a hole in it (stopped up with bread) and was no doubt the one Pidgon lost ...

We strolled down Little Bourke Street and outside Mrs Morris' boarding house we saw Wallace talking to some prostitutes. I went up to him and told him to get into the cab which was following us.

He cursed dreadful and fought like a demon, but Hartney and I got him in, and although he struggled violently all the way, we landed him in the detectives' office where we stripped and searched him. In his socks we found Pigdon's seal and some of the sovereigns, and in his pocket we found the other rupee.

I never let on to him that I had the other rupee, but he swore mortal vengeance against the nigger who he said has put him away because he had done him with changing a rupee.

I pretended not to know what he meant, but he swore he would get even on the nigger some day when he met him. At the same time he did not have the slightest idea that I was identical with the darkie.

I took him to the watchhouse and charged him with assault and robbery on John Pigdon, and next morning I was in waiting at the watchhouse to see if any of his pals would bring him some breakfast. I was right in my conjectures as a notorious character named Kate Laurence called at the watchhouse with some breakfast for him.

After she had departed I shadowed her house and on searching the house I found a quantity of stolen property including Pigdon's watch and chain, all of which was concealed in a hole under the hearthstone which I had to raise.

Both were tried and convicted for the robbery. Wallace got seven years and Laurence two years. And I got a 25 pound reward from Mr Pigdon.

The Shock Horror Truth about John Norton

*N*obody could write John Norton's history – 'not even John Norton', the *Bulletin* said when the owner of *Truth* newspaper died, an alcoholic, in 1916.

'Freak big man, small man, philanthropist, scoundrel …one of the few orators the New South Wales Assembly has known … a writer with a powerful punch … a muck-raking journalist for the money that the muck-rake brings … an editor who prostituted his paper … a proprietor who money could not buy when the matter had the right appeal to his boiling mind.'

The *Bulletin* might seem to have summed him up nicely. But John Norton was also, a jury found, a blackmailer, a thief, a wife beater, and a murderer. A pugnacious pipsqueak with a Napoleonic complex – he was just 150 centimetres – completely bald and beady-eyed, Norton was a scoundrel of the highest order. A ratbag possibly without peer.

The *Bulletin* also said that 'he was the personification of heredity's problems', and here there can be no dispute. Norton had a certain genius, but his tumultuous life, from the very beginning marked by torment, denied him the chance to make something good of his exceptional talents. Like almost all villains, he was an exceptionally nasty piece of work whose life – seen from the safe distance of time – is hugely entertaining.

John Norton was, he used to claim, 'the bastard son of a parson – a child of pure love like Napoleon and all other bloody men with brains.' He also claimed to be the bastard son of a military officer and, sometimes, the illegitimate offspring of an English aristocrat.

What is undeniable is that he was brought up in England by a Bible-bashing cleric, 'a man of almost inconceivable ignorance on matters of morals and religion, especially as they related to children,' Norton wrote.

His mother was 'half mad ... in neurotic moods was more worthy to be in charge of kind keepers than to have charge over a singularly sensitive and stubborn son, whose innate stubbornness and sense of shame and wrong were deepened and intensified by the severities and the harsh discipline – often extended to whippings and solitary confinement – of a puritanical stepfather ...'

The next incontrovertible fact about Norton fast-forwards his life to exotic Constantinople, a city perfect for the on-the-make young man he now was, and which Sydney was about to come to grips with. He arrived in Sydney in 1884, a sub-editor from Constantinople's Levant Herald, and a 'stringer' for the *London Daily News*, a man fluent in French who may have spent a good deal of his formative years in Paris. We will never know.

But, from the time Norton stepped ashore from the schooner-rigger steamer *Haverton*, we know much – but certainly not all – about him. Typically, he played up on the voyage out. Once he urged his mates – one of them a man named Grohn – to a lark that could have had tragic consequences: 'We'll holler down the hatches "The ship's going down!"' He got into fights, he was usually drunk and obnoxious, he broke into the stores and stole food, he mocked and disturbed religious observances, he threw biscuits down the cabin ventilators, and finally he was told that he would be clapped in irons if he continued to cause trouble. The voyage out was more or less the way Norton's life was to go for the next three decades.

Norton had a flair for words, the more and the more florid the better, and a talent for alliterative invention – he described Queen Victoria, for instance, as 'this flabby, fat, and flatulent looking scion and successor of the most ignoble line of Royal Georges,' – he was charged with sedition for that – and Winston Churchill as 'a witless wild ass ... a bulgy-eyed, frothy-mouthed, loose-tongued, leather-lunged, British half-breed ... a demi-demented decadent ... the blatant, mad-brained bounder ... this sibilating shyster.'

And Norton invented the word 'wowser'. He didn't know what it meant, he confessed, but it suited the sentence in which he was condemning kill-joys, and wowser came to be a synonym for them in the Australian language.

Within six years Norton had somehow managed to describe himself on the imprint of *Truth* newspaper as 'the Proprietor', although he had not a penny invested in it. In time he actually seized control of the paper. By the time of his death, he had an income of $30 000 a year – an immense amount at the time – and owned a chain of newspapers. As well, thanks to *Truth* and his demagogic gift, he had been four times elected to the New South Wales State Parliament despite the fact that he had celebrated his election by urinating in the House. Norton was careless where and when he relieved himself.

How Norton got control of *Truth* is, naturally, not certain. But one published account of Norton's life claimed: 'Willis was the original proprietor of *Truth*. This was at the time when Norton might have been seen hanging about King Street the whole day, cadging threepence from anyone who could bear the range of his breath. By some means or other Norton wormed into *Truth* office and finally, by theft and fraud and conspiracy, obtained a hold upon the proprietary.'

This would hardly have disturbed Norton, he had been called worse – and called others, and done, much worse – but then the account went on: 'Norton is an active inciter to crime. Whether he is an actual murderer we do not know, but there is in the hands of the Inspector-General of Police, a statutory declaration, which asserts that Norton, in his house at Randwick, killed a man named de Groen [sic]. De Groen, it seems, came out from England with Norton on the same boat. Norton stole his money, and reduced him to a state of beggary, and de Groen, as a hanger on, lived with Norton during several years. De Groen "died suddenly" three or four years ago; but the allegation is that Norton hit him on the head with a beer bottle.'

Norton, a man accustomed to talking to libel lawyers, took the author to court. The jury was asked to consider a number of claims and concluded that Norton had illegally gained *Truth*; that he beat his wife; that he published untrue accounts of her infidelity; that he blackmailed people; and that he had killed Grohn (wrongly called de Groen in the alleged libel). They threw out Norton's defamation claim.

(The murder allegation – it was substantiated by a bodyguard of Norton's who was in the house at the time of Grohn's death – was investigated. A body said to be Grohn's was exhumed – there is a real possibility that it was the wrong body – but it was too decomposed to determine the cause of death. Norton, however, admitted that he had said to the police when they called next morning after Grohn had allegedly been found dead in bed: 'Shift that ****ing carcass out of here.')

The master of yellow journalism lived an extraordinary, alcoholic and increasingly megalomaniac life, and eventually died in a Melbourne hospital in April 1915. John Norton would have gone raging against that dark night. The little man who idolised Napoleon was never happier than when he was at war. And hardly a day went by when he wasn't. Here is Sydney's *Evening News*, recounting a day in the life of John Norton.

High Life in King Street
An M.L.A. a Journalist and the Premier's
Ex-Secretary
Indulge in a Lively Mill
Willis and the Policeman

Now that the legislature have abolished prize fights and boxing competitions, anything in the shape of a mill is heartily welcomed by the sporting fraternity.

A cheap display of fisticuffs, and a remarkable one at that, under no particular rules, was witnessed in King Street last evening about 6 o'clock, the contest being somewhat after the style of Marryatt's triangular duel, was of a novel character.

The combatants were Mr. W. N. Willis, the member for Bourke, Mr. John Norton, ex-editor of Truth, and Mr. W. B. Melville, ex-secretary to the Premier, who, it is understood, is to contest Molong constituency at the next election.

How trouble arose in the first instance is not yet known, but it is hinted that an article which lately appeared in a weekly paper had something to do with the matter.

The first thing that attracted the attention of passers-by was the sight of the ex-secretary and the ex-editor (the latter in a somewhat excited state) engaged in a scuffle on the footpath outside the Metropolitan Hotel, which resulted in both measuring their length on the pavement.

A crowd soon gathered and the combatants were separated, Norton faring somewhat the worse of the two.

An attempt to renew hostilities was prevented, and after an exchange of compliments decidedly unjournalistic, Norton was rushed into the hall of the Metropolitan Hotel followed by Melville and a number of onlookers, where the first person he encountered was the member for Bourke, Mr. W. N. Willis.

With a fierce gesture he approached the legislator and having expressed his opinion of him in terms more forcible than polite, exclaimed "I'd like to fight you, you ****, I would."

Bourke's representative however, did not appear to court an engagement, but next instant the newspaperman let drive at him and landed him a blow on the throat.

With a howl of rage Willis raised a heavy cane which he had in his hand and aimed a blow intended for Norton that landed on the head of an unoffending bystander whose back happened to be turned towards his assailant.

The fun was now fast and furious, all the parties being mixed up in a state of inextricable confusion.

The party who had received the blow from Willis' cane, with a yell of pain, was heard enquiring "Who struck me?" and next instant, after vainly endeavouring to divest himself of his coat, was observed grappling with and pummeling another individual whom, in his excitement, he regarded as his assailant.

Meanwhile the other combatants had not been idle.

With a cry of "Let me get at him" Willis rushed at Norton and commenced belabouring him about the head and body with his stick. Getting to close quarters, however, he lost his weapon and next instant Norton had his antagonist by the throat and amid the excited cries of partisans they went at it hammer and tongs, raining blows on each other's head and face.

At this juncture the presence of the crowd from behind forced the combatants from the passageway through the doorway of the private bar where Willis, getting his opponent's head in "Chancery" to use a sporting phrase, landed heavily on his face.

A moment later locked in an octopus-like grip, journalist and legislator were rolling on the floor, Willis being underneath.

Biting and hitting, over and over they went, Norton having Willis' ear firmly between his teeth, Willis yelling "Pull the ... off; he's biting me."

All efforts on the part of onlookers to separate them proving futile, a policeman appeared on the scene and having made his way to the struggling combatants on the floor, seized hold of Willis who happened just then to be uppermost, and tried to drag him off.

His task was anything but an easy one for Norton had not relaxed his hold on Willis' ear and Willis held Norton by the throat in a vice-like grip.

In despair, the constable seized hold of Willis who kept grasping out "Don't take me I'm Willis" and succeeded in dragging him to his feet.

Then, recognising his man, the constable released his hold of Willis and turned his attention to Norton who by this time had also regained his feet and had stationed himself behind a table in one corner of the room.

Seizing him behind, high and low, the constable ejected him into the street.

Visible signs of the encounter were prominent on the features of both combatants, Norton's face being a gory red, while he was minus his hat and his collar was in shreds.

Blood besmeared the usually florid features of Bourke's representative which was also embellished by a gash over the eye.

Norton subsequently was driven away in a cab while Willis, surrounded by some of his friends, remained in the hotel.

Long after the affair had ended, it continued to form a theme of discussion for a number of spectators who had gathered about the scene of the encounter.

Later in the evening Norton further distinguished himself by walking through a plate-glass window in J.F. Collins & Coy's outfitting establishment in Pitt Street. The window is valued at 50 shillinga and is uninsured.

10 | Wild, Wild Women

A Saturday Arvo's Entertainment with Sweet Nell of Tooth's Brewery

*I*t might have been a scene from the worst excesses of Caligula's Roman Colosseum: two half-naked whores circling, hissing hate and spitting threats, flinging themselves at each other as the spectators bellowed for blood.

The younger of the two was a ferocious fighter. Quicker and crueller and prettier than the older one, she relished violence. Usually the spectator as men fought it out for her, this time she had an appreciative audience – Nellie Cameron was a stunner – and it was over all too soon for them. Nellie dropped Big Aggie with a succession of sickening stomach punches, jumped on her and raked her face and body with long, painted fingernails. In the backyard of a Darlinghurst pub in the Sydney of the 1920s, Black Aggie was finished. Her William Street beat was lucrative – for streetwalkers, it's position, position, position in more ways than one, and now Nellie had won the position.

Nellie Cameron – Sweet Nell of Tooth's Brewery, some droll souls called her – lived for and with violence. Like Sweet Nell of Drury Lane, the mistress of King Charles II, Nellie was a stunning, sexy redhead, but unlike her 17th century counterpart, who aimed high and won a monarch's favours, Nellie Cameron aimed as low as she could go. She moonlighted in cocaine running, theft and receiving stolen goods. She packed a revolver and a razor (razor slashing was then in vogue) and she herself was slashed, shot and beaten so often that in the last year of her life, in hospital with a bullet in her stomach, doctors came across another two bullets from bygone days and gaped at the crosshatching of knife and razor scars across her shapely figure.

Today, we find it incomprehensible that such a highly intelligent, devastatingly attractive woman would want such a life. Yet Nellie, like her only peer, Pretty Dulcie Markham, delighted in the milieu of killings and savagery that accompanied her for most of her 41 years.

Nellie was born in 1912, a year earlier than Pretty Dulcie, and like her was raised in middle-class comfort on Sydney's North Shore. Dulcie left home aged 16 to sell herself on the streets of King's Cross. Nellie, despite her private school education, started at 14. (As a 12-year-old amateur, she had got off to an even earlier start.)

What drove Nellie to the seamy world of sex and brutality in King's Cross? Lillian Armfield, a famous woman police officer at the time, believed Nellie became a prostitute 'for no other reason than she wanted to be one. But she wasn't content with the sordid thrills of the life of a prostitute. She wasn't happy unless she was associated with violent men, and it is beyond any doubt that she encouraged them to violence. And if gangsters held a lure for Nellie, she also held a lure for them.'

Nellie was beautiful, with a 'hubba hubba' figure. She was sunny, full of life and loved a drink.

'Dulcie – 'Pretty Dulcie' Markham – was prettier than Nellie, but Dulcie's features didn't have the rare and curious indestructibility of Nellie's,' Lillian Armfield said. 'Right to the finish Nellie retained her attractive appearance and the assured poise that set her apart from all the other women of the Australian underworld. Even after being badly wounded or bashed up, she maintained her air of rather disdainful nonchalance and she continued to queen it over men.' Above all, Nellie had a sexual aura and reputation that, as Lillian Armfield said, 'turned out to be a fatal lure for some … Jealousy over her was responsible for more than one murder.'

The murders started very early on. Nellie had barely been on the streets when she was installed as mistress by a Melbourne gangster who had a meteoric rise in the underworld of Sydney. Norman Bruhn had fled a shooting charge in Melbourne and quickly distinguished himself as an expert garrotter. Bruhn may have learned his macabre skill – the garrotter would creep up behind his victim with a leather thong looped around his wrist and strangle by tightening it with one powerful hand – fighting with the AIF at Pozières in World War I. Certainly Bruhn saw enough horrors at Pozières to immure him to death. More than 23 000 Australians were killed, wounded or missing at Pozieres, 'a place so terrible,' one digger wrote, 'that a raving lunatic could never imagine the horror.'

This frightening thug, an ugly man in every way, bashed 15-year-old Nellie regularly and lived off her earnings, while his devoted wife chose to ignore Nellie.

What did a vivacious, highly attractive girl like Nellie Cameron see in this brute?

'When I wake up in the morning,' she said, 'I like to look down on someone lower than myself.'

Bruhn's gang members were scarcely less palatable than their overlord. His right-hand man was the infamous Melbourne criminal Snowy Cutmore, a vicious psychopath who, while still a teenager, murdered his first man. Snowy himself was to be bumped off by Squizzy Taylor – and return the favour, mortally wounding Squizzy.

Then there was razor specialist George Wallace, known as the Midnight Raper for his modus operandi – sexually assaulting prostitutes who would not share their takings with him. And there were henchmen and hangers-on such as Razor Jack Hayes, Nigger, a black homosexual with flowing platinum blonde locks, and 'Sailor the Slasher' Saidler, soon to be shot dead in a standover that misfired badly. (Sailor the Slasher had his razor out and was promising 'I'll carve you up. I'll slice off your smeller with this little beauty!' when his mark took out an equaliser – a pistol – and terminated the discussion.)

For a while, this wolf pack terrorised the underworld, preying on its own kind: sly-grog merchants, drug pushers and street walkers. But in 1927, in a bid to become the unchallenged boss of Sydney's crime scene, Bruhn made the mistake of setting Razor Jack Hayes on to Sid 'Kicker' Kelly. Razor Jack slashed Kelly's throat but bungled the job. Kelly lived, and on 6 June Hayes was gunned down. (Sid's brother, Jack Kelly, was later charged and acquitted when witnesses gave wildly different evidence and alibis.)

But, sixteen days later, while Hayes was recovering in hospital, Bruhn himself was shot twice in the stomach and lay screaming in agony outside Macks, a cocaine den in Darlinghurst. He died a few hours later. For 15-year-old Nellie Cameron, the brief and brutal liaison with Norman Bruhn established a way of life and death she was to follow for the next quarter of a century. Norman's corpse was scarcely cold before she had taken up with Frank 'the Little Gunman' Green. One of the most poisonous criminals ever to haunt King's Cross, Green's only rival for the position of the most feared man in Sydney was Guido Calletti.

Naturally, both men wanted Nellie. Naturally, too, Nellie wanted the top dog – whoever he might be at the time. At first it was Green. Then, when he was gaoled or in hospital, it was Calletti. When Calletti was lying low, incarcerated or otherwise out of action, it was 'the Little Gunman'.

Of course, Nellie couldn't ever be true to any man. Briefly, she lived with another thug, Eric Connolly, until Calletti shot him on 16 February 1929. She immediately went back to Calletti where the police found her with him at his home the following morning. They also found a revolver, which Calletti had been trying to hide under a sofa cushion when they burst in. Nellie could explain that. She appeared in the lounge room, all sleepy eyed and tousled haired, but anxious to help the police in their investigations. She had found the gun in the street, she said, all wrapped up in brown paper, and she had planned to hand it in to the police station that very day. When two witnesses got cold feet after Calletti got to them, the police gave up any thought of prosecution.

On 16 June 1931, 'the Little Gunman' Green, fresh from acquittal on a murder charge, went with Nellie and another man to the home of Big Jim Devine, the husband of Tilly Devine who ran a score of brothels in inner-Sydney. Green worked for Tilly as an enforcer and was of the opinion that Big Jim owed him twenty-five pounds. He wanted it, one way or another. In fact, one thing led to another, as they had a habit of doing in those circles, and Big Jim Devine got the drop on them, blasted away at Green and Nellie as they fled in a taxi and shot dead the driver, a man named Moffitt.

At the inquest into Moffitt's death, patrons in the public gallery rocked with laughter as Nellie told the coroner: 'I don't know James Devine, and have never been to his house.' She did, however, know Green, she thought. 'I have heard of him ... I think.' Big Jim's subsequent trial (he was acquitted) put Nellie in the public eye and the public was enthralled. Here was a 19-year-old girl who had been in at the kill at Tilly Devine's, who had once been the mistress of the murdered gang leader, Bruhn, and who had caused two gunmen, Connelly and Calletti, to ventilate each other in their eagerness to claim her. Soon she was making headlines again. This time, it was Nellie who was plugged.

It was a sensational story that had the tabloids slavering. Nellie was shot leaving St Vincent's Hospital with another man and woman. They had been to see 'the Little Gunman' Green, recuperating after being shot by a musician, Charles Brame, whose lover was a well-known Sydney socialite. Green had been her lover, briefly, two years before, when he had taken up with Nellie. In turn, Nellie and the musician had an affair. Green couldn't stand for that nonsense and shot Brame.

Brame survived and Green had another try. This time he razor slashed him. Again, Brame survived. Finally, 'the Little Gunman' decided to do the job properly. He got Nellie to arrange to meet Brame outside St Vincent's, but as they stood talking and Green walked up to them, Brame saw him coming, pulled a gun and shot 'the Little Gunman'. Badly wounded, he was taken to St Vincent's where he slowly recovered, and from whence Nellie and her two companions were leaving after visiting Green when a man stepped out and aimed a sawn off shotgun at them. Nellie was shot in the side.

Nellie and Green survived and, in 1933, were fit enough to bring the Calletti–Green grudge match to a head. For years, the two men had fought over Nellie; now they agreed to one final fist fight, the winner to take her. The two fought for an hour, watched by a crowd of 500, until neither could go on. It was a draw, and Nellie settled things by choosing to go off with Calletti. A few months later, in 1934, when Calletti went to Long Bay Gaol for six months, she moved back to Green. When, in turn, Green was gaoled, Guido Calletti, now out on the streets, took Nellie Cameron to Melbourne and married her.

Guido kept out of trouble for some time, but three years later, he was back in the dock, charged with consorting. Nellie was outraged. 'It's only for me that he goes out and does bad,' she told the magistrate. 'I don't know how you can send men like my husband to gaol and then go home and have some sleep!' Unmoved, and certainly not suffering from insomnia, the magistrate sent Guido down for six months. When he got out, Nellie wasn't home to comfort him. She was working in Brisbane, and Calletti picked up with 'Pretty Dulcie' Markham, Nellie's only rival. Pretty Dulcie, even more than Nellie, was a femme fatale. Half a dozen of her lovers had died violently, and Guido was about to join them. On 6 August 1938, he and Dulcie invited themselves to a party thrown by rival mobsters, the Brougham Street gang.

Calletti, then at his peak as a gangster to be feared, evidently thought he was invincible. He strutted and taunted until the inevitable brawl broke out. A lamp light was smashed, and in the dark two shots were fired. Calletti's funeral was one of the most spectacular Sydney has known. His wife couldn't make it, but she sent flowers from Brisbane.

During the 1940s, Nellie Cameron and Dulcie Markham led quieter lives. The war years were prosperous for prostitutes, and in the 1950s both women were entering middle age.

In 1952, neighbours called the police when Nellie was discovered with a gunshot wound in her stomach, crawling and weeping with pain, outside her Darlinghurst home. As always, Nellie kept to the code of the underworld and refused to say who had shot her – police suspected it was the man she was living with. But, now, for the first time in her life, Nellie's indomitable spirit failed her. She fell into a depression, convinced she had cancer as a result of surgery to remove the bullet, and on 8 November 1953, she turned on the gas and put her head in the oven.

Nellie Cameron would have liked to have gone, there's no doubt, guns blazing, like Bonny and Clyde. But she never found her Clyde.

You Always Hurt the One You Love

*M*en fell for 'Pretty Dulcie' Markham in the worst possible way. At least eight men who loved her met bloody ends, stabbed to death or shot. Yet she was at a loss to know why the Sydney tabloids dubbed her 'The Angel of Death', 'The Hoodoo Girl' and 'The Black Widow'.

As Dulcie told the press, widening those big, grey eyes and tossing her flowing platinum hair in irritation: 'Because men who've loved me have died I've been called these silly names. I've even been sketched in one newspaper, feet apart, hair flying loose and holding a smoking gun. But I'm not a gun girl. I've never touched a gun in my life! It's just unfortunate that these men have died. Believe me, at heart I'm just an ordinary girl.'

Dulcie may or may not have had a heart, but she was no ordinary girl. And it may or may not have been unlucky to have been Dulcie's lover, but it was certainly unhealthy. 'Pretty Dulcie', she was best known, was the most desired and one of the most notorious woman in the underworlds of Sydney and Melbourne. She had pin-up looks: a stunner, with a lissom figure, beguiling grey eyes and full lips begging to be kissed. Irresistible to most men – and she had known thousands – Pretty Dulcie had a fatal attraction for gangland 'identities'. She had only one rival, Nellie Cameron. [See A Saturday Arvo's Entertainment with Sweet Nell of Tooth's Brewery, page 248.]

Pretty Dulcie should have led an uneventful, anonymous life in suburbia. She was born to middle-class parents on Sydney's North Shore in 1913 and grew up a spoilt little madam. (Much later, she would actually become a madam.) By the time she was in her teens, she had grown into gaol bait for boys of all ages; too wilful and wild for her parents to handle. At the beginning of the Great Depression, she walked out of home, and at 16 she began her working life on the streets. For the next two decades, in Darlinghurst, King's Cross and St Kilda, she worked in the vice trade and made her name as gangland's femme fatale.

At first and for years after, Dulcie called herself Mary Eugene. But, on the police files, she had various aliases, some absurdly exotic – Tasca de Marca, Tasca Damarene, Tosca de Marquis – and some prosaic – Dulcie Taplin, Dulcie Johnson, Mary Williams and, in 1950, Dulcie Markham. To the underworld she was 'Pretty Dulcie'.

In 1934, aged 21, Dulcie married Frank Bowen, a thug who operated out of the Cross. Bowen, a robber and an extortionist, took Mary Eugene to have and to hold in sickness and in health and he stayed in good health when she moved out two years later to live with another notorious crook, Alfred Dillon. Her passion for Dillon cooled quickly – a characteristic of Pretty Dulcie's love life – when she met William 'Scotty' McCormack, a 21-year-old standover man not long out of gaol. The two began a flaming affair. Dillon quickly found out. He was only 18, and when he swore that he would do for McCormack, no one took him seriously.

Raging jealousy drove Dillon to follow Dulcie and her new love one day until he cornered them in a shop doorway near the notorious Fifty-Fifty club in William Street. Without a word, Dillon rammed a long needle between McCormack's ribs and into his heart. Dulcie ran for her life and hid in a cinema nearby. McCormack lurched along the street and, when a passer-by asked him if he was all right, replied 'I'm okay' and fell down dead.

Dillon got 13 years for manslaughter and, as he was led away, yelled out his love for Miss Markham. In the gallery she waved farewell and wiped the tears from her eyes.

Dulcie was front-page news now, the seductive young vice girl who had gangsters fighting to the death for her favours. Mary Eugene decided to take her business to Melbourne and under the name Dulcie Bowen worked the streets of St Kilda. There she took the notorious Arthur 'The Egg' Taplin as her lover – briefly – until he made a very bad error of judgement.

Taplin was a pimp, a fellow Sydneysider laying low down South. On 15 December 1937, 'The Egg' and two mates were whiling away a pleasant afternoon in the Cosmopolitan Hotel, Swanston Street, teasing a mild-mannered male hairdresser who was nearby at the bar. The three thugs invited the man to buy them a round, and then another, and another. When 'The Egg' left, the man plucked up the courage to refuse to buy any more. Taplin's mates left and came back with their enforcer who opened the debate by smashing a beer glass on the hairdresser's head.

The hairdresser went down, but to Taplin's astonishment, got back on his feet, pulled a gun from his coat and shot his tormenter in the chest. Taplin lingered for a week in Royal Melbourne Hospital, and Dulcie was chief mourner at his funeral. But, after his death, she hurried back to Sydney, not anxious to be involved for a second successive year in a murder trial. (The hairdresser pleaded self-defence and was acquitted.)

The year 1938 passed without incident. The following year, however, Dulcie took up with yet another murderous criminal, Guido Calletti, believed by police to have been involved in a number of killings. It was reckoned that by the time of his death – which, Pretty Dulcie's form guide should have warned Guido, was not far off – he had killed four men.

A gunman, razorman and garrotter, Guido also made a living from pimping. He recruited his team of prostitutes by the protection plan: 'You pay me and I'll protect you from other pimps. Otherwise I'll give you a hiding.' Violence ended almost all discussion with Calletti. On the dance floor, he would break in on couples if he fancied the woman and if her partner objected give him the choice of backing down or settling it in the lane outside where Calletti always left his adversary bloodied and bowed.

Calletti led the Darlinghurst Push, a gang of up to a score of men who were quick to sort out any who infringed on their territory. When the Ultimo Push tried to move in on the Darlinghurst prostitutes, Calletti and his boys turned up in their rivals' favourite bar and beat and razor-slashed them into submission.

Guido, then, should have known the dangers of venturing into another gang's territory. The Brougham Street Gang was selling protection to illegal bookies in King's Cross and Woolloomooloo, and Calletti saw an opportunity. He would let the Brougham Street thugs collect their takings, and then he would stand over them. Things were going beautifully. He was admired and feared by all, he had Pretty Dulcie as his moll and business was expanding. On Sunday, 6 August, he was so cocky that he decided to drop in on a birthday party for one of the Brougham Street prostitutes.

Calletti and Dulcie stopped the show when they walked in, but when he assured all that he only wanted a friendly drink a truce was called. Inevitably, a fight flared, Calletti went for his gun, a man grabbed his wrist and another shot out the lights. More shots and Dulcie, drinking outside with the girls, rushed in to find Calletti's bloody body in the empty room.

The men had all fled when police arrived, leaving Dulcie and four other women to attend the gangster, writhing in agony from bullet wounds to the stomach. 'Who shot you, Guido?' they asked, and he answered, 'I don't know.' He died in St Vincent's Hospital two hours later. His body was laid out in his best gaudy suit in the Reliance Funeral Chapel, Darlinghurst, and buried two days later.

Guido Calletti's funeral, fondly remembered as Sydney's grandest gangster send-off, would have done him proud. 'The Hoodoo Girl' was among 5000 mourners at Rokewood Cemetery's Catholic Chapel, weeping copiously. But then it was time, once more, to skedaddle. Two men had been charged with the killing, and Dulcie decided Melbourne's autumnal climate was better for her health.

A few months later, in 1940, Frank Bowen, Dulcie's first husband, with whom she was still friendly, was shot dead on his home turf, King's Cross. Not long afterwards, her latest lover, John Charles Abrahams, followed in much the same way. John Abrahams fell heavily for Pretty Dulcie, but he was soon to pay the price. Frederick Anderson, a towering criminal known as Paddles, was also smitten, and the two fought over her one night in a two-up school in Collingwood. Anderson pounded Abrahams and left with Dulcie on his arm. Abrahams staggered out at 2.00 a.m., and a man whom witnesses said was 'tall and hiding near a car' stepped out and opened fire. The first shots missed and Abrahams ran for his life, but he was chased and shot down.

The next day, true to form, Dulcie moved in with Paddles who, a month later, police later charged with Abrahams's death. He was acquitted, but by then Dulcie had moved on to fresh fields, the busy Sydney brothel of Tilly Devine.

The 1940s went smoothly for Pretty Dulcie. Business was never better, with big-spending American servicemen in Brisbane, Sydney and Melbourne waiting to be serviced, and only two of her lovers – Sydney's Donald (The Duck) Day and Melbourne's Leslie (Scotland Yard) Walkerden – bumped off.

Day was a former jockey, but he could handle himself. On 29 January 1945, he got stuck into a man who owed him money. He promised that he'd be around that night to get the money – or else. When he went to the man's flat, he was greeted by a volley of shots, through his nose, both cheeks and his chest. The killer got off after he told the court, 'It was him or me.'

In Melbourne, Leslie Walkerden had a reputation for violence that almost guaranteed Dulcie's interest. He was a standover man for a Richmond baccarat club and was shot at by three men who emerged from the shadows when he was changing a flat tyre on his car outside the club. Asked who shot him, he replied: 'Don't waste your time. I'll fix it my way.' Minutes later he died.

In 1951, Dulcie was drinking with two men and another woman drinking in her Fawkner Street, St Kilda house, with her boyfriend, Gavan Walsh, a 23-year-old pug, his brother, and Len 'Redda' Lewis, when there was a knock at the door. Walsh opened the door and two gunmen burst in, spraying the room with bullets. Walsh was shot dead, hit in the stomach. His brother was shot in the hand, and Dulcie took a bullet in her hip. In court, on a stretcher, she looked at the two charged with Walsh's murder and swore that police had got the wrong men. They were acquitted.

The judge was at a loss to understand the world of the Walsh brothers, Dulcie, Redda and co. 'She, in fact practically all the witnesses, moves in somewhat queer circles. As far as one can gather, the men seem to spend the greater part of their day in hotels, and a good part of their night drinking from place to place. The women seem to join them in their drinking, and to change the people with whom they sleep from month to month without anyone worrying about it or doing anything about it.'

The bemused judge was mostly right, but in Dulcie's case, people frequently did things about it when she changed partners.

Dulcie was still in bed recuperating from the shooting, and recovering from the loss of her lover when, three months later, she married 'Redda' Lewis. The wedding guests crowded into her bedroom to hear Redda and Dulcie swear 'till death us do part'. But part they did; Dulcie took off back to Sydney after a few domestics, and in April 1952 a caller at Redda's mum's house in Prahran almost made the parting permanent.

Redda answered the front door to a gunman. For a split second, he must have thought of young Walsh making the same mistake seven months before. The gunman fired three shots into Lewis's stomach and another three when he dropped. He lived – 'I'll cop it sweet', he told detectives – but when he was shot again, in another incident he told reporters from his hospital bed, 'It's past a joke. And I don't like you fellows calling my wife "The Angel of Death". It's not fair!'

Redda's resolute defence of Dulcie – she was now in her forties and could no longer be called Pretty Dulcie – wasn't enough to save the marriage.

In 1955, Dulcie was in the news once again. This time she was the victim. A man flung her over the balcony of her first-floor flat in Bondi, and she was taken to hospital with internal injuries and broken ribs. Dulcie told police she'd fallen down the stairs. Whatever, it was all downhill from here. Too injured to work, she shacked up with an Irish sailor. In 1964, he opened their East Sydney flat door, always a worry when Dulcie was around and was badly bashed. No doubt he counted himself lucky.

Finally, Dulcie settled down with a third husband, Martin Rooney, a man who had no criminal connections and lived happily with him in a neat semi-detached in Moore Street, Bondi, until April 1976 when she fell asleep with a cigarette in her hand and was asphyxiated in the flames it ignited. 'The Angel of Death' had finally met her namesake.

La Lola's Excellent Australian Adventure

*H*ad Lola Montez not existed, Hollywood would have had to invent her.

In fact Lola Montez is constantly invented, reincarnated in thousands of television and feature film dramas and scores of Mills & Boon bodice rippers. Lola – or a woman very like her – can be seen in a multitude of movies made over a century and more. She is the shady lady with the flaming temper, the spitfire with the heaving bosom and tossing hair, the wench with the big eyes and the grand flounce, the scarlet woman who makes men of steel melt, the Spider Lady who lures men into her fatal web. Invariably, the lavender water heroine triumphs over this tumultuous temptress, but only after a great deal of anguish. And, without the Spider Lady, the movie would be exceedingly dull.

Naughty Lola Montez is an irresistible character in history, the most flamboyant woman Australia has seen, a beauty who enthralled almost all men and who was capable of taking a horsewhip to those who resisted. She lived for only 42 years before syphilis claimed her. But how she lived! By the time she arrived in Australia, Lola was 37. Behind her were four marriages and so many affairs that she was known as 'The Fair Impure'. Her lovers included such luminaries as the composer Franz Listz and King Ludwig of Bavaria who was infatuated with the raven-haired dancer, draped her with pearls and diamonds and made her Countess of Landsfeld.

In reality, the Countess of Landsfeld was not Lola Montez, but Marie Dolores Roseanna Eliza Gilbert, from Limerick, Ireland, who by the time her teenage charms began to take shape realised that her long raven hair, brilliant blue eyes and voluptuous figure were magnets to men of all ages. Marie decided the best way to take advantage of these God-given gifts was to display them to as many men as possible on the stage. And, as Lola Montez, to that end she choreographed a daring Spider Dance during which she attempted to dislodge hundreds of wire spiders from 'numerous short petticoats of different colours' which she wore – sometimes – over flesh coloured tights.

Lola took this temperature-raising dance to the goldfields of California, where it caused a sensation. In 1855, she decided that the Spider Dance should be enjoyed by their Australian compatriots. Lola sold some jewels to the madam of a San Francisco brothel and, with $20 000, put together a company of out-of-work actors and set sail for Sydney.

In August 1855, at the Old Victoria Theatre in Sydney, Lola and her company had their Australian premiere of *Lola Montez in Bavaria*, 'a drama of an entirely political nature'. 'The eccentric and much advertised Lola Montez pounces on us direct from California and the excitement of her visit is emptying the opposition theatres. Last night the Countess looked positively charming and acted very archly,' the *Sydney Morning Herald* reporter wrote. The reporter 'found her, much to my surprise, to be a very simple mannered, well behaved, cigar-smoking young lady.' But, while he purred, the Melbourne *Argus* correspondent pouted: 'She is sometimes graceful for a moment or two but coarseness and vulgarity is sure to follow.' (How right he was.) What's more, in a bold critical judgement, he found the play 'the greatest piece of trash and humbug ever introduced before an English audience ... profligate and immoral in the extreme.'

Certainly the play was dramatic. But not half as dramatic as the off-stage goings-on. By the time *Lola Montez in Bavaria* opened, Lola's travelling company of thespians were warring among themselves and taking their quarrels on stage. 'A regrettable fracas recently occurred at the theatre where Madame Montez has been playing. The uproar continued for some time and was much increased by the actors and actresses squabbling among themselves.'

Madame Lola herself was causing much consternation and commotion. Charles Folland, her leading man, was incensed by her romance with the besotted younger brother of the Duke of Wellington, who had followed Lola to Sydney from Calcutta. Folland flung himself into Sydney Harbour and was dragged out wet, bedraggled and unhurt except for his broken heart.

Three weeks after opening, La Montez decided to sack some of the cast and move the show to Melbourne. But the redundant actors sued for damages totalling $12 000, and a bailiff from the sheriff's office, a Mr Brown, boarded the ship on which she and the company were sailing and demanded the money. Lola offered him $500. Brown waved this aside and announced she would have to leave the ship in his custody. The press gleefully reported her reaction: 'Madame Lola, ever ready for the fray, retired to her cabin and sent word that she was quite naked, but the sheriff could come and take her if he wanted. Poor Mr Brown blushed and retired amid roars of laughter.'

In Melbourne, in September, Lola opened at the Theatre Royal. The Spider Dance bought the wrath of the *Argus*. 'We do not intend to go into details ... if scenes of the kind are ever to be repeated we consider that the interference of the authorities is imperatively called for.' The details that the *Argus* did not intend to reveal to its readers included the fact that, at some performances at least, Lola neglected to wear underclothing, an oversight all too apparent during the Spider Dance. An outraged reader, Dr Milton, demanded that the police stop the 'extreme of indecency', but a swift writ from Lola piped down Dr Milton.

Henry Seekamp, the editor of *The Ballarat Star*, didn't get off so lightly. The show was to open in 'the new and elegant Victoria Theatre' on 16 February 1856, and Lola, a publicity genius, had sent the paper a press release on the Spider Dance. 'This dance, on which malice and envy have endeavoured to fix the stain of immorality, has been given in the other colonies to houses crammed from floor to ceiling with rank and fashion and beauty.' Seekamp begged to disagree. The dance, he told the *Star's* readers, was 'not only shameful but indecent'.

Lola was one of those readers. That evening at the United States Hotel as Mr Seekamp was relaxing with a friend over an ale – and possibly glowing with satisfaction at putting the shameless self-publicist in her place – Madame Lola came in steaming. Seekamp had got her Irish up. In her right hand, she gripped a short whip with which she proceeded to thrash him.

Seekamp, too, had a whip and attempted to retaliate. Needless to say he was no match for Lola and quickly fled the field, leaving Lola shaking her whip 'in defiance and contempt' at his fast-retreating figure. A writ was to follow. Ticket sales for the show boomed, and when Lola appeared on stage, the diggers from the goldfields showered her with gold nuggets, a gesture to warm Lola's heart.

Bendigo was the next stop, and once again the diggers were enthralled by the Spider Dance and the whip-wielding femme fatale who was able to give better than she got. Lola left Australian men nursing warm memories. 'Her popularity was not limited to the stage,' wrote William Kelly, a squatter who saw her. 'She was welcomed with rapture on the gold fields, and the more for the liberal fashion in which she "shouted" when returning the hospitality of the diggers. Her pluck, too, delighted them, for she would descend the deepest shafts with as much nonchalance as she if she were entering a boudoir.'

Celeste de Chabrillan, the wife of the French Consul, saw Lola's Theatre Royal show on the eve of her trip to the goldfields. She wrote:

In the fifth act she also makes a speech to the audience. She asks for their support, for their protection. They can prove their goodwill by coming to her plays every day. She blows kisses to everyone.

"Reduce the price of the seats," shouts an Irishman, lording it in the stalls. Lola answers him and they argue back and forth for half an hour. Others call out to her; she replies with remarkable presence of mind. She speaks English very well. They clap and whistle. There is an infernal din.

The play is followed by a ballet composed and danced by Lola! It consists of moving about a lot while frantically shaking the folds of an extremely short gauze skirt. There is a spider hidden between the folds; it's called the spider dance. I don't know why, but all the women walked out before the end of the ballet, although there is nothing improper about it. However, the police have banned a second performance.

Lola says that all the nations are rising up against her: they fear her influence, politically speaking, that is. People say she's mad, but she is simply very excitable. She came to see me. I don't really remember what she said to me. She speaks very quickly and her ideas have no logic to them. She was leaving that evening to perform on the goldfields. She promised to come and see me on her return. She's counting on making a fortune here. I hope she does but I don't think it will happen.

Celeste de Chabrillan was right. After her Australian tour, it was all downhill, and in the last years of her life the celebrated courtesan embraced religion. Five years later, she died in New York.

The Days of
Julia's Lives

Parkinson's Disease. Alzheimer's. Hodgkins' Disease. Gladstone's Despatch.

Gladstone's Despatch? Gladstone's Despatch has the distinction of having afflicted only one man, Sir John Eardley-Wilmot, the Governor of Van Diemen's Land. But that fatally.

A 62-year-old baronet, Sir John died in Hobart Town in September 1846 – officially – of peritonitis, or ulceration of the bowels. But the knowing ones gave the cause of death as Gladstone's Despatch. This devastating malady came in the form of two letters sent from London to Sir John. They were written by William Gladstone, the Secretary of State, and the future sanctimonious prime minister who so bored Queen Victoria. The letters advised Sir John, until then a jolly old gentleman, that Her Majesty's Government was dispensing with his services.

Gladstone, an Anglican prude fond of prowling London's East End seeking fallen women to preach to before giving himself a whacking good whipping, began the first letter by deploring the lowering of civilised standards in Van Diemen's Land. This letter was public and announced that nameless sins – he was referring to the love that then dared not speak its name – were, he was given to understand, a commonplace among the convicts. Sir John, Gladstone raged, had utterly failed to show enough 'assiduity', 'anxiety' and 'prudence' in moral reform, and because of this lack of diligence he was dismissed.

The second letter was private. In it Gladstone warmed to his theme, that nothing could be done to curb the immorality or to reform 'these depraved creatures' when Sir John's own private life – the details of which it was 'perhaps unnecessary' for Gladstone to discuss –

disqualified him from exercising any sort of moral control. As an added admonition, Gladstone warned Sir John that he must never expect another official post.

Sir John was undone. His career was over. In vain, 'the battered old beau' protested against 'the grossest falsehoods that ever oppressed an English gentleman.' It was no use, and within nine months the flirtatious old boy had died, it was said, of a broken heart. 'Gladstone's despatch,' said a Hobart newspaper, 'was to an old man, a husband and a father, like a poisoned knife.'

But perhaps the real problem was the cause of Gladstone's Despatch ... the ladies of Van Diemen's Land and in particular the lip-licking lovely Julia Sorell. Julia Sorell's story, and the story of her tempestuous and passionate family, would make a *Days of Our Lives* scriptwriter blush at its sheer audacity and improbability. A more appropriate title for a television series starring this celebrated beauty could be *All in the Family* because, for three generations, the Sorell family managed to scandalise the good folk of Tasmania – among whom, until he got Gladstone's Despatch, was Sir John Eardley-Wilmot.

The Sorells took the view that life is for living and didn't give a damn what people thought. And for three decades they gave people much to think about. The family stemmed from French Huguenots who had fled to England to escape persecution, and the first Sorell came to Van Diemen's Land, as Tasmania was known until 1855, in the dashing form of another Governor – Lieutenant-Governor Sir William Sorell who arrived there in 1817 with his mistress, whom he passed off as his wife.

The Sorell family men were noted soldiers who found employment in the almost incessant conflict of the 18th century: in Scotland and Ireland, in wars on the Continent against the arch foe Napoleon, and in Canada and America. The young Sir William himself was a dasher, a gallant, the son of a General in the Coldstream Guards, and a soldier who had distinguished himself. In 1807, his military record was awarded with his appointment as adjutant-general to the British forces at the Cape of Good Hope.

William had fathered seven children by this time, to a woman – Harriet – he had only just got around to wedding. Harriet Sorell came from the wrong side of the tracks, and when William got his appointment he had few qualms about leaving her and the children in London, and practising his amorous art with the ladies of the Cape.

The lusty fellow was bound to fall in love with another man's wife, and he duly did. Mrs Louisa Kent was the daughter of a general and the sister of a fellow officer. When Mr Kent hurried his wife back to England to get her away from Sorell, her lover followed and moved into quarters with her. Kent divorced his wife, and the couple were forced to assess their future. He couldn't expect to progress in the Army in England, and since he was already married, he couldn't expect to introduce Louisa into polite society. Van Diemen's Land, on the other hand, was the ideal place to start afresh, a place where he and Louise could live together as man and wife without frightening the horses, and a place where his connections would see him very comfortably off.

William managed to do better than that. In 1817, aged 42, Sir William and his 'wife' sailed for Van Diemen's Land. He was to take the reins as the new Lieutenant-Governor of the colony. The colonists welcomed the 'Old Man', as the grey-haired Governor became affectionately known, and the fact that he was not married to his pretty partner, 12 years his junior, didn't seem to matter a whit.

Except to Anthony Fenn Kemp.

A former officer in the Rum Corps, Kemp was a wealthy grazier and magistrate whom Sir William had dismissed from his post for various 'irregularities'. Kemp began a poison pen campaign in retaliation. In letters to people in power back in England, Kemp painted a lurid picture of 'Sorell and his paramour publicly parading together in the government carriage, living in a state of open concubinage to the vile example of the rising generation.'

This comment blithely ignored the fact that the rising generation of Taswegians were exposed daily to the horror and depravity that accompanied the lives of those men and women convicts and their keepers in the penal settlement. Nonetheless, it had its effect and eventually, through a process of attrition, Kemp's railings against the sinful Governor began to persuade those in London of the need to pay heed to him.

Finally, Lord Bathurst, the Secretary of State, as Gladstone was later to do, picked up his quill and began writing a letter of dismissal. It was somewhat rueful because Sorell had been a success. He had broken the Howe gang of bushrangers who had terrorised the settlers and had made the farmlands around the Derwent and Clyde safer. He had overseen the fourfold growth of population in Van Diemen's Land from 3114 to 12 464, and he had established the penal system of 'perpetual reference and control' over convicts that was seen as the model for future settlements such as Macquarie Harbour (which Sorell established), Norfolk Island and Port Arthur.

Sir William got his despatch in late 1823. It was couched more circumspectly than the Gladstone Despatch of 23 years hence. Nevertheless, the meaning was plain. Lord Bathurst found himself under 'the painful necessity of appointing a successor to you.' And, at this painful point, the *Days of Our Lives* scriptwriter bows low to the superior inspiration of Fate. Because the only substantial difference between the letter that Governor Sir William Sorrel got and the Gladstone Despatch of Governor Sir John Eardley-Wilmot was that Sir John's letter of dismissal was initiated by Sir John's relationship – if there was one – with Sir William's granddaughter, Julia. There was one last turn of the screw: Julia was the child of Sir William's son and his wife, the tempestuous daughter of the man who brought about Sir William's sacking – Anthony Kemp.

All this was in the future, taking embryonic shape when, before Sir William and Mrs Kent had sailed, his 23-year-old son turned up, quite out of the blue. Young William Sorell brought news of his mother and the other six children Sir William had left behind. Mrs Harriett Sorell, he told his father, was struggling, making a meagre living selling apples and pears from a cart in south London. He expected Sir William to make some amends by finding him a position in the colony.

Sir William was honour bound to oblige, and the young man was made registrar of the Supreme Court. It was an ideal position for William who, unlike his father and his grandfather, had no interest in the world of the warrior. But he did like the ladies. In that regard, he was a chip off the old beau, and within a year he was courting a 17-year-old, Julia Kemp, described by a contemporary diarist as 'the most beautiful woman you ever saw.'

Julia Kemp was the daughter of Sir William's nemesis, Anthony Fenn Kemp. And she was trouble. 'The very devil incarnate,' the diarist hissed. She fell pregnant to young Sorell and had a dark-eyed daughter – Julia – before marrying him that same year, 1825. They had another girl and then, while on the Grand Tour of Europe with the two girls, Mrs Sorell ran off with an officer. William never saw her again. But the two children were brought back to him in Hobart Town where young Julia grew up into a mirror of her mother.

By the time the 60-year-old Sir John Eardley-Wilmot became the new Governor of Tasmania, it was said that Julia had been pursued by every officer in the garrison. Sir John could not help but be beguiled. He and Julia spent a stolen weekend together at New Norfolk and provided the ammunition for his enemies that led to the Gladstone Despatch.

One final twist. Julia, perhaps not surprisingly, went on to become the mother and the grandmother of three international celebrities. Not long after the New Norfolk weekend, Julia became engaged to Sir John's son, Chester, but broke off the engagement and continued her busy social life until in 1850 she married the most unlikely of men.

Thomas Arnold the younger was the son of Dr Arnold, the author of the famous Victorian novel, *Tom Brown's Schooldays*. Thomas was quiet, sensitive, soulful – everything, apparently, that Julia, passionate, capricious and tempestuous, was looking for in a man. The marriage lasted three uncertain decades. Arnold was a man with a gift for choosing the right path at the wrong time. Thus, when his conscience told him he should become a Catholic, Julia was infuriated: Thomas held the post of Inspector of Schools in Tasmania. There were 75 schools on the island and 71 of them were Anglican. The remainder were Catholic. He had to resign his job, and Julia, in her fury, smashed every window in the local Catholic church. They had eight children. The four boys were brought up as strict Catholics. The girls were allowed to decide for themselves what they were. The family went to England, to Ireland and back to England where Thomas had a conscience crisis that forced him to resign his job as classics master at a Catholic school. His belief in Catholicism lay dormant for 11 years, and then returned just as he was on the point of getting a professorship at non-Catholic Oxford University.

In 1888, as Julia lay dying of cancer, her eldest child Mary, writing under the name of Mrs Humphrey Ward, published *Robert Elsmere*. It sold a million copies and she was the dominant English author of the 1890s. Julia's third daughter married the scientist Leonard Huxley and gave birth to the biologist Sir Julian Huxley and the even more famous author, Aldous Huxley.